Save Me from the Waves

Save Me from the Waves

An adventure from sea to summit

Jessica Hepburn

Aurum

First published in 2024 by Aurum Press,
an imprint of The Quarto Group.
One Triptych Place, London, SE1 9SH,
United Kingdom
T (0)20 7700 9000
www.Quarto.com

A catalogue record for this book is available from the British Library.

ISBN 978-0-7112-9130-0
Ebook ISBN 978-0-7112-9132-4
Audiobook ISBN 978-0-7112-9390-8

10 9 8 7 6 5 4 3 2 1

Typeset in ITC Giovanni Std by SX Composing DTP, Rayleigh, Essex
Printed by CPI group (UK) Ltd, Croydon, CR0 4YY

Contents

Overture

*'I hope to become a better human being.
A kinder, wiser, funnier, more courageous human being.
For me.'*

–Maya Angelou, *Desert Island Discs*, 1987

I've noticed that the older I get, the less I care about what other people think of me. Today, I said to a stranger sitting next to me on the Tube: *'Do you like lists?'* He looked at me as if I was mad and then went back to what he was doing on his phone. Undeterred, I turned to the woman on my right. *'Do you like lists?'* This time changing the intonation of my voice so it cadenced up and was softer, less interrogative.

'What sort?' she said. *'Shopping lists?'*

You see, I've been wondering whether the world is divided into people who like lists and people who don't. I thought I'd conduct some market research on my way home.

I love lists. Shopping lists – yes – especially ones with carbohydrates on them. To-do lists, although mainly if I've ticked everything off. I've got lists of all the books I've read; all the shows I've seen; and all the countries I've visited. I keep them in colourful notebooks by the side of my bed. There's also my 'Blessings Book' which lists the (mainly) little things

1

that make life worth living each day, like a great cup of coffee and the first sight of spring blossom. There are my lists of 'New Year Resolutions' and my 'Bucket List' – which I'm starting to accept has one thing on it that will never happen . . . I also keep lists of people through history I admire (mainly women, sorry men) and lists of words that I like. Oh and a long list of reasons why I hate social media, and then another list about why I should still do it . . .

But there's one list that, for me, has always stood at the summit of all lists. My *Desert Island Discs* list, inspired by the UK's most beloved radio show. The programme (now also available as a podcast because everything's a podcast these days) was first created by Roy Plomley for the BBC in 1942 and recently celebrated its eightieth birthday. During all these years it has only had five presenters. Roy himself (1942–85), Michael Parkinson (1986–88), Sue Lawley (1988–2006), Kirsty Young (2006–18) and Lauren Laverne (2018–). Guests on the show are invited to pick eight music tracks which they would take to a desert island, plus one luxury and one book (along with the Bible and *The Complete Works of Shakespeare* which are set text reading, although some people do refuse them). And at the end, they have to choose just one of their tracks to '*save from the waves*'.

For many people, being invited to be cast away is a lifetime ambition and the show is sometimes referred to as the UK's unofficial honours system. From pop stars to prime ministers, Oscar winners to Olympic athletes, it has become a kaleidoscope of British social history of the last hundred years. With credentials like that, who wouldn't want to have a go at composing their own list?

This story is a mountainous musical adventure for list lovers like me. But it's not your average adventure story, so the aim of this overture is to make sure you're not in the wrong place. Life's too short to read on if you are. It starts on the streets of London and finishes on top of the world – literally. It has inspired my new list book of all the mountains I've climbed: from Box Hill to Ben Nevis; Elbrus to Everest. There is disappointment, danger and derring-do like all good adventure stories should have – in fact it culminates with a series of horrible events which nearly ended everything for me . . . But what's different is that it is also a journey from sea to summit in song, after I made the decision to take on the challenge of listening to every episode of *Desert Island Discs* while walking up 8,848 metres (well, technically currently 8,848 metres and 86 centimetres high – Everest is growing – but most mountaineers still round the number down).

Why? You might ask. If I were a real mountaineer I might say: *'Because it's there.'* (in the legendary words of the real mountaineer George Mallory). Plus, the archive of *Desert Island Discs* is now freely available and, at over 3,000 episodes, it's an Everest of listening. But I'm not a real mountaineer. I'm a middle-aged, unlikely athlete who, in her forties, started taking on massive endurance challenges to try and exercise her way out of heartbreak.

In 2015, I swam the English Channel. In 2017, I ran the London Marathon. And in 2022, I summitted Mount Everest – although I call her *'Chomolungma'*, her original Tibetan Sherpa name. In fact, I am the first and (at the time of writing) only woman on the planet to have done all three of these things. I'm also possibly the first and only person to have ever listened to every available episode of *Desert Island Discs*. But that feat is impossible to certify.

While an adventure about music and mountains might be unusual, what is true is that music and movement are closely associated and you can't get up a mountain without moving. However, before you make your final decision about whether to read on, let me say that this is also a story about music and memory which I think is the essence of *Desert Island Discs* and why it has and will always endure. And like so many memories, at its heart it's about family and friends. The ones we have and find, but also the ones we've lost or will never have; all of whom make us who we are. Everyone has ghosts in their lives and, like ghosts, they can surprise you, especially when you find them in the most unexpected places. Sometimes you find them in music on a mountain. I did.

What I hope above all is that this story will encourage you to go on your own adventure – whether that's high and far away or closer to home and in your head. Because sometimes we all need to be saved from the waves, and an adventure – whatever it looks like, wherever it is – will always change your life for the better.

So, are you coming along? If you are, read on.

– Jessica Hepburn #livebigandbrave

PS. A footnote on the endnotes. Firstly, apologies for them. I hate footnotes and endnotes myself. This is formal permission from the author to do any one of these three things. 1: Read them as you go along. 2: Read them at the end if you don't want to interrupt the flow of the story. And 3: Don't read them at all. They're not essential – even though they are an important part of this adventure for me. If you're a list lover yourself, you might even enjoy them. But now we've got to begin – so tie up your reading shoes and let's get started.

Songs of Childhood

1. Diana Ross and the Supremes: 'Baby Love'

2. Joe Jackson: 'Is She Really Going Out With Him?'

3. The Style Council: 'My Ever Changing Moods'

4. Gilbert & Sullivan: 'Pour, Oh Pour the Pirate Sherry', from *The Pirates of Penzance*

5. Tracy Chapman: 'Fast Car'

6. Frank Loesser: 'Sit Down, You're Rockin' the Boat', from *Guys and Dolls*

7. The Lord's Prayer

8. Alan Parker and Paul Williams: 'You Give a Little Love', from *Bugsy Malone*

1

'What do you want? That strikes me as the most important question in life. What do you want? Finding out how to get it is comparatively easy.'

–Jimmy Carr, 2017

If you'd told me that Jimmy Carr would change the trajectory of my life on Sunday 19 March 2017, I wouldn't have believed you. I would have said: 'Who's Jimmy Carr?' No. That's not quite true. I did know who he was. At least, I knew what he looked like. In fact, I once saw him on Regent Street with his Christmas shopping. Obviously I don't know for sure it was his Christmas shopping. But it was just before Christmas. It was dark, there were twinkling lights, the evening was dry but biting and he was carrying a Hamleys bag. I suppose he could have been in to buy something for himself. He might like train sets or model aeroplanes or have been lured by those colourful boomerang toys they're always demonstrating at the entrance to entice you in. But I think it's fair to assume that he'd probably been in to buy presents: for a niece or nephew; a godchild; maybe his own kids if he has them. After all, why else would you brave Hamleys at Christmas? So, yes, I did know who Jimmy Carr was. The tall, dark, slightly toffy-looking comedian off the telly. But I don't watch his show and

9

I've never been to one of his gigs. I don't think I'd get his jokes. He seems too clever for me. So . . . if you'd told me that he would change the trajectory of my life on Sunday 19 March 2017, well, I wouldn't have believed you. But life's funny like that.

I was running down Sloane Street at the time. I say running because it's not cool to use the word 'jogging' any more, but the truth is my body was not built for speed. In fact, a week or so before this a stranger had shouted out at me: *'You must be exhausted running like that.'* At first, I thought he was being kind. I *was* exhausted. Then I thought, how rude. I can't help it that small dogs and toddling children overtake me. At least I'm giving it a go. I'm doing my *best*.

Anyway. I was moving somewhere between a walk and a run down Sloane Street. I'd already done nearly six miles but still had twelve to go. I was in training for the London Marathon, and was trying to put in enough work not to have to face the ignominy of reaching the finishing line at the same time as the rhinoceroses. Or should that be rhinoceri? What is the plural of rhinoceros? I've never had much use for the word before. The point is I'd given up on the thought of 'sub four' and even 'sub five' was looking dodgy; but please, let it not be 'plus six' – Save the Rhinoceros and me.

You see, I've never been very good at sport – always one of the last to be picked for the rounders team at school – I've certainly never embraced my inner runner or even shaken her hand. But at least I looked the part. I was wearing a new pair of trainers. A group of friends – all real runners – had been aghast when I told them I was planning to do the marathon in ones that were several years old. I was a bit short of cash and hoped that I could avoid buying a new pair because I wasn't planning on running a marathon again. Why would you? But when I casually enquired whether they thought my trainers might be responsible for the fact that my little left toe felt like it's broken whenever I put them on, they immediately sent me off to a running shop near Victoria Station. A lovely shop assistant measured my feet and then brought out a pile of boxes. When I tried the first pair on, I felt like I was Cinderella. So even though she told me to break them in and not to do a long run in them the next day, I ignored her. My new trainers looked like jewels next to my old ones, which were muddy and falling apart at the vamp and (according to the shop assistant) half a size too small.

It was only because I went to buy trainers that I had also acquired an aquamarine armband thing. When I was paying, I noticed them hanging behind the cash tills like Christmas decorations. I'd seen other runners wearing them so I knew they were for encasing iPods and smartphones and had wondered what people listened to while they ran. Music, obviously, but I'd also considered whether some people multi-tasked and learnt a new language or finally got through Tolstoy or Proust. It would be quite good to do something constructive, and might take my mind off the pain. But I'm part of the 'didn't-grow-up-with-tech' generation and, back in 2017, I hadn't even mastered listening to music while running (not helped by the fact that running wasn't something I'd ever really done) so until then I had been training in 'let's-just-get-this-over-with silence'.

However, there in the shop, emboldened by a new pair of trainers, I recklessly decided to buy an armband thing. In my favourite colour: aquamarine. I thought I had a pair of old headphones somewhere. I'd recently moved back to my child-hood home in north London and a lot of stuff was still in boxes. I couldn't bear to unpack them. Too many memories. I didn't want to remember. But if I could find some headphones, I could plug them into my phone and find something to listen to. The combination of this and wearing new trainers might help with the horror of the obligatory five-weeks-out, eighteen-mile-training-run.

I was just passing Harvey Nichols when Jimmy Carr changed the trajectory of my life. I had decided to listen to him being interviewed on *Desert Island Discs* – my all-time favourite radio show/podcast. For his fourth track, he picks Death Cab for Cutie's 'I Will Follow You Into the Dark'.[1] Such a weird name for a band. Just before it plays, Jimmy describes how he lost faith in religion – he'd been brought up as a strict Catholic but is now an atheist. He says: *'You've got this one life and we're so privileged to be alive and it's not going to last forever. Try and enjoy it, spend it with nice people and when it's over, this seems like a beautiful sentiment.'* At the end of the show, it's the track he chooses to save from the waves if he can take only one. I've always thought this a mean final twist to the show – as if choosing eight tracks isn't hard enough.

After the song plays, the presenter, Kirsty Young, enquires why Jimmy decided to upend his career working for the oil and gas company Shell to becoming a stand-up comedian. And Jimmy says it was because he was 'sad'. Not because he was depressed, he wants to make that clear. Depression is an illness, a chemical imbalance in the brain. Sadness is something else. It's circumstantial. He reckons you can more easily do something about it. So Jimmy did. And then, as if he were talking to me, he says through my headphones into my heart: *'What do you want? That strikes me as the most important question in life. What do you want? Finding out how to get it is comparatively easy.'*

His words made me think: *'What do I want?'*

My mind was blank.

'What do I want?' I asked myself again.

Still nothing.

It was only then that I realised how sad life had got because in the past I'd always had a plan. I made myself focus on the question, hard. *'Jessica, what do you want with this one life of yours that is not going to last forever?'*

And the only answer I could find? *'I want to choose my list of eight tracks and leave everything behind for a desert island.'*

2

'I love music more than any other of the arts . . .'
–Clive James, 1980

———————————

The magic of *Desert Island Discs* is in the music. That's what makes it more than your average autobiographical interview. The linking of memory with music can be very moving and often makes its castaways reveal things about themselves they never have before. Long before the confessional interview became a thing, it offered a glimpse into the souls of the UK's most famous and high achieving people. That's probably why the programme has endured for eighty years (and counting). It's one of the UK's longest running radio shows.

I got through five episodes on that run – the run that changed the trajectory of my life. Most of them were recent episodes but I also listened to the broadcaster Clive James from back in 1980. The BBC were repromoting his interview with the show's creator, Roy Plomley, as part of their Classics series. I don't think I'd have listened otherwise. I'm a sucker for the new.

Clive chooses eight discs, all of women's voices, on the basis that if he was alone on a desert island that's what he'd miss the most. He saves from the waves Diana Ross and the Supremes' Motown track, 'Baby Love'.[2]

I hadn't heard or thought about this song in years but when the bells started dinging at the beginning, it immediately reminded me of my sister and my seventh birthday.

I say 'my sister' although technically she is my 'half-sister' because we share a mother but have different fathers. For years, I did describe her as a fraction until I realised what a weird phrase it is – half-sister, half what? So now I just call her 'my sister'. However, what is true is that we didn't really grow up together, so we weren't conventional siblings. She's twelve years older than me, and left home when she was sixteen and I was four to live with her boyfriend. The only memory I have of living with her is the time she was left to babysit me and climbed out of the back window, slid down the drainpipe and went to see the boyfriend that she left to live with not long later. So I guess even that is a memory of absence.

But Clive James reminded me of when she came to my seventh birthday party and gave me a Diana Ross and the Supremes' album on which 'Baby Love' was the second track on side one (in the days when music had sides). I was sure I must still have that album somewhere – in a box, in a room, in the house where I grew up and had recently moved back to live again. I could still visualise the cover – three ruby red lips singing into microphones suspended in a black background. And when the bells started dinging as I ran along the Thames Path towards Richmond I was seven again, listening to it.

My sister and her boyfriend had arrived late to the party. In those days they were always late and you couldn't ring them too early in the morning because they were never up. Although my mum always did ring them too early – I think just to prove she was still my sister's mum. It was already getting dark outside when they arrived at our house. I'm a November baby, so it could have been about four, but I feel like it was later. The sitting room was infused in a warm orange light; remnants of wrapping paper from pass-the-parcel lying around and leftover food which always seems to taste better after its first appearance. My friends were starting to leave and going-home presents were being given out.

Then my Motown-loving sister and her boyfriend arrived with the gift of music. I remember lying on the sofa listening to it playing on our record player, thinking how glamorous Diana Ross sounded and that one day I was definitely going to leave this house and travel to a place called America where she was from. And I recall thinking that birthdays were great because it meant you were getting older and becoming an adult was getting nearer, and that sisters (even 50% of one) were a pretty special thing.

It was Clive James and his music that had brought back all these memories. And although I wasn't sure that 'Baby Love' would make it to my own final list of eight tracks to take to my desert island, it's definitely a song from my childhood that says something about who I am.

Roy says to Clive at the beginning of the episode: *'Is music important to you?'*

Clive replies: *'It plays a profound part . . . I love music more than any other of the arts.'*

Personally, I'd much rather listen to music than run. If the world is divided into sports people and arts people – which it was when I was young – then I was the arty and not the sporty one. However, in my forties, I started trying to exercise my way out of heartbreak, when my life didn't go to plan. That's basically the only reason this unlikely athlete was attempting to run a marathon.

3

'You just think: why? I'm trying everything and why does someone keep knocking me down?'

–Kelly Holmes, 2006

————————

The day before the London Marathon (on the sofa, eating pasta), I decided to have a *Desert Island Discs* medley of runners. Consider it motivation. Sebastian Coe, Kelly Holmes and Roger Bannister. Coe and Holmes have two Olympic gold medals each and Bannister will forever be the first man on earth to run a mile in less than four minutes. One Lord, one Dame and a Sir. It's amazing what you can achieve when you put your trainers on.

So I did. On Sunday 23 April 2017, I put my (new) trainers on and ran 26.2 miles from Greenwich to the Mall.

This should be cause for celebration, right? So how comes the track I couldn't get out of my head was 'A Foggy Day (in London Town)'[3] – chosen by Sebastian Coe – self-confessed lover of jazz – as his most treasured track on the first time he appeared on the show.

It wasn't a foggy day. In fact, conditions were pretty much perfect and the atmosphere amazing. It was like being at a carnival, crowds lining the route, cheering my name (because – top tip – I had it printed on my T-shirt). The song I *should* have had in my head was Vangelis' 'Chariots of Fire'.[4]

For the first half, I felt pretty good. As I crossed Tower Bridge onto the north side of the Thames, I was even confident about achieving my target time of under five hours. Then the four hours, forty-five minute race pacer passed me. I couldn't keep up and felt a pang of regret. Shortly after this the five-hour pacer passed me as well. I struggled for the rest of the race, eventually crossing the finishing line in five hours, twenty-seven minutes. OK, it wasn't 'plus six', but a rhinoceros (female) pipped me on the home straight.

Perhaps you'll be reading this and thinking: what are you moaning about, woman? You've told us you're an unlikely athlete. Who cares in what time? And, of course, you'd be right. I am shit at sport. And who cares but me? Except, the thing is, I knew I could finish it. I knew because I can do endurance. I'd already done several things to prove that over the previous decade. So my time had become the important goal: running a marathon in under five hours was what I told myself I needed to do in order to face the hard times I'd been going through recently. So that's why it felt like a foggy day in London town (although Louis Armstrong and Ella Fitzgerald do sing about it beautifully – with Oscar Peterson on the piano).

In the week following the marathon, I found myself thinking a lot about Kelly Holmes. Her life story is remarkable. She was cast away in 2006 with the programme's third presenter Sue Lawley. Kelly tells Sue that she knew from an early age that she wanted to do something significant in her life. Born in the same year as me (1970), Kelly was fourteen when she decided that thing was to become Olympic Champion, after watching Sebastian Coe win gold at the Los Angeles games in 1984. I bet she was the 'sporty' one in school. But it would take her twenty years from that moment to do it. Of course, it can take a long time to reach the top of a career but in sport that sort of duration is highly unusual, especially in athletics. Kelly was constantly plagued by injury and eventually, she admits, it got the better of her and she went through a very dark period in which she started to cut herself with scissors. She says she was losing hope: *'You just think: why? I'm trying everything and why does someone keep knocking me down?'*

Kelly describes the moment when she finally achieved her dream as being like a fairytale. She was in her room at the 2004 games in Athens when suddenly she felt a big gust of wind swoop around her neck, even though the doors and windows were closed. She says it felt like it was a sign she was going to do something special. And she did. Gold. Double gold. First in the 800 metres, and then in the 1,500 metres, too. She not only achieved her dream, she surpassed it, and the delight, gratitude and something that sounds a bit like disbelief is unmistakable in her voice as she talks about it.

Then Sue asks: *'And what do you think the gust of wind was?'*

Kelly replies: *'Well, I really don't know, I just don't know. I just believe that after over all the years I've been fighting, something said: right it's her time.'*

My heart heaved at these words as I thought of all the years I had been fighting, all the times that something said, 'It's not your time.' Like Kelly, I have often wondered who keeps knocking me down.

Whoever it was, they couldn't even let me run a marathon in under five hours.

For a while I seriously thought about running a marathon again. I thought about Kelly's perseverance. Although Jimmy Carr had said that working out what you want in life is the hard bit and getting it is relatively easy, this wasn't the case for her. She worked out what she wanted early on; getting it was what proved hard.

I think I am more Kelly than Jimmy – nothing I have wanted in life has ever been easy. But I didn't even know what I wanted anymore – except going to a desert island with my eight discs. But that was just a quip.

Wasn't it?

I found myself asking Jimmy's question again: *'What do I want?'*

There was a time when I knew the answer to that immediately.

'What do I want?'

Still nothing.

But I did know this: running a marathon in under five hours wasn't *really* it.

4

*'I just wanted to go somewhere different
and try different things.'*

–**Paul Weller, 2007**

———————

On *that* day – the one that changed the trajectory of my life – after Jimmy Carr but before Clive James – I also listened to the British historian Sir Antony Beevor on *Desert Island Discs*. I was struck by the fact that he chose not one but two Blondie records to take to his island. He was also very keen on trumpets and chose four classical tracks in which they featured. If I were going to the island, I would *never* choose the same artist twice – that seemed like a waste. I'd want to mix up my instruments too. But that was Sir Antony's prerogative – he was going, not me – and his passion for Blondie had reminded me of Nicky, my first love.

Nicky was seven when I was eleven. We would dance together in the school playground to Blondie's 'Sunday Girl'.[5] I chose the song and taught him the words and the moves. But it was Nicky who taught me how good it feels when boys are interested in you, and how much it hurts when they get bored and want to play football instead.

I was thirteen when I fell in love again – this time with Matthew. I was wearing a burgundy T-shirt when he kissed me and put his hand down my top to the sound of George Michael singing 'Careless Whisper'.[6] Sadly, though, we weren't careless whispering for very long. I played hard to get the next day at our local adventure playground. It backfired badly, and the song that ultimately defined us was Joe Jackson's 'Is She Really Going Out with Him?'[7] Matthew had moved on.

In fact, thinking about it, all the men in my life have come with their music. After Nicky and Matthew came Dan. And Dan came with David Bowie.[8] He bought me Bowie's album *Scary Monsters (and Super Creeps)*, and inscribed on the cover a line from 'Ashes to Ashes', a song from side one: *'I'm happy, hope you're happy too'*. Dan had gone to great effort to copy the same spindly typeface as the album's title. And we were happy – for nearly four years – until I ended it on a payphone from my university halls of residence. Over twenty years later, I wrote to Dan on the day that David Bowie died and said that I would never forget how much he loved him. Dan wrote back: *'. . . I did . . . I still do . . . rarely a week goes by when I don't listen to one of his albums.'* If Dan were ever on *Desert Island Discs* maybe he would choose more than one David Bowie song, just like Sir Antony Beevor did with Blondie and the trumpets. For some people, one musician, one instrument, one genre of music defines them.

But as important as Dan was to me, the time came when I needed to look for another piece of music in my life.

Blondie, Joe Jackson and David Bowie could all be contenders for my *Desert Island Discs* list of eight. But it would be very hard for me to choose between any of them and my other childhood love, Paul Weller.[9] The Style Council were the first band I saw live and I'm pretty sure on that occasion he was singing 'You're The Best Thing' to me, even though we hadn't met yet. Later, I did meet him. Once. On a CND protest march where I got him to sign the sleeve of my top. I treasured that top for years. I'd make my mum wash it with the sleeve hanging over the baby blue bowl she hand-cleaned our clothes in, so it didn't get wet and the ink fade.

Paul Weller was on *Desert Island Discs* in 2007, interviewed by Kirsty. I remember hearing the episode live, sitting on the bedroom floor one Sunday morning, sorting out the washing. For years that was my day and location of choice for listening to the programme. I've never been the best washer of clothes. I would let them pile up in a corner like some bacterial growth for the joy of moths until I totally ran out of clean knickers. I'm also possibly one of the only women in the world who is terrible at multitasking. But one day, I discovered that sorting out the washing and listening to *Desert Island Discs* seemed to be one of the few combinations I could manage. If I worked slowly it could take me a whole show to divide the pile into blacks, colours and whites, then change the sheets on the bed and pick up all the items hung on the floor. For several years, Sunday mornings with *Desert Island Discs* and dirty washing was my 'happy place'.

The one thing I still recall from that programme was Paul Weller talking about his decision to break up his first band, The Jam, at the height of their success. I didn't know the story before and it surprised me. Kirsty asks Paul what his dad – who was the band's manager – said when he told him what he was going to do. Paul tells her he can't repeat the words because they wouldn't be broadcastable on the radio – basically his dad thought he was crazy.

'And what was the future that you saw that you didn't want?' Kirsty asks.

'I didn't know and I didn't want to see one to be honest. I just wanted to go somewhere different and try different things . . .' It was after this that he formed The Style Council and in doing so

alienated many of his Jam fans who hated the new group and its music.

Paul Weller's bravery inspires me. I've always wanted to be someone who goes somewhere different and tries different things. Maybe his transition from The Jam to The Style Council is a bit like my own version of trying to become 'sporty' after years of being 'arty'. I reckon The Jam was Paul Weller's sporty side: fast, boisterous. And The Style Council was his arty side: slower, more soulful. He'd gone Jam then Style Council – and in my youth I was definitely a Style Council girl. But then life happened and you could say, I had to go out and find my Jam.

5

*'She's travelled with me all my life
and is a rock in my life.'*

–Kay Mellor, 2017

———————

Six months on from the marathon and I was still listening to *Desert Island Discs* on my headphones – in fact, I'd invested in a new pair. Those big ones that people used to wear before fashion became small. And then re-emerged when fashion decided big was better again. I loved my new headphones – they shut out the world, although I did nearly get run over soon after I got them. A police car stopped and told me not to walk in the road but they're just too big for narrow pavements.

I'd stopped running though. Five hours, twenty-seven minutes will be forever imprinted on my soul/sole. I listened while I was walking to places. I've decided that human beings were born to walk not run – with apologies to Bruce Springsteen[10] (cast away in 2016, great episode). Walking and listening on my big headphones was fast becoming a rival to *Desert Island Discs* and dirty washing.

One evening I was walking home from Kentish Town, having just had my nails done (my regular game of colour roulette, not always won), and decided to listen to the TV scriptwriter Kay Mellor, interviewed by Kirsty in October 2017. Towards the end of the programme she chooses a track to remind her of her best friend, Linda. Kay says: *'She's the one I met at school when I was three years old with her big curly hair, who I absolutely adore. I've known her all my life and she's travelled with me all my life and is a rock in my life.'*

I've noticed over the years that friendship doesn't get much of a musical look-in on *Desert Island Discs*. With only eight tracks allowed, people's parents, partners and children generally take preference in their musical memories. So Kay's choice for Linda is unusual and it made me think of the two friends who have travelled with me all my life. I wouldn't want to be without them on a desert island either.

First there's Beth – like Kay and Linda we've known each other since we were three. And the music that will always remind me of her is Gilbert & Sullivan's opera *The Pirates of Penzance*[11] – in which I played Frederick to her Mabel in Gospel Oak Primary School – the same school where I danced with Nicky to Blondie.

If I'm honest it's always been a slight source of discomfort to me that whenever I was cast in school plays, I was given the part of a man. It started with the Angel Gabriel in the infant nativity, although admittedly I didn't know that Angel Gabriel was a man because I thought all angels were female. (Aren't they? Calling Robbie Williams!)[12] But now I realise it initiated a trend. It wasn't even as if it was necessary – there were plenty of boys around who could have donned a white sheet and a cardboard halo, or later played a young man indentured to a band of pirates.

That said, the one compensation about being cast as Frederick in *The Pirates of Penzance* was that my dearest and oldest friend, Beth, was my love interest, Mabel. Beth would never be cast as a man. She's far too beautiful and who couldn't love her when she sang 'Poor Wandering One' while I was 'Pour, Oh Pour(ing) the Pirate Sherry'.

I guess I could also take our audition piece to my island, 'Whiskey in the Jar' – the Irish folk song about a highwayman betrayed by his wife (before you ask, *yes*, I was the highwayman). It was a rather bizarre choice of song for two ten-year olds from London in the 1970s but our music teacher, Mr Hayes, taught us all sorts of repertoire. I remember sitting in assembly belting out The Beatles and 'Right Said Fred',[13] loud enough to make Bernard Cribbins proud.

Beth is more musical than me. In 'Poor Wandering One', she could reach the necessary top D. When we were sixteen, she went to Japan to study with the violin guru Dr Shinichi Suzuki and then went on to do a music degree. And in our twenties, she'd say stuff like: 'I love Benjamin Britten' and I'd think 'Who he?'

The other friend who has travelled with me all my life and I'd want to take to a desert island is Tara. We met at secondary school – where our assembly singing was a bit more formal. Think 'The Lord is My Shepherd'[14] rather than John, Paul, George and Ringo.

Tara is the opposite of me. She's the sort of girl who was the first to be picked for rounders at school and was in the county athletics team. She moved to Australia when we were in our twenties and became a fire fighter and a national champion surfboat rower. I could never compete with her strength and her speed and when you've got a friend like that it doesn't really encourage you to get out of breath. But as teenagers we set out on life in Tracy Chapman's 'Fast Car'[15] and have been driving together ever since.

The moment I hear the opening bars of that track I'm taken back to the little cream Mini we bought together when we were seventeen (and I crashed on Day 1), to setting the world to rights with a Silk Cut and a glass of Lambrusco, to back-packing together in Greece after our A levels. I can't hear Mikis Theodorakis' theme tune to *Zorba the Greek*[16] without thinking about Tara too, but even though that might be a more suitable track for desert island-hopping, I'd take a fast car with her in it playing instead.

As I walked and listened (and occasionally nearly got run over – clearly I've never been safe on the roads), musical memories were coming back to me that I hadn't thought about for years. It just confirmed how hard it was to choose your ultimate list of eight tracks. But as a committed list lover, I still wanted to try.

The song that Kay Mellor picks for her Linda is 'Ain't No Mountain High Enough' – the Diana Ross version, not the original sung by Marvin Gaye and Tammi Terrell. While it wasn't on the album my sister bought for my seventh birthday, so doesn't bring her to my mind, I did start thinking about the lyrics – how no mountain would be unclimbable if the person who Diana is singing to ever needed her. I guess that's what Kay is saying to Linda. And I feel the same about my friends Beth and Tara. So, I smiled as I listened, and thought about music and mountains. I could feel a new plan starting to formulate.

6

'I'd just sit there quite quietly with my lovely records,
and think about my very, very happy life.'

–Peter Bull, 1983

———————

I will never be as musical as Beth, but I did learn the piano
and the oboe when I was little. The problem is that like most
children I didn't practice enough. I played second oboe in the
school orchestra but that was mainly because there wasn't
much competition for the place. When it got to the difficult
bits, I'd have to put the reed in my mouth and pretend to
blow. I was better on the piano – but at a basic level, it requires
less skill than a woodwind instrument. My piano teacher was
called Roger and he used to come to our house on a Tuesday
evening and I would hastily play through my pieces for the
only time all week just before he arrived. I think Roger liked
me though. Not in *that* way. There were no hands on knees
while I was at the piano stool. I didn't practise enough but I
felt the music deeply. I think that's what he liked.

Our house in north London was originally bought and
owned by my paternal grandparents. I never knew them – they
both died long before I was born. My uncle and aunt (and
cousins) lived in the basement of the house, my mum and dad
(and my sister and me) on the ground floor. The top two floors

were let out to lodgers. It was an unconventional set-up and when I describe it people often say: *'how bohemian'*, which I think is basically the equivalent of saying 'how lovely' in the arty circles I generally move in. But as a child, I didn't like it and longed to get away. I wanted to travel the world and then I wanted my own home, with my own family.

My uncle and aunt were both formidable figures who did the discipline in our house when I was growing up. I remember once having a row with them, and then immediately going upstairs to the piano and pouring my heart into playing Beethoven's 'Moonlight Sonata'.[17] Within hours, they capitulated and gave me what I wanted. It was the Beethoven that did it! I've always been a strategist and I've also always known the power of music to move people – which is probably why I love *Desert Island Discs*. My family were all Radio 4 listeners but when I was a child this was the only programme that they liked which I liked too.

And after *that* day – the one where this story began when I realised all I wanted to do was write my list of eight tracks to take to a desert island – I started to explore the back catalogue of the BBC archive in detail for the first time. I found out that the programme premiered on 29 January 1942, with Roy Plomley, who devised it, presenting. His first guest was the actor and comedian Vic Oliver, who was also married to Winston Churchill's[18] daughter. The first piece of music taken to the island was Frederick Chopin's Etude in C Minor[19] (Chopin was also in my piano repertoire and equally effective for getting what I wanted).

The sixteenth guest, I discovered, was the comic actress Beatrice Lillie[20] who had been a friend of my late grandmother's. Family legend has it that when my grandmother was invited to go to Buckingham Palace with my uncle to collect the military honours that had been bestowed on him for his service during the Second World War, Beatrice wanted to buy her a new outfit from Selfridges on Oxford Street. My grandmother would have none of it – she wasn't one for dressing up, not even for royalty. She's reported to have said somewhat defiantly: *'I will go as I am.'*

Sadly, Beatrice Lillie's episode hasn't survived because in the early days of *Desert Island Discs* the radio broadcasts weren't recorded. However, after a little more research, I discovered that the actress had been chosen by several castaways as one of their discs. And that's how I wound up listening to actor Peter Bull – a man I'd never heard of – who chose one of her songs when he appeared on the show in 1983. I listened to his episode on a long walk through Regent's Park (a week before the marathon when I was officially 'tapering' – the practice of reducing your running to give your legs a rest before the big day. And let me tell you there's nothing better than the taper).

It turns out Beatrice Lillie was Peter Bull's friend too, and he had me captivated from the beginning when he describes going to a party dressed as a tomato. But, for a while, I did wonder how he had made it onto the show because his career seemed so full of failure. He tells Roy – without any false modesty – that he was sacked from the Royal Shakespeare Company because his Sir Toby Belch was more burp than belch; cut out of his first Hollywood movie because his American accent wasn't up to scratch; and once when he was cast in a musical, he was relegated to the chorus and asked just to mouth the words. However, it transpires he was in the first UK production of Samuel Beckett's seminal play *Waiting for Godot* – although even this was a challenging experience. The play was denigrated at first; audiences would shout at the actors and walk out. Peter describes a night when a lady sitting in the front row said loudly: *'I do wish the fat one would go.'* She was referring to him.

He observes simply: *'You know, it's a bit disconcerting while you're at it.'*

I already adore him but, even more so after Roy introduces the subject of teddy bears. Peter collects them, and he declares proudly that they are a great comfort to him and he isn't ashamed to admit it. In fact, I was expecting him to take his favourite teddy as his luxury but he doesn't. He takes a crystal ball, explaining he's just opened an astrology shop (although what he really wanted was a gypsy tearoom). Then the piece of music he saves from the waves is a Greek song by Λόλα Τσακίρη called 'Slowly Slowly'[21] because he just happens to own a piece of land on a remote Greek island which he bought for £40 and loves going to. He comments that it's good experience for his desert island. When Roy asks whether he could build a shelter, Peter says he doesn't think he'll try: *'I think I'd just sit there quite quietly with my lovely records, and think about my very, very happy life.'* He repeats the word *'very'* twice.

I listened to the programme walking through the park in the dappled light of its central avenue of trees, then through the rose garden not yet in bloom and past the lake with the black swan. All these things seemed more beautiful to me than usual as I got to know a stranger who followed his passions and who seemed to be able to wear the disappointments of life so lightly. Something I myself seemed to find so difficult to do.

When I reached my destination – breakfast on Marylebone High Street – I opened my laptop and googled Peter Bull. I figured he must be getting really old now but maybe I could find a way of contacting him to tell him how much I'd loved his interview. So it was a shock to see that just a few months after appearing on the show he had died suddenly of a massive heart attack. I felt a rush of sadness. He had seemed so alive. But then I felt something else. Something hard to describe. Maybe I'll just call it 'gratitude' – to whatever strange and marvellous thing it was that had led me to listen to Peter Bull on a sunny morning tapering through Regent's Park. Because he had reminded me that life is always lighter when you find and follow your passions, and that we should try and enjoy it as much as we can because death is always following close behind.

'Slowly, slowly' I thought about Peter Bull while I ate my eggs. I had inadvertently discovered what has become one of my favourite *Desert Island Discs* episodes of all time.

7

'I think all of us see what moves our parents.'
–Lin-Manuel Miranda, 2019

———————

My dad wanted to be an actor. He was always the first at a party to get up to dance and sing. He adored the Great American Songbook and musicals. In fact 'Sit Down, You're Rockin' the Boat' from *Guys and Dolls*[22] is him in a song. If you already have a picture in your head of Nicely-Nicely Johnson, the character who sings this show-stopping number, then let that be your image of my dad. But if this doesn't immediately conjour anything up then you could also *Google* Stubby Kaye, the actor who originated the role on stage and film, and then you'll understand.

My dad was born in the house where I grew up – and he lived there for the whole of his life until he died, aged ninety-two. He wasn't a man who ventured on adventures. He was a man consumed with regret for what he hadn't been and done. In fact 'My Father,'[23] the wistful song by Judy Collins which several castaways have chosen to remind them of their dads, could also be a song for him.

Just like Nicely-Nicely, my dad was a small-time gambling man. He didn't do dice, but he loved a bet on the horses and towards the end of his life became obsessed with winning the

National Lottery. Every week he would write out the winning numbers and pore over them for hours, convinced there was a system that he had a chance of working out. He never staked more than a couple of pounds, and he never won much more than that either, but he left behind rows and rows of numbers neatly written out.

And just like Nicely-Nicely, my dad was also a small-time drinker and a big-time eater. There was nothing he loved more than a full English breakfast and, later in the day, a half a pint of bitter. In fact, 'Food, Glorious Food' from the musical *Oliver!*[24] was another of his favourites that also sums him up in a song. For the time it took him to finish his plate and sink his glass, my dad was a contented man. Then he'd take to the stage with delight to sing you a song. But he'd break off after a few bars to bemoan the fact that he should have been an actor and tell you all the things he wished he'd done.

The composer Lin-Manuel Miranda – creator of the musical hit *Hamilton*[25] – was cast away by the show's fifth presenter, Lauren Laverne, who took over from Kirsty. His first track choice is Liza Minelli singing 'Cabaret'[26] from Kander and Ebb's musical of the same name. He says it makes him think of his mother, in their Subaru, turning the dial all the way up to the top and screaming along with Liza. That's how he fell in love with musical theatre: *'I think all of us see what moves our parents,'* he says.

I saw what moved my dad and that's probably why I fell in love with the theatre too. It might also be why the only thing I really like about exercise is what I can consume on the sofa – guilt-free – when it's over. Like my dad, I love food and booze.

If I were going to choose a song from my youth to remind me of my dad, then I would also need something for my mum. The problem is that Mum, unlike Dad, never really showed any interest in music. When I was a child the only thing she seemed to care about was the Bible. She'd take me to church on Sunday (my dad never came, declaring mischievously he didn't believe in God – like Nicely-Nicely, he was always rocking the boat to heaven). I wasn't sure I believed in God either and I hated sitting through the boring service. I also thought it was unfair I didn't get to taste the bread and wine during Communion. I only ever got pressed on the head.

Thinking about it, there isn't even a hymn that reminds me of my mum. Which is strange really because I do remember her singing loudly in church, an embarrassment as she had such a terrible voice. I would try to hush her, even though I felt bad doing it – I knew from an early age that my mum struggled with life and here at least she was doing something with gusto.

My mum's struggles were different from my dad's. He knew what his sadness was. He spoke it. She didn't. That made it harder to understand. I think she thought God had the answers. She's in her nineties now and one of the by-products of returning to my childhood home is that I've become her main carer. She hardly ever goes to church these days and if I ask her whether she thinks God exists, she'll say simply: 'God's within you.' I don't think she believes he's waiting for her in heaven with my dad.

Although there isn't a hymn that I associate with my mum, the one thing I would often and still hear her reciting by heart is 'The Lord's Prayer'.[27] Thanks to *Desert Island Discs*, I now know that it was set to music by the American musician Albert Hay Malotte. One idle afternoon, I decided to play my mum a selection of versions that have been chosen on the show to see which she liked best: Gracie Fields, Mahalia Jackson, Perry Como and the Roger Wagner Chorale. She seemed bemused at this game at first – she said she'd never heard it sung before and it was difficult to make out the words. But that's partly because she's going deaf.

We listened to all four versions and my mum held her head close to the sound in thought. I was secretly hoping she'd choose the Mahalia Jackson version. Mahalia was taken by the writer Maya Angelou when she was on *Desert Island Discs*, although Maya didn't take 'The Lord's Prayer' – she took 'How Great Thou Art',[28] and saved it from the waves. I love Maya Angelou. She's the person who makes me think it's OK to write autobiography. (This is my third and she wrote seven. I promise I won't write seven. I know I'm not Maya Angelou.)

Of course, my mum didn't deliver on the Maya/Mahalia front. She's her own woman. Instead she started singing along with Perry Como, her voice still terribly out of tune. And I was immediately taken back to standing next to her in church. But this time I didn't want to hush her. I wanted her to keep singing with Perry.

Forever and ever. Amen.

8

'This song is about the fact that not everything you do will succeed, and that's OK.'

–Emma Thompson, 2010

—————————

When I was a young child I wanted to be an actress. It's hard to know now whether that was just about pleasing my dad or whether it was what I really wanted to do. But I dreamt of performing on the West End stage. I wanted to be in a musical with kids – like *Annie*.[29] Or *Bugsy Malone*.[30] I knew playing Annie herself was a long shot (for one thing I wasn't a redhead and didn't know anything about wigs). In *Bugsy Malone*, I would ideally have liked to play Blousey, the girl who ends up with the man and the happy ending, but I was more like Tallulah – strong and slightly sad. Although if I had been cast, I probably wouldn't have been either, I probably would have been the baddy, Dandy Dan.

The thing is, I've always been tall. Tall and sturdy. I remember when I was a teenager, the boys I used to hang around with out of school recorded this infamous tape on which they described each of the girls in our group. We used to congregate at the Lido on Hampstead Heath – by the pool when the weather was good, outside on the steps when it wasn't. And the girls got hold of the tape and listened to it on the steps and I remember the boy I fancied at the time describing me as 'horsey'. It's not the sort of thing you forget. *Horsey*. I can't run like a horse that's for sure. I'm definitely not a racehorse.

That said, I think I have always been good at knowing the things I am, and the things I'm not. The actress Emma Thompson attended the same secondary school as me and I followed in her footsteps onto our school stage (playing a policeman, a cad, etc.). But I knew I wasn't as good an actress as she was and there wasn't going to be an Oscar with my name on it. And that's because I'm only really good at playing me. So I adjusted my acting dreams quite early on and decided I wanted to 'run' a theatre instead.

Emma Thompson was cast away in 2010. It's a great interview. I first listened to it in my *Desert Island Discs* and dirty washing days. She's thoughtful and truthful, witty and warm – all the elements that make for the best type of guest. She talks openly about her first marriage breakdown and about going through miscarriages and IVF, and says it's the 'activist' in her that believes it's important to talk publicly about such stuff because they are shared experiences. She immediately made me feel less alone. And although I'd never heard it before, I loved her seventh song choice, 'Some of Your Planes' by Richard Lumsden[31] – which she says helped her through her toughest times. The lyrics are so true: *'Some of your planes will come down—'*. Or, as Emma says: *'Not everything you do will succeed.'*

So my dream of starring on a West End stage never materialised. But I did do everything that the pupils at my suffragette-founded comprehensive, Camden School for Girls, were told to do. I went to university, climbed the career ladder and by my early thirties I was Chief Executive of one of London's largest theatres, the Lyric Hammersmith. But to be honest, I blame my school a bit for encouraging me to think I could 'have it all' – that terrible phrase that has become a noose for women. Just like that other terrible phrase 'career woman' – which is never used in the masculine – you never hear 'career man'. I'm not sure it *is* possible to have it all. At least it wasn't for me. Some of my planes just never got off the ground.

I ran the Lyric for ten years. It was one of my acts of endurance. It made my dad proud. Then he died and I resigned. The very last show we produced while I was there was *Bugsy Malone*. There are pictures of me on the internet standing next to its creator, Alan Parker, in a sparkly dress. He's jockey-sized next to me. I hope I don't look too horsey.

Alan Parker was cast away twice. He was the first guest of Michael Parkinson, the show's second presenter, in 1986. And then he was cast away again fourteen years later by Sue Lawley. He says that each of his films have been written in the spirit of a piece of music, even though that piece of music might never feature in the film itself. When he went to the island first he asked to take a song by Roger Daltrey (he of The Who) called 'When the Music Stops'.[32] He says that within it there is the most beautiful love story that one day he wants to write. If he takes it with him to the island then maybe he'll get round to doing it there.

I think this story I'm writing is a love story as much as it's an adventure. After I've written it, I intend to go to a desert island with my discs and then the music can stop. But, for now . . . here's a shortlist of songs from my childhood that are all contenders for my ultimate list of eight tracks.

My Songs of Childhood Shortlist

1. Diana Ross and the Supremes: 'Baby Love' – for my sister.

2. Joe Jackson: 'Is She Really Going Out With Him' – with apologies to Blondie and Bowie but I think this is the song that ultimately defines young love for me.

3. The Style Council: 'My Ever Changing Moods' – my favourite song on my favourite album, *Café Bleu*.

4. Gilbert & Sullivan: 'Pour, Oh Pour the Pirate Sherry', from *The Pirates of Penzance* – even though my dear friend, Beth – playing Mabel – wasn't in this number it will still remind me of her and I'll be able to sing-a-long on the island and not have to try and reach a top D.

5. Tracy Chapman: 'Fast Car' – for my dear friend, Tara, and our cream Mini.

6. Frank Loesser: 'Sit Down, You're Rockin' the Boat', from *Guys and Dolls* – for my dad.

7. The Lord's Prayer – spoken, not sung, although I'm still smiling at the thought of my mum and Perry Como.

8. Alan Parker and Paul Williams: 'You Give a Little Love', from *Bugsy Malone* – Alan Parker wrote and directed the film; Paul Williams composed the music. I adore every song on the soundtrack but I'm choosing the final number just because it all comes back to love.

PS: Sorry to Beethoven for not choosing 'Moonlight Sonata'. But Beethoven will be back.

Songs of Home

1. Ralph McTell: 'Streets of London'

2. Billy Bragg: 'Jerusalem'

3. 'Amazing Grace' played by the Scots Dragoon Guards

4. A mash up of 'Myfanwy' and 'Danny Boy/Londonderry Air'

5. Kate Bush: 'Wuthering Heights'

6. Charlie Rich: 'I Feel Like Going Home'

7. Flanagan and Allen: 'Underneath the Arches'

8. Eric Coates: 'By the Sleepy Lagoon'

   (Hidden Track)

1

'And what a reminder of home would be those
wonderful bells peeling.'

–James Blades, 1977

———————

'Our house'[33] stands on London clay at the top of
Parliament Hill. It's one of the highest points in the city.
If you carry on past the end of our street, you come out onto
Hampstead Heath and then it's less than a five-minute walk to
the summit – which when I was little was the destination for
tobogganing in the snow, flying kites in the wind and watching
the fireworks on Bonfire Night and New Year's Eve.

There's a lovely legend that the hill got its name because
Guy Fawkes planned to watch the explosion of the Houses of
Parliament from here in 1605 – his failed 'Gunpowder Plot'.
Now every sunny summer weekend, you will find hoards of
people up there eating picnics, smoking dope and looking at
the view. There are plenty of other places on the heath that they
could have all to themselves but instead they crowd together
on the summit. That's because summits are special. It's not just
the vista (there are better skylines to be had on the heath), it's
that the climb-destination-view-combo makes people glow.

I've always had a complex relationship with the four stories
of red Victorian brick that I grew up in. I agree with Burt

45

Bacharach that 'a house is *not* a home'.[34] So, if you'd told my childhood self that, in my mid-forties, I would find myself living back there again as a single woman caring for my elderly mother, I would have considered that a failure of everything I left the house to achieve.

However, if a house is not my home then London is. The sprawling mass of grey streets and coloured Tube lines is where I was born – in University College Hospital on Gower Street on 21 November 1970, the day after the newly formed Women's Liberation Movement famously stormed the Miss World Contest at the Royal Albert Hall.

Apparently my dad – who was at my birth – said to the midwife as I arrived: *'Here comes a future Miss World'* (in a display of first-time-father-love-at-first-sight).

And she snapped back: *'Surely you want more for your daughter than that?'*

My dad always told me this story with uninjured pride – because he knew the midwife was right. And I think he felt his mother (my grandmother) wouldn't have approved either, and he adored his mother, so his telling of the story was a way of putting that right.

One of the things I will always credit the London Marathon for is how much better I got to know the city while training for it. (*Note to runners everywhere: avoid Hampstead Heath (it's hilly); approach the Regent's Canal with caution (fabulously flat but crazy cycler-ry). A loop round Hyde Park and Kensington Gardens or along the Thames Path is probably better, still flat but more runner-friendly.*) Contrary to what you might think, London is also full of trees. In fact, it has a higher percentage of public green space than most of the cities of the world. It's not as good as Moscow. But it's better than New York.

As I started to listen to more of the back catalogue of *Desert Island Discs*, I was introduced to several songs about London that I'd never heard before. In fact I created a 'London Playlist' – which I now listen to when I'm gadding about town.

It opens with the chimes of 'Big Ben',[35] which the percussionist James Blades chose when he was on the show. James (*Jimmy* to his friends) says they will remind him of home and I reckon he must know a thing or two about good bells when he hears them. I've also got Maxine Daniels singing 'The London I Love'[36] and Noel Coward with his 'London Pride'.[37] Plus all my own personal favourites. 'Waterloo Sunset' by the Kinks[38] – which is about London's best bridge (on account of the fact it offers the best view of London there is). And Flanagan and Allen's 'Maybe It's Because I'm a Londoner'[39] – because I do love London so.

However, there is another song of theirs that I like more which reminds me of home just as much. I used to think it was a song about London, but apparently it's not. It's about the city of Derby. I know this because I looked it up on Wikipedia the other day. It doesn't matter though – it's not really London which makes the song sing home to me (read on, you'll see). Suffice to say though, I've had to take it off my 'London Playlist', although it's still on my shortlist of 'Songs of Home'. I need both lists in my life. They do different things.

I think perhaps my all-time favourite London song is Ralph McTell's 'Streets of London'[40] – which we also sung in my primary school. And even though it's a song about the poverty and loneliness which exists in the city, I love it for its beautiful melody. And as I walked the streets of London with *Desert Island Discs* in my ears, I stopped feeling lonely. I love London. '*I love the bones of it*' (as actress Helen McCrory told Lauren on the show in 2020). '*It's the sun in my sky*' (as writer Peter Ackroyd told Kirsty in 2012). I think everyone needs a place that feels like home and a song that takes them there when they're away.

Like when they're on a desert island.

Or a mountain.

2

*'I think there's a sense of destiny inside of people
that tells them what they are.'*

–Alan Plater, 1989

———————————

When I moved back to our house in Hampstead, it felt as if everyone had died or deserted it. The only people left were me and my mum. But the ghosts of my family were still around. I could feel them, and I started to meet them wherever I went.

After the London Marathon – in the time I now think of as my cooling down period – I started regularly heading out onto the heath with my headphones, and revisited all the places I'd known as a child. The climbing tree which seemed no longer climbable; the hollow tree which was just as I remembered it, except the bark was even smoother now from thirty more years of children clambering inside. I walked past the ponds and said hello to the ducks, apologising for not being able to bring bread anymore because it's not good for them. And up to Kenwood House and its bridge that's not a bridge. I'm kind of amazed it's still there and hasn't fallen down (the bridge, not Kenwood House).

The cool down from a big physical challenge is nearly as good as the taper. Not quite because it's always tinged with the inevitable anti-climax that comes on the completion of a goal, especially when you didn't quite score the goal you wanted. But it was good to focus on something else and I liked walking (much more than running). I'm sure it's what human beings were designed to do over long distances – move slow. I'd also found my perfect walking companion – the back catalogue of *Desert Island Discs*.

In fact, I had been inspired to create a new list – of all the episodes I had listened to since that life-changing one with Jimmy Carr (him being Number One on the list). I created an Excel spreadsheet (the original list lover's software) and wrote the name of the castaway, their profession, the date and location I'd listened to them. Then I listed their luxury, book and the track they had saved from the waves.

I also created another list with all eight tracks that they'd chosen so I could start to sort and see which artists and music were most popular over the years. I was becoming a walking database of *Desert Island Disc* trivia. Now I can tell you who took and saved four minutes and thirty-three seconds of silence as one of their tracks (although you could hear the castaway's tummy rumbling in the quiet).[41] Or who took and saved a song about new potatoes (great choice – I love a potato myself, preferably with butter or fried).[42]

I also created a Word document and wrote notes on each castaway – the things they said that had inspired me, the name of artists or tracks they'd introduced me to and I liked. And then with my favourite track choices from each episode, I started to form different playlists. Like my 'London Playlist'.

Sometimes a castaway would remind me of a piece of music that I knew but had completely forgotten about, or introduced me to something I had never heard before and loved immediately. I'd download it, add it to a playlist. I have so many now that Apple Music must have me down as a lifer.

Some of these new and refound songs have even risen up as contenders for my own ultimate eight tracks to take to my desert island, which has made the process of compiling my definitive list even harder. But I started having fun with it. That's what mattered.

One day out walking on Hampstead Heath I met the writer Alan Plater (not in person, on *Desert Island Discs*). Following on from what I now call my 'Beatrice Lillie Adventure' (the one which had introduced me to Peter Bull), I went on a 'Dylan Thomas Adventure' – listening to every castaway who had taken him to their island in track or book form.[43] This was a much bigger adventure than my Beatrice Lillie one because Dylan Thomas is the most chosen writer on the show, bar Shakespeare.[44] It took several months to complete it, but I was keen to do it because Dylan Thomas was also a friend of my grandmother's. Like him, she was a poet. Her name was Anna Wickham but you probably won't have heard of her because how many twentieth-century female poets have you heard of? Except Sylvia Plath. And she's not Sylvia Plath. Apparently, my grandmother once said to someone who snubbed her at a party: *'I may be a minor poet but I am a major woman.'*

In the 1930s, before the outbreak of war, our house in Hampstead was one of the centres of London's creative life. At the front door there was a sign which read:

> *Stabling for Poets, Painters and their Executives.*
> *Saddle your Pegasus here. Creative moods respected.*
> *Meals at all times.*

And the kitchen walls were covered in the musings of some of the greatest writers of the day. Dylan Thomas visited often: he and my grandmother had drunken arguments which ended in her throwing him out of the house. My grandmother, like Thomas, was a big drinker and known all over London for her bar fights.

Alan Plater appeared on *Desert Island Discs* in 1989, interviewed by Sue – episode number 73 on my list. I was walking past the 'Stone of Free Speech', just up from the café and the bandstand, when he chose Dylan Thomas reciting his own poem 'Do Not Go Gentle Into That Good Night' as the second track on his list of eight. I used to like going to the bandstand on Sunday afternoons much more than church on Sunday mornings. Mainly because there was ice cream living in the café nearby. Alan says he heard the poem on the radio when he was a teenager and it was his first and most powerful lesson in the strength of the spoken word – he calls it his *'Damascus Road Choice'*. He became a writer himself and there's a bit in the programme that I love where he says that he always wears his grandfather's signet ring and his dad's retirement watch so that when he's writing at the typewriter he's got two generations sitting on his left arm saying: *'Don't tell any lies, Alan, because we're watching.'*

And towards the end of the show, Alan says something else which basically took my Jimmy Carr moment on Sloane Street and raised it by ten. Musing on the fact that the miracle of nature is that every human being comes out differently, he says: *'I think there's a sense of destiny inside of people that tells them what they are.'*

To which Sue enquires: *'It's just that you have to be able to hear the voice when it calls?'*

And without missing a beat Alan replies: *'And have the courage to respond. That's the tough bit.'*

It made me think about how life had brought me back to the house that my grandparents bought in 1919: the house where my dad was born and lived until he died aged ninety-two because he didn't have the courage to leave it. Two generations of my family now gone – but through the walls and the floors and the windows and the doors they seemed to be saying: *'Don't tell any lies, Jessica, because we're watching. You know what your destiny is. Have the courage to respond.'*

The time had come to leave my streets of London and head higher than Parliament Hill.

3

'The mountains wept tears for me that day.
It never stopped raining.'

–Alfred Wainwright, 1988

———————

I arrived at The Swan in Grasmere at 7 p.m. I'd taken the train to 'Oxenholme Lake District' – which seems an odd name for a station. Why does it need the Lake District suffix when other stations in the area don't? It's as if it's got an inferiority complex – like it needs to tell the Keswicks and the Kendals that it's in the Lake District too.

Originally built in the seventeenth century as a coaching inn, The Swan is one of the oldest and most famous hotels in the Lakes, mentioned in Wordsworth's poem 'The Waggoner' – *'Who does not know the famous Swan?'*. And I do, but not because of Wordsworth,[45] but because of my grandfather – Patrick Hepburn – the man who bought the house which I struggle to call home – who died on the fells on Christmas Day 1929. I went to the Lakes to retrace his final footsteps and then climb Scafell Pike – England's highest mountain – for the first time.

The Swan has changed since Wordsworth and my grandfather's days. It's now carpeted throughout and has instant coffee on the bedroom tea tray – but it's still low-ceilinged, with winding corridors and nooks which whisper its history.

According to my grandfather's obituaries, on Christmas Eve he left his office in Lincoln's Inn in London – he was a solicitor by trade – and travelled north by train. He arrived at the Swan at 7 a.m. on Christmas morning and had a bit of breakfast. The hotel proprietor said that he spent a few hours pacing around restlessly until at around 1 p.m., when he asked for some sandwiches and said that he was going to walk to Borrowdale – a distance of about 10 miles cross-country. He was advised not to go – the weather was bad, the hour getting late. Yet in spite of this he still set out, dressed in a knickerbocker suit with a small rucksack, wearing shoes that were by all accounts too light for the journey.

The morning after my own arrival, I set out for Borrowdale myself. It was early November but defying both the season and the Lakes' reputation for rain, the day was clear and there were glimpses of blue in the sky and the sun even made an appearance. On a day like this, my grandfather might have been fine.

The route up the Easedale valley is direct and straightforward and I listened to the Lakes legend Alfred Wainwright along the way. Wainwright – whose guidebooks are the companion of any serious walker in the Lakes – was eighty-one when he was on the show and, at the beginning of the episode, he admits to music being an irritation not an inspiration for him – he says what he'd much rather hear is the *sound of the earth*.

The first time he went to the Lake District, Alfred says he couldn't believe that such beauty existed. There weren't many walkers at the time so he had the fells to himself. Nor were there any guidebooks, so he started to write them. He worked on them every night. He became obsessed. Nothing mattered except getting them done and eventually his wife walked out on him, taking the dog. He doesn't blame her for this; he says he doesn't know how she stuck it for thirty odd years.

When he'd finished the first guide, a local printer agreed to do a run on tick and let him pay off the bill as he sold them. He sold them all, and ultimately millons more. Then Sue asks him what makes a good walker and Alfred says that he doesn't think there's any art to it. But on the fells you have to take care to watch where you're putting your feet. There's a temptation to look around and that's the way accidents happen.

My grandfather was a frequenter to the fells long before Wainwright. But why he was there on Christmas Day in 1929 in an agitated state and not at home with his family in London is a mystery. My grandparents were known to have a fractious marriage. He didn't approve of her writing poetry and their struggle over this was the subject of a lot of what she wrote. Maybe their relationship was on the rocks at the time. Or maybe he just wanted to be alone in the Lakes that he loved on his few days off from a job that, by all accounts, he loathed.

As I reached Greenup Edge and began the descent into the Langstrath Valley towards the mountain stream known as Greenup Ghylll, where my grandfather was found dead on Boxing Day by a local shepherd, a man appeared from below. We stopped for a moment to exchange fell pleasantries. He said the way ahead was steep and hazardous: he didn't mind climbing up but he wouldn't want to climb down. Regardless, I continued my descent feeling sure that this was where my grandfather died and that I needed to retrace his steps. Maybe he looked at the view when he shouldn't; maybe the light was fading because he set out too late; maybe the weather was harsh not clear like it was that day. Back in those times, there was probably snow. Nobody but him will ever know, we only know the ending. A body in a stream at the foot of the fell.

Writing this now after everything that would happen to me on this journey later feels prescient. Almost spooky. It's as if the ghost of my grandfather has been with me throughout.

When the shepherd found my grandfather's body, it was almost hidden by big boulders, only his hand visible. At the inquest, the coroner's verdict was a case of 'accidental death by drowning'. He noted that the fells get a bad name because people do foolish things; and that this was an occasion where a man took a risk which very few people who know them well would have taken.

Alfred Wainwright knew them intimately. He didn't die on the fells. He died three years after his appearance on *Desert Island Discs* from a heart attack. He had stopped walking in his late seventies, when his eyesight started to fail. In the most moving moment of the whole episode, he says: *'The last time that I did a fell walk it was a pouring wet day. And I was stumbling and slipping all over the place and it wasn't because my glasses were misted, it was because I couldn't see where I was putting my feet. And that's the last time I did a fell walk. And the mountains wept tears for me that day. It never stopped raining.'*

Despite the treacherous trail, I reached Borrowdale and St Andrew's Church where my grandfather is buried in the graveyard. I doubt there's a more pleasing place to rest. He was fifty-six years old when he died. My dad had just turned ten. I've always felt there's a double cruelty to the story – the first blow that he wasn't with his dad on Christmas Day; the second that on that same day he lost him forever.

My dad would often lament that if he'd had the opportunity to know his father better then his life might have been different. He could only recall one memory of him, which was his father taking him to the Lord Mayor's Show. I was lucky enough to know my dad. I had him until I was forty-one and have many memories. He was never a keen walker himself (bar a short stroll to the Magdala pub at the bottom of our hill). Yet, I think a small part of the reason for this whole journey has been to reclaim the fells for them both.

I spent the night at the Scafell Hotel in Borrowdale and the next day I climbed Scafell Pike. I looked at my feet all the way, and listened to the sound of the earth.

4

I feel I have an 'Englishness' which I've inherited from my grandfather, and I like it.

Over the last eighty years, Edward Elgar[46] has been the most chosen English classical composer on *Desert Island Discs* – for many castaways he reminds them of home. Some have taken his Proms anthem 'Land of Hope and Glory' (now a somewhat controversial choice because of its association with Britain's colonial past). Others say his music evokes for them the English countryside, his *Enigma Variations* being a particularly popular choice, especially the ninth variation known as 'Nimrod'. In 2011, social entrepreneur Victor Adebowale chose it in honour of his father who he says was invited to come to Britain from Nigeria to *'add value'*. But when he did he faced significant prejudice. Victor says he associates the pain and struggle of the piece with his dad. It's a poignant reminder that Elgar and Englishness is not 'white', although the reason I like the piece myself is because it says: 'Green' – rolling Malvern hills of them. I went there to walk. I got the train to Worcester and then the bus to Tenbury Wells and then I followed my

Ordnance Survey map to a fantastic restaurant called Pensons. There's no public transport – you have to drive or walk to get there. I ate and spent the night, and the next day I went to 'The Firs' – Elgar's birthplace in Lower Broadheath – and spent five hours discovering everything there is to know about the most famous of all English composers.

The other classical composer often chosen for his 'Englishness' is Ralph Vaughan Williams.[47] When there was a vote to choose listeners' favourite 100 tracks, his piece 'The Lark Ascending' beat Elgar's *Enigma Variations* to the top spot. And the more I have listened to the show, the more I've fallen in love with his music. So one weekend, I went and visited his childhood home – Leith Hill Place, just below Leith Hill Tower in Surrey, which is officially the highest point in south-east England. As I walked up the long road from Dorking I listened to a playlist I had created of Vaughan Williams' greatest hits and as the light dappled through the trees and his version of 'Greensleeves' tinkled in my ears, I threw my arms up in joy and said: *'This is my England'.*

Gustav Holst – who sounds German but isn't – is another English composer who seems to invoke people's patriotism, particularly his suite *The Planets*.[48] Of the seven movements, most people take 'Jupiter: the Bringer of Jollity' which he also set to the poem 'I Vow To Thee, My Country' by Cecil Spring Rice. It's perhaps a more palatable patriotic piece than Elgar's 'Land of Hope and Glory' or that other paean of patriotism, 'Rule Britannia!', which has been selected by some guests, including Princess Margaret in a Roy Plomley classic from 1981.

Holst's music especially makes me think of my grandfather who, as well as being a hill walker, was an amateur astronomer, a world expert on the planet Saturn and Secretary of The

Hampstead Observatory. He would often stay up all night with a telescope watching the stars.

One day, I was on Hampstead Heath and over halfway through listening to an episode with the musicologist Imogen Holst when I realised she was Gustav Holst's daughter. Roy hadn't mentioned her famous father in his introduction (being of the 'needs none' school of interviewing) and it wasn't until she got to her sixth track, a record of her father conducting the Planets suite in 1926, that I realised the connection. Imogen says she's chosen a few bars from 'Saturn: the Bringer of Old Age' which was Holst's favourite movement. I smiled and thought that my grandfather Patrick would have liked that – Saturn being his favourite planet too. The recording was made just three years before my grandfather died on the fells and I decided then that if I were compiling his *Desert Island Discs* list, he would have this on it. Imogen specifically chooses the bit moving towards the climax of the piece where old age approaches in a loud dissonant clashing of bells; then gradually these fade and the music becomes lighter as if a resistance to death becomes reconciliation. I thought about how the bells must have crashed when my grandfather slipped and fell and how the music would have become lighter when he stopped and was still. The landscape resettling and resuming its natural music. The babble of the ghyll.

After I'd listened to Imogen's episode, I went and visited the house where her father was born in Cheltenham, and then her own house in Aldeburgh, Suffolk – where she lived for many years when she was working with the composer Benjamin Britten.[49] I visited his Red House nearby too – the one he shared with his partner, singer Peter Pears. It's an amazing place – full of art and atmosphere.

Britten is the second most chosen English composer on *Desert Island Discs* (after Elgar and just ahead of Vaughan

Williams) and because of this adventure I can now confidently hold a conversation with my dear friend, Beth, about how *Peter Grimes* is my favourite of his operas. That's because it includes another 'Home Song' for me. Although it's nothing to do with England, it's for the same reason that I like that Flanagan and Allen song I mentioned . . . I promise I'll explain about this soon but for now I'll just say I walked the 'Sailors' Path' from Aldeburgh to Snape when I was in Suffolk. And that's a kind of clue.

My own favourite England home song, though, would be 'Jerusalem'[50] – words by the poet William Blake set to music by the composer Hubert Parry. Some people have called it an alternative UK national anthem. My favourite version is sung by Billy Bragg.[51] I was a big Billy Bragg fan when I was younger. I wanted Paul Weller as a lover, but I wanted Billy Bragg to be my brother. I first heard him while I was standing in a tent at Glastonbury and from that muddy moment on, I idolised him for his poetry and politics. Many years later, he came to my theatre for a meeting (not with me, with some colleagues). He actually sat in my chair. I came back from an appointment elsewhere and could see him in my office chatting away. My lovely assistant said I should go in and say 'hello'. But I didn't dare. I didn't want to risk any 'Levi Stubbs' Tears'.

I then went on a 'Jerusalem Adventure' and listened to every castaway who had chosen it and was struck by all the different associations the song has for people. For many it does say 'England' but it's also chosen because of its association with the labour movement, the women's institute, with Israel – because it is, after all, a song about a city in the Middle East. No one has picked Billy Bragg's version of 'Jerusalem' yet, but he has been on several castaways' lists although he's never been a cast away himself.

The comedian Jo Brand chose 'Waiting for the Great Leap Forwards', describing Billy as the perfect Englishman. I listened to Jo walking home from a shopping trip to Sainsbury's in Camden town. She says that these days it's difficult for English people to say they like being English because *'it always has connotations of racism, little Englanderishness and Daily Mailness'*. But Billy Bragg manages to *'achieve being English without sounding like he wants to send everyone back home'*.

I have an 'Englishness' which I've inherited from my grandfather, and I like it. So I've created an 'England Playlist' for whenever I take an English country walk. It opens with Vaughan Williams' 'Lark Ascending' and then it breaks into Billy Bragg.

5

———————

To Wales. To Snowdon. To the second highest mountain in the UK.

My first ever two-day trip there didn't start well. When I got to Bangor on the train, I made a misstep and ended up going to Llandudno rather than Llanberis. I blame the Welsh comedian Rob Brydon for this. I was listening to his *Desert Island Discs* at the time and his last three tracks reminded me of someone I was trying to forget. And while I was remembering what I was trying to forget, I forgot what I needed to remember – which is why I ended up going to Llandudno on the coast, and not Llanberis at the foot of Snowdon.

As I was staring out the window, trying to make sense of what had gone wrong in my life, the sea suddenly surprised me and I realised something had gone very wrong again. By the time I got back to Bangor, it was late and dark so I took a taxi to Llanberis which set me back thirty quid. The driver was sweet though: he said it didn't help that there were so many towns in Wales that start with a 'Double L'. But I still blame Rob. I only forgave him because he took Dylan Thomas' collected works as his book, and I like people who take Dylan

Thomas because of my familial connection. Rob says he wants it to remind him of Wales – which seemed a good way to begin at the beginning of my Welsh adventure.

If Wales is your home and you are compiling a list of tracks to remind you of it, then Dylan Thomas is definitely a contender. Although Rob took him in book form, most people have taken recordings of his poems and prose. 'Under Milk Wood' is the most popular, and if you have it narrated by the Welsh actor Richard Burton in the iconic 1954 BBC radio recording, you get two for the price of one.

I was nearing the end of my 'Dylan Thomas Adventure' when I went to Snowdon (which I should probably call by its Welsh name – Yr Wyddfa – so please forgive me if you're Welsh and reading this). Before leaving home I'd googled 'famous Welsh people' and cross-referenced them with interviewees on the show. My list of listening also included Tom Jones (I couldn't take Shirley Bassey because her episode is unrecorded) and actor Anthony Hopkins (I couldn't take Catherine Zeta-Jones because she's defected to Hollywood and never been on it). I also had a bunch of people I'd never heard of before.

The next morning, after a Welsh breakfast, I set off. Boots on feet. Headphones on ears. In case, you're not yet a seasoned mountaineer, like I wasn't, let me just make it clear that Scafell Pike in the Lake District and Snowdon in Wales are not at all like Parliament Hill in London. Forget five minutes to the summit, you're going to need at least five hours, although on Snowdon if you're really not feeling it you can take the train. Both have an up that feels like forever, and a down that can feel just as bad. A lot of 'real mountaineers' will tell you they prefer ascending mountains because descending them can be so hard on the legs. On balance though, I prefer the coming down because you can relax a bit knowing you're over halfway and the delights of bath and booze are coming.

After getting my glow on Snowdon's summit, on the final bit of the down when it had started to rain, I listened to the organist and choir director George Guest in an episode from 1976. He was a Welsh somebody who I'd never heard of before. I had got through quite a few episodes by then and my head was pounding from all the listening, all the learning. And if I'm honest, I didn't have particularly high hopes for George. That's probably why I'd left him to the end. The first track he chooses is a traditional Welsh folk song called 'Cyfri'r Geifr'[52] which translates as 'Counting the Goats', and its sound in my ears came as a shock because it was unlike anything I'd ever heard before. He describes it as a 'quick patter song' and there was something about its strange and rhythmic sounds, increasing in speed with each verse which in the rain felt transcendent.

In fact, in the end I enjoyed everything about this episode – the gentle lilt of George's Welsh accent, the stories and thinking behind each track choice, and I started hoping he was going to choose Dylan Thomas as his book just to make my day on Snowdon perfect. But he doesn't, he choses the complete works of Saunders Lewis – who I'd never heard of either. George says he's one of the most important writers of the twentieth century who has been cruelly neglected. I admit, I was still a bit disappointed. I really wanted him to choose Dylan Thomas.

The next morning when I was writing up my list of listening in bed at the B&B in Llanberis (not Llandudno), I googled Saunders Lewis. I discovered he was a Welsh nationalist and one of the most prominent figures of Welsh language literature who was nominated for a Nobel Prize in 1970 (the year I was born). Somehow it then felt like it was the perfect conclusion to my Snowdon/Yr Wyddfa(!) adventure – sent to me by whoever created those green hills. If I was Welsh, 'Cyfri'r Geifr' would definitely make the shortlist for my songs of home. I'd sit on my island and count the goats.

6

'If you love the world, then you hurt more.
But you also rejoice more.'

–Gillian Clarke, 2013

_____

Other Welsh home songs are available. You could also have 'We'll Keep a Welcome'[53] – in the hillside, for all Wales-loving walkers, including Shirley Bassey. Or Tom Jones singing 'Green, Green Grass of Home'.[54] Or a Welsh Male Voice Choir with 'Land of My Fathers' (the unofficial Welsh National Anthem).[55] Or my own personal favourite, 'Myfanwy',[56] another of my *Desert Island Discs* discoveries. The singer Bryn Terfel called it *'one of the most beautiful, haunting pieces of music that has ever come out of Wales'*, when he was on the show in 2003, and I agree. It was also chosen by the former Welsh National Poet Gillian Clarke. In fact, I think it was Gillian who first introduced it to me.

I didn't actually listen to her episode in Wales. I listened to her in London on Hampstead Heath when I was on a 'Poetry Adventure' – a continued voyage around my grandmother. It was a significant episode for me. Shortly before appearing on the show in 2013, Gillian had written a poem about five-year-old April Jones from Machynlleth in Wales who had been abducted and killed. And Kirsty asks her why she writes poetry about melancholic subjects like murder and suicide. Gillian says that your heart hurts when you hear about a suicide; and it hurts at people suffering at the death of a little girl. But it's a heart that hurts because it loves the world and if you love the world then you hurt more, but you also rejoice more.

I stopped walking when she said this, momentarily stunned, and took a breath.

My grandmother killed herself. In our house on Parliament Hill. She hanged herself in the French windows leading out into the garden. I only found this out when I was a teenager and after that I could never get the image out of my head – of her hanging there. That and the fact that my dad was the person who found her. I remember asking him what he did when he saw her and he simply said that he went out into the street and howled like a dog. After that my dad never found the courage to leave the house where he'd lost and found his mother – which is why I grew up there. The ripple effect of that loss radiating downwards into a new generation. And what made me stop walking when I heard Gillian's words was they felt so true of my dad. Maybe he hurt so much because he also loved the world. His pleasure in musicals and singing, food and drink, even his love of the Lottery, was how he rejoiced.

On Snowdon I also listened to another episode which made me think of my grandmother's suicide – it was with the Welsh Rugby referee Nigel Owens from 2017. It's an extraordinary episode so I was glad I listened on the ascent because it really helped take my mind off the long climb up. He's such a lovely man and talks about how he struggled with the shame of being gay for years, so much so that he tried to take his own life when he was in his early twenties. He left a note and went up into the mountains above his house in Mynydd Cerrig in South Wales with a shotgun and took an overdose. It was only because he slipped into a coma before he could pull the trigger that he survived. He says that refereeing the Rugby World Cup final in front of 85,000 people, with millions more watching at home scrutinising every decision he made, was nothing compared to the challenge of accepting who he was. And accepting who he was saved his life.

Kirsty says in response to this: *'Nigel I have nothing to ask, and nothing to add, I just want you to tell me about this next piece of music.'*

And with that Nigel introduces Bryn Fon's *'Angen y Gan',*[57] which he translates from Welsh into English as 'I Need The Song'. Then he explains the lyrics: *'Turn to the song and the song will get you through'* and it did get him through the darkest time in his life. At the end of the show this is the song Nigel saves from the waves.

I think I am someone who loves the world but hurts more. Like Gillian. Like Nigel. Like my grandmother. And my dad. But walking and listening to *Desert Island Discs* had started to help get me through. Music and mountains were gradually becoming entwined in my feet and my head and my heart, and I know that doesn't make this your usual kind of adventure story. But come with me, and rejoice.

PS. If you're unaccustomed to climbing mountains then here's something to know. If you summit Snowdon on Day 1, and then you try Tryfan on Day 2, you won't be able to walk down the stairs to the platform at Bangor, and the moment the train starts rolling eastwards, your head will start nodding southwards. Then you'll get to the end of your episode of Desert Island Discs *and the closing bars of the show's theme tune – 'By the Sleepy Lagoon'[58] – will wake you up, and you'll realise you're going to have to listen to that episode all over again.*

7

'I love Scotland . . . I will play "Amazing Grace"
like so loud. It's not hip-hop but it rocks me.'

–Lemn Sissay, 2015

I've collected a whole bunch of classic 'Home Songs' now for almost everywhere in the UK. So if you need inspiration, then I'm the woman to call.

I went to Northern Ireland to give a talk and walked for hours up and down the River Foyle in the rain listening to all the Irish castaways I could find. From that time, I've decided that my favourite Irish Home Song is 'Danny Boy'[59] (although when I told an Irish friend this the other day, she responded disdainfully: *'You do know that was written by an Englishman?'*). It's also called 'The Londonderry Air', which is the Irish folk tune that the Englishman Frederic Weatherly set his lyrics to. I now call it 'Danny Boy's Derry Air'. My talk was in Derry/Londonderry where I learnt the difference between the two. But if it's still too Anglican a choice for you, then how about the triple Irish whammy of the Chieftans and James Galway's version of 'Carrickfergus'?[60] Or here's another good one: Val Doonican singing 'Paddy McGinty's Goat'.[61] (Especially if you enjoyed the George Guest goats from before.)

If you're a Liverpudlian – then the obvious choice is The Beatles or Gerry and the Pacemakers' 'You'll Never Walk Alone' (although technically this is not a scouse song, it's from the Rodgers and Hammerstein's musical *Carousel*).[62] It's still legitimate Liverpool though. If you're a Mancunian, then there's obviously anything Oasis or Joy Division/New Order.[63] And if you're more north-east than north-west there's the 'Blaydon Races',[64] the Geordie unofficial anthem, or if you're just more Yorkshire then there's 'On Ilkla Moor Baht 'at'.[65]

But my own personal favourite northern song is by a girl from south-east London – Kate Bush and her 'Wuthering Heights'.[66] I love it not because of the northern boy who broke my heart and set me off on this whole adventure; but because of the north London girl you'll find out on the moors in her big headphones.

As my adventure progressed and I started walking and listening across the UK, I increasingly felt that the whole of the country was home to me. I wasn't just an English Londoner. Part of me felt Welsh, part of me Irish. Even before I went tramping across heathered moorland, part of me was Yorkshire (I went to university in Leeds). And part of me was from Newcastle (the city of my first job in theatre – where I started out as an usher selling interval ice creams).

And then there's the massive part of me that's Scottish. According to my dad, our ancestors came from the Borders. He would proudly proclaim they were cattle raiders who 'hopped over the burn' with their stolen goods inspiring my surname 'Hep-burn'. I've no idea whether this is true, but I liked believing my dad's stories and I've long felt a calling to the Borders and beyond. However, it wasn't until this adventure started that I went to the Highlands in winter, and I'm still recovering from the shock. I just had no idea how much snow there is up there between the months of December and March.

In fact, I think most people living in the south of the UK are oblivious to what it's like at the top of the map in winter. If they weren't, there's no way the whole of the English transport network would grind to a stop whenever's there's a smattering of snow. Or, even more embarrassingly, allow it to become headline news. People would be too ashamed to even mention it if they knew how much snow Scotland gets. So if you've never been to the Highlands in the winter then you should at least know this: professional mountaineers say it's one of the best places on earth to train for Everest.

During the course of this adventure, I went many times and my 'Scotland Playlist' now has more tracks than my English one. Many of the show's Scottish castaways have helped me compile it, introducing me to music I'd never heard of like 'The Skye Boat Song'[67] and reminding me of things I had like Mendelssohn's 'Hebrides Overture'.[68] But it's the Mancunian poet Lemn Sissay who I'll always credit with giving me what has become my ultimate Scottish home song – 'Amazing Grace' played on the bagpipes by the Scots Dragoon Guards.[69]

Lemn was another of my 'Poetry Adventure' listens. On Hampstead Heath. And, yes, before you think it, I do know the lyrics of 'Amazing Grace' were written by an Englishman, but in the bagpipe version there aren't any words. I was just walking up past the Ice House – the small stone circular building which is about as wintery as the heath gets – when Lemn chose this track for magical memories of holidays with his Scottish grandparents. He plays it loud with the roof of his car (a little Peugot) down. *It's not hip-hop but it rocks me,* he says laughing. Then the bagpipes soared, and they rocked me too as I reached Whitestone Pond, which is officially the highest point of Hampstead Heath. I closed my eyes and imagined I was on Ben Nevis.

*

One Scottish castaway in particular made me think deeply about 'home' – and that was the actor David Tennant.

The first track he chooses for his list is by a band with another definitive Scottish sound – The Proclaimers.[70] I adore their music – they wrote one of the best songs about long-distance walking ever written as well as the glorious 'Sunshine Over Leith'. Anyone who can write a song about your heart being broken that is bold enough to say 'sorrow' four times in a row is making my kind of music.

And yet it wasn't The Proclaimers that made me think about home. It was David's seventh track choice, Tim Minchin's 'White Wine in the Sun'.[71] The song is a love letter to Tim's baby daughter, telling her that when she grows up, wherever she is in the world, she'll always find her brothers and her sisters and her aunts and her uncles and her grandparents and her cousins and her dad and her mum drinking white wine in the sun on Christmas day (presumably in Australia where Tim's from). I guess it could make for a good Australian Home Song, along with 'Waltzing Matilda'[72] or 'Tie Me Kangaroo Down, Sport'.[73] David says that both times he's heard it sung live, it's left him in floods of tears: *'It starts off as what seems to be a funny song before becoming just a simple, heartfelt ballad to the importance of family.'* Right at the end of the programme, when David has to save one of his songs from the waves, he says he wasn't planning on it, but that he'll take the Tim Minchin because he's suddenly feeling sentimental.

That's what *Desert Island Discs* does to people.

I guess the pinnacle point I'm trying to make here is that sometimes a house is not a home and sometimes a place isn't either. Sometimes your home is something else entirely. And I think Tim Minchin's song is essentially about 'family as home', and that's why David Tennant saved it and let The Proclaimers get washed away by the waves.

8

'So this song is called "I Feel Like Going Home".'

—Tim Minchin, 2012

Tim Minchin's 'White Wine in the Sun' is not one of my 'Home Songs'. It's on my 'Sad Songs Playlist' because it makes me cry – for the same but different reasons that it does David Tennant. A family as home is not something I seem to have been able to create for myself and that's a sadness. And yet, at the same time, the sadness did create another sort of home for me – water, specifically the sea. But in the absence of salt, any natural open water will do. Rivers, lakes, ponds, puddles. I'm not fussy.

Back in the first chapter of this section of my story, I mentioned another Flanagan and Allen song that reminds of me home. (I like a book that makes it easy to reference back because I'm a reader myself and have lost a lot of life looking through pages for characters and plot twists I'd forgotten about.) That song is 'Underneath the Arches' and the reason is *the sea*. If you know the song, you might be confused because it's about homeless men living under railway bridges in the land-locked English city of Derby. But midway through, Bud (who was Flanagan) and Chesney (who was Allen) break-off from singing to read the headlines of a newspaper from 1926: *'Gertrude Ederle. Eighteen-year-old American. First woman to swim the Channel.'* And *that* is the sea reference for you.

My dad was a big Flanagan and Allen fan, so I grew up listening to them. He loved music hall as much as he loved musicals. But it wasn't until I was on this adventure and heard the song again that it meant something more. Back in Songs of Childhood, Chapter 3, when I ran the London Marathon, I told you I was disappointed in my time. I told you it was because I knew I could do endurance. That I'd done several things to prove it . . . Well, one of those things is that in 2015, two years before I ran from Greenwich to the Mall, I swam the Channel – the 21 miles from England to France. Gertrude Ederle was the first woman to do it. I was the 491st woman.

I promise I'm not being disingenuous when I describe myself as an 'unlikely athlete'. I'm not a very good swimmer, like I'm not a very good runner. A few laps in my local pool or a splash in the shallows on holiday was all I'd swum for most of my adult life. But I did enjoy swimming as a little girl, even though I was always at the back and everyone used to joke that my best stroke was breast stroke legs. And once, when I failed to get into the school swimming team, I remember consoling my dad by telling him that it didn't matter because I was going to swim the English Channel instead (it was always harder managing his disappointment than my own). Thinking about it now, maybe I even got that idea from my dad listening to 'Underneath the Arches'. But the key thing is I didn't think about the Channel or, indeed, the song again for over thirty years. Not until my dad died. Not until I'd been through eleven rounds of unsuccessful IVF in a bid to create my own family (that was another of my endurance tests).

I lost a decade of my life to 'Project Baby'. All those pictures of me standing smiling alongside famous directors and actors at press nights in the theatre were a lie. Behind the smiles, I was shooting up fertility drugs and miscarrying in the public toilets. For a long time nobody knew – not even my closest family and friends, let alone colleagues. I was so ashamed my body could not do what every other woman seemingly found so easy to do. And I was appalled with myself that after women like my grandmother had fought so hard for me to become more than a wife and mother, my brilliant career just wasn't enough. In fact, my deepest fear was I would never be happy if I couldn't have my own children.

Then, when I turned forty-three – after yet another unsuccessful cycle of treatment – I decided I needed to do something completely different. That thing became the English Channel, an attempt to swim my way out of sadness.

To begin with I had no idea what was involved. I didn't know how long it would take or anything about the cold. And if you want to be an official 'Channel Swimmer' you can't wear a wetsuit. That's because 'A Shopshire Lad',[74] Captain Matthew Webb, the first man man to make the crossing in 1875, didn't wear one, and you have to adhere to the same conditions today.

After two years of hard training – which included learning to swim the crawl, navigating myself in open water and with-standing the cold – I miraculously managed to do it. It took me 17 hours and 44 minutes. So running for 5 hours and 27 minutes (my marathon time) was nothing. When my feet left the pebbles on 'Dover Beach'[75] and touched the sand in France, it changed my life forever. In fact, it felt like my own version of giving birth – euphoria eclipsing all the pain. And from that moment on, water became a home to me. It makes me feel safe and loved, which is what home does. It doesn't mean I want to swim the Channel again. Like I said, a puddle is enough.

There's been so much music written about water and there are pieces that objectively I like even more than 'Underneath the Arches', although this will always have a special place in my heart. Like I love the 'Sea Interludes' from Benjamin Britten's opera *Peter Grimes* (Songs of Home, Chapter 4 for that reference – remember my Sailors' Path clue?). I started regularly going down to the Channel coastline and walking along the cliffs – eastwards from Dover to Deal, or westwards from Eastbourne to Seaford, up and down the Seven Sisters (both excellent training for mountains, if you need it). I would look at the sea and listen to my 'Sea Playlist'. It felt like coming home.

The English Channel healed my heart in so many ways but after I'd swum it my heart got broken again (*sorrow, sorrow, sorrow, sorrow*). The family I had so wanted to create was already minus a baby, and then it became minus a man. I left my job. I moved back to my childhood home alone. I ran the London Marathon in the hope that it would help. But it wasn't enough. I needed something bigger to save me from the waves of life again. Something, it turned out, that was 8,848 metres high and eighty years of episodes wide . . .

And so a new adventure emerged, which I will always trace back to Jimmy Carr on Sloane Street. He asked me what I wanted, and I decided what I *'really, really wanted'*[76] was this: to listen to every episode of my favourite radio programme while walking to the top of the world. An Everest of listening needed an Everest-sized mountain to climb. And at the end of it, I decided I would write my definitive list of eight tracks and go and relax on a desert island. Somewhere like Madonna's 'La Isla Bonita'[77] or Harry Belafonte's 'Island in the Sun.'[78]

My Songs of Home Shortlist

1. Ralph McTell: 'Streets of London' – because I love the bones of this song, it's the sun in my sky.

2. Billy Bragg: 'Jerusalem' – because he makes it OK for me to like being English.

3. 'Amazing Grace' played by the Scots Dragoon Guards – because it rocks me and I love Scotland.

4. A mash up of 'Myfanwy' and 'Danny Boy's Derry Air' – because I love Wales and Ireland too.

5. Kate Bush: 'Wuthering Heights' – just because.

6. Charlie Rich: 'I Feel Like Going Home'[79] – it was Tim Minchin who introduced me to this great track when he was cast away himself. In fact, it could be a definitive home song for whoever you are, wherever you're from, whatever home is to you. Have a listen and see what you think – maybe while sipping a 'white wine in the sun'. This, by the way, is not only on my 'Sad Songs Playlist', it is on my 'Christmas Playlist' too – although come December, I do prefer snow and a wee dram to the beach and a glass of Chardonnay.

7. Flanagan and Allen: 'Underneath the Arches' – because of Gertrude Ederle who made the sea a possible home for me.

8. Eric Coates: 'By the Sleepy Lagoon' – which has been the theme tune of *Desert Island Discs* since it first aired in 1942. The show, like the sea, has started to feel like a home to me. And a sleepy lagoon after the wide-awake English Channel is the cosiest of homes there could be.

And this list has got a hidden track – Dire Straits' 'Brothers In Arms'. But it's too soon to explain why. We've got to get to the top of the world first. Then we can go home.

(If You Still Believe in) Love Songs

1. Nick or Nina
2. Marlene or Mozart
3. Rodgers and Hammerstein
4. Rachmaninov
5. Joni Mitchell
6. Marvin Gaye
7. Bette Midler
8. Carole or Cole/King vs King

1

'Because at the end of everything love is the answer.
So I'm going to go with a love song.'

–Anne-Marie Duff, 2018

————————————

It was March 2018 – one year after all this started – and I was on a train from Manchester travelling back to London. I'd been speaking at an event there. I didn't have what felt like a 'proper job' anymore. I'd written two books (in which I went from telling no one about my infertility to telling the world). I had also founded a small arts festival – Fertility Fest – about the science of making (and not making) babies. But I dreaded being asked the question, 'What do you do?' because none of this earnt me much money or felt like a legitimate job. It was almost as bad as that other party question I had hated for years: 'Do you have children?' No. I didn't have any dependents and had moved back to live with my mum so I didn't have a mortgage or rent to pay either. And that meant I could make this new adventure my vocation.

I put on Anne-Marie Duff. My episode 310. Her luxury: beautiful underwear. Her book: George Eliot's *Mill on the Floss*. And the track she saves from the waves: Nick Cave and the Bad Seeds' 'Love Letter'.[80] It's only because of Anne-Marie that I started creating a playlist of 'Love Songs'. Although I call it my '(If You Still Believe in) Love Songs Playlist'.

Kirsty was interviewing and midway in she risks a loaded question and asks what's the toughest thing Anne-Marie has been through in her life, not 'on stage' but 'off stage'. And Anne-Marie admits candidly that she's been through a lot recently – it's been all over the papers – clearly referring to the breakdown of her marriage. But, she says, however awful it feels, she also believes you've got to get your face out of the dirt and feel the sun on it, and that's what she tries to do.

'And so tell me then about this next piece of music,' Kirsty says.

And Anne-Marie replies: *'I am a hopeless romantic. You know, I am. And that means sometimes I'll burn with pain as well as burn with desire. I will. Because that's the nature of opening your heart up to someone else. But I refuse to believe that there's a scarcity. I absolutely believe that there is love, and more love.'*

And then 'Love Letter' starts to play with its piano, and violins, and the gravelly yearning of Nick Cave's voice as Anne-Marie says these final words: *'Because it tells me, yeah, I can love, and I can hurt, but I can love again.'* And I looked out of the train window, rain lashing at the speeding glass, and thought for the first time in a long time it might be possible to still believe in love.

The eighth and last track Anne-Marie chooses on the show is by the Irish singer–songwriter Declan O'Rourke. It's a track to celebrate her heritage. Her mum's from Donegal and her dad's from Meath, but they met in London's Shepherd's Bush in the 1960s, *'as a lot of Irish people did'.* She says that one of the things she adores about the Irish culture is the tradition of standing up in a group of people and singing a story-song unaccompanied – it alarms all her nerve endings. And the song she chooses Declan to sing is 'Marrying the Sea (Til Death Do Us Part)',[81] which I've never heard before but immediately think must go on my 'Sea Playlist'.

At the end of Anne-Marie's episode, she mulls for a moment on which record she'll save from the waves and then says suddenly in a rush: *'I'm going to go with "Love Letter". Because at the end of everything love is the answer. So I'm going to go with a love song.'*

As I've said, Anne-Marie Duff is the inspiration behind my '(If You Still Believe in) Love Songs Playlist' and it will always include a love letter from Nick Cave and a love story from Declan O'Rourke. Like Anne-Marie, I want to believe that I can love, and I can hurt, and I can love again. And if I can't, well, at least I'm married to the sea. *Till death do us part.*

2

'If it's not frightening then it doesn't change you.'
–Christina Dodwell, 1994

———————

Back then (in 2018), I wasn't anywhere near being married to the mountains yet. We had only just started dating and I wasn't sure it would last. I'd rashly made the decision to walk to the top of the world and only then started learning exactly what was involved. While 'real mountaineers' might tell you that Everest isn't the hardest or most dangerous mountain to climb, it would take me well beyond my comfort zone. I didn't know how my body would perform at high altitude. I'd never put on a helmet and harness and tied myself to a rope. I didn't even know what crampons were, let alone crossed a crevasse wearing them.

But I did have form in taking on big physical and mental endurance challenges that I knew nothing about. I'd swum the English Channel. I'd run the London Marathon. I'd proved I could do long, and cold. I don't mind the long but I still hate the cold. One of my mottos in life is that you can never be too cosy. I'll put the central heating on at the beginning of September if you'll let me. But at least in the mountains you can wear more than a swimming costume. You've got fleece, and PrimaLoft, and like all good geese you've got down.

Soon after my mountainous musical challenge evolved, I listened to (nearly) all the men who had climbed Everest who had been on *Desert Island Discs* – Bear Grylls, Chris Bonington, Conrad Anker, David Hempleman-Adams, Ranulph Fiennes (although Fiennes didn't summit until after he was cast away). I wasn't able to listen to Eric Shipton and John Morris who had both been involved in the early pioneering attempts to climb the mountain. Their episodes had been lost but I still listed their choices on my spreadsheet. The only person I didn't listen to immediately was Edmund Hillary – the first man along with Sherpa Tenzing Norgay – to reach the top of the world on 29 May 1953. I decided to save him until just before I was due to go. That seemed like good poetry to me. I may have wanted to reclaim the hills for my grandfather, but I am my grandmother's granddaughter too.

I admired all the male mountaineers who I listened to but I also knew I was not of their species. They were sporty. They relished risk and danger. Most of them had lived their whole lives in nature. But I hoped that there might be a place in the mountains for another type of adventurer who had a different sort of relationship with nature. She might not be the fittest or the fastest. The thing she might most like about training is what she's listening to on her headphones and compiling playlists. And even though there are men out there who think she should probably stay at home walking the streets of London – because I've met them – I hoped the mountains would be still happy to welcome her.

All I knew about Jan Morris was she was a writer and she'd been on the show twice – once with Roy in 1983, once with Sue in 2002. I always tried to listen in chronological order if a person has appeared on the show more than once. I like to see how their musical life story has evolved. So I put on Roy's episode first. He introduces her, briefly, as Ms Morris and a little way in I thought I must have misheard the 'Ms' because they start talking about Jan's days as a choirboy called James. I was confused. But I was getting tired. I had already done a lot of mileage that day and my energy was flagging.

And then something unexpected and exciting happened – they started talking about Everest. It turns out that Jan/James (I was still unclear at this point) had been *The Times'* correspondent (and only journalist) on the 1953 expedition, and had been responsible for getting the news of Hillary and Norgay's successful summit back to the UK. At that time there weren't any radio transmitters on the mountain and dispatches had to be sent back to Kathmandu by human messenger. And because of the danger of the news leaking out, they had developed a code. The final message read: '*Snow conditions bad; advance base abandoned; all well*' – which meant: '*Edmund Hillary and Tenzing Norgay have reached the summit and indeed we are all very well!*' This landmark news arrived in the UK on 2 June 1953, which also happened to be Queen Elizabeth II's coronation.

Then after all this surprising and fascinating Everest stuff and without any preamble and a bit out of the blue, Roy says: '*Since the age of about four you had the idea that you were encased in the wrong body.*'

I'm immediately taken aback – not by the idea itself, but by the fact that Roy has uttered these words because his interviews rarely stray into personal territory. Jan responds that it was '*more than an idea*' and they then briefly discuss the subject of hormone therapy and genital surgery, the whole James/Jan thing now clear.

Sue's episode is markedly different in that she refers to all this in her intro. It turns out that Jan was one of the first public figures to ever write or talk openly about transitioning. Even so Jan says it's only a small aspect of her life and something that she finds difficult to define – like a piece of Debussy.[82] But Sue is much more interrogative than Roy and won't leave the subject alone. She asks why, if Jan felt like a woman, she joined the army, married and fathered five children. It starts to feel a bit uncomfortable, so much so that at one point Jan says: '*I'm not enjoying this.*'

I felt bad for Jan. I liked her. And I was impressed by the fact that she was part of that first successful expedition to Everest in which no other women were involved. She says she climbed to 22,000 feet (which is nearly 7,000 metres). And even though no one thought this at the time – maybe not even her – she did it over twenty years before the first woman would successfully summit Everest in 1975 – Junko Tabei from Japan. Jan was the first trans woman to get anywhere near the top of the mountain.

Eventually, towards the end of the episode, Sue's interrogation subsides and, as if she's finally found the explanation to the conundrum of her guest, she conjectures that Jan has played her life as an artist might – with swagger, bravado and a little bit of danger.

For the first time, Jan's voice noticeably relaxes: '*That's the nicest thing you've said in this programme. I do like to think that I've played life like an artist. Not always successfully believe me. But I like to think that I've played it as if I were composing a book.*'

And I thought when I heard this: I want to be like Jan. I want to play my life like an artist. I want to write about my unique mountainous musical adventure. Snow conditions bad. Advance base abandoned. All well. Heading to a desert island. With my music.

At the time of writing this, there isn't a woman who has been on *Desert Island Discs* who has climbed to the summit of Everest. At least, in all my listening I haven't found her and I think I'd know. But there have been a few women adventurers, including Christina Dodwell, Dervla Murphy and one of the first icons of female exploring Freya Stark – whose episode from 1970 is sadly also not available.

I admire their spirit and bravery – although Dervla Murphy says she isn't brave, she's fearless. There's a difference: *'If you don't feel fear you don't have to be brave, you're brave when you're overcoming fear.'* She says she taught herself to repel pain by putting her feet in very hot water and tying string round her finger and pulling it tighter and tighter. So perhaps she was brave in the beginning and just trained herself to be fearless.

Christina Dodwell describes an occasion when she took part in an initiation ceremony in Papua New Guinea where her shoulder was cut in the pattern of crocodile skin so deep it left a lasting scar: *'But if it's not frightening then it doesn't change you. If you go through something that's the most horrible and terrifying experience of your life, then for the rest of your life you have that extra strength.'*

I turned to the challenge of swimming seas, running marathons and then climbing mountains to heal a heartbreak. But there could be nothing more challenging than going through eleven rounds of unsuccessful IVF in my pursuit of motherhood, and then losing the man I loved at the end of it. That taught me what bravery is and I've faced it. But I think I'm drawn to these hard physical and mental challenges to make me stronger still. Because I want to change. I want to live a *fearless* life.

3

'I am frightened of nothing.'
–Marlene Dietrich, 1965

———————

The episode with Marlene Dietrich – the inimitable German chanteuse – opens with Roy asking her whether she would be frightened of anything on a desert island, and her defiantly replying: *'I am frightened of nothing.'*

I'm not entirely sure whether she'd been fully briefed on the show's format. She takes umbrage at many of the questions and the ever-amiable Roy starts to sound a bit defeated. At the end of the show, recorded from the dressing room of a theatre on London's Shaftesbury Avenue where Marlene was performing, he even concedes to choosing her last track for her, and then lets her take *two* luxuries, *two* books and save all *eight* records from the waves. Poor Roy, I bet his postbag was full after that one. *Desert Island Discs* fans hate the rules of the show being flouted.

After I listened to her episode (while walking from Specsavers in Swiss Cottage back to South End Green at the bottom of our hill – and I have a feeling there are several things about that statement Marlene wouldn't approve of if she was still alive), I began thinking a lot about my mum's mother, the only one of my four grandparents I met. We all called her Mima – a name made up by my sister when she was little because she couldn't say her real name. And Mima lived in Germany, with her husband. He wasn't my mum's father. Mima had met him on a cruise when she was in her fifties. And she wasn't German but I always thought of her as my German grandmother because that's where she lived all the time I knew her. When I was little, my mum and I would occasionally go to visit her in the spa town of Bad Pyrmont where they lived. My dad never came – he wasn't a traveller. We only ever holidayed in England as a family – mainly Whitstable in Kent long before it got chichi.

Everything about Mima seemed glamorous and exotic to me. In Bad Pyrmont, she had flavoured water delivered to her door (not boring milk like we did at home and where the only water we drank came from a tap). She dyed her long hair red and coiffeured it in an updo, wore floral dresses in pinks and purples, white high heels, jewellery, lipstick and perfume. In her matching handbag, she carried little packets of scented moisture wipes and boiled sweets wrapped in colourful cellophane. Marlene would have approved of my grandmother. (My grandmother definitely didn't go to Specsavers.)

Whenever we visited Mima, she would encourage my mum to care more about her looks, but my mum was always falling short. If she ever tried dying her hair, the colour never looked right. The only jewellery she wore was her wedding band. And if you looked in her handbag all you'd find was a blue Biro without a lid, a small old man's comb and a purse with a couple of coppers. It was as if my mum didn't quite know how to be a woman, whereas my grandmother definitely did.

Mima would write long letters from afar and send newspaper cuttings about the latest vitamins and superfoods before blueberries were ever a thing. And I remember her telling me once that you needed to start using moisturiser when you were very young if you wanted to stand any chance of avoiding wrinkles. She sounded as if she was implying it could already be too late for me. I think I was about thirteen at the time. My mum never told me to use moisturiser or used it herself. And she had pots of it, given to her on birthdays and christmases, all unopened on the shelf.

Mima was never married to my mother's father, my grandfather. In her twenties, my grandmother had worked in a bank as a teller. My grandfather was the manager. She was young and beautiful. He was titled and rich. Lust must and my mum, born in 1932, was 'illegitimate' at a time when that was a terrible label of shame.

Desert Island Discs has been my corroboration of this. I was walking along a very muddy path in the Peak District – when Peggy Makins affirmed it for me. Cast away in 1988, she was one of the first ever 'agony aunts' and when her column started in 1937 (five years after my mum was born), it was one of the subjects she often received letters about because having a child out of a wedlock was a *'very bad thing'*. The novelist Pat Barker – cast away in 2003 and born illegitimate during the Second World War – reaffirmed this to me back in London on an unmuddy pavement. She says that the stigma was *'gigantic'*, that it *'darkened'* her mother's life.

Then one day, a while later, I was walking past the Hill House Pergola, a dilapidated folly, which is in one of the most romantic and hidden parts of Hampstead Heath when the popular scientist Jacob Bronowski chose Marlene Dietrich's 'Falling in Love Again'[83] – her signature song from the 1930 movie *Blue Angel* (*Der blaue Engel*) which made her a star. I didn't even know the Pergola existed when I was growing up. I only stumbled on it when I started walking with a pack and a purpose. Apparently people get married there – that's if they know where it is and can find someone to marry them.

Jacob asked for the original German version of the song, and when Marlene started singing it I thought of my grandmother. It was around this time that I had begun playing a game with myself – composing playlists for members of my family inspired by my listening. My paternal grandfather, Patrick, had Holst's *The Planets* on his list. And I immediately thought this would be a good track for Mima.

I've always wondered why she went to Germany. Was it because she'd fallen in love again or just because she'd finally found someone to marry her? After my grandfather got her pregnant, he married somebody else of better social standing. My mum spent most of her early years in a children's home while my grandmother worked to survive. When I first found this out, I was shocked and sad for my mum. But it explained a lot about her that I hadn't been able to make sense of. It's probably the reason she seems to live her life as if she's playing it on catch-up but still doesn't quite know who she is. It could be an explanation for the lid-less Biro, the man's comb and the all-but empty purse. And even The Lord's Prayer. But Mima was like Marlene. She was a flame to a moth. And the fire she started delivered a daughter – her only child – and although my mum never knew her father, Mima never let her forget who he was.

Jay Blades – presenter of the BBC's *Repair Shop* who was cast away in 2022 – would probably say I should refer to my grandfather as the *'man who contributed towards my mum's birth'*. That's what he calls his because he believes you can't call yourself a 'father' if you don't do the job. But I still think of the man who contributed to my mum's birth as my grandfather. One of the few things I know about him is he was from Holland, so I've put Wagner's 'The Flying Dutchman'[84] on his playlist.

In 2021, another siren of the screen appeared on *Desert Island Discs* – the Italian actress Sophia Loren. Born in a ward for unmarried mothers in 1934, she's two years younger than my mum. She says she only met her father two or three times and that she's not sure whether he ever loved her mother, yet Sophia believes: *'If you love somebody, you take care, you are with a person, especially if you have children. My God, it's a miracle to have a child. It's wonderful to have a family.'*

I will never know if my grandfather loved my grandmother. But I know he didn't take care of her, or my mum. I also know for certain that it's a miracle to have a child.

4

'And that was the most beautiful love song,
sung by the most faithless rogue ever born.'

–Liz Lochhead, 2017

———————

Sophia Loren took a pizza oven as her luxury (a woman after my own stomach). And Marlene, as I said, insisted on *two* luxuries – a ballet shoe from Russia and a bunch of white heather she'd been given by the people of Scotland which, she says, she takes with her wherever she goes.

So, maybe this is a good moment in the story to go and climb Ben Nevis – not only the highest mountain in Scotland, which stands at 1,345 metres, but the whole of the British Isles (FYI Snowdon is 1,085 metres and Scafell Pike is 978 metres high). And Ben Nevis is not just a mountain. Ben Nevis is a *Munro*: the title conferred on Scottish mountains with a height over 914.4 metres (which seems a weird number but the definition was set in pre-decimal days, so in 'old money' that's anything over 3,000 feet). There are officially 282 Munros in Scotland, plus another 227 'Tops', that is mountains still over 914.4 metres, but not formally classified as Munros because they are not of sufficient distance away from one that is. A total of 509 Munros and Tops makes Scotland the undisputed mountain capital of the UK. And 'the Ben' – which is what locals fondly call him – is King.

I mainly think of mountains in the female – as I do with the sea. But Ben Nevis is not a woman: he's a man. And the first time I climbed him was one of the most terrifying experiences of my life. I had enlisted the support of Adele Pennington, first among mountaineering royalty. At the time she had climbed more 8,000 metre peaks than any other British woman. There are fourteen mountains in the world over this height, which denotes the altitude known as 'the Death Zone', since there's not enough air to survive. And Everest is the highest of them all.

Adele, or 'the pocket rocket', as she's also known – she's just 4 feet, 11 inches and mighty – has been on many of them. She was also the first British woman to summit Everest twice. I couldn't have had a better guide. However, it was the first time we'd met and she'd clearly over-estimated my ability when I told her my aspiration to get to the top of the world. So we didn't take the tourist track, we climbed by the Tower Ridge Route which is classified as the highest grade of scrambling – i.e. at the cusp of walking and rock climbing. I suspect she deeply regretted that we had. When we reached the infamous 'Tower Gap' – the clue is in the name – you have to lower yourself down to a tiny pinnacle of rock in order to cross a gaping hole with a long drop. And we had a row.

'*I can't,*' I said.

'*You can.*'

'*I can't.*'

'*You can.*'

'*I can't.*'

'*Lady, get down on that rock. Now.*'

I did. I didn't want to, but I didn't dare not to. I crossed the gap and clung onto the face of the rock on the other side, panting.

'*You want to climb Everest?*' she scoffed. '*You're going to have to get better than that.*'

It took us ten hours to get up and down Ben Nevis that day.

I look back now and think of it as 'Type 2' fun. Horrible at the time. Hilarious afterwards. It cemented my relationship with Adele who became my mountain mentor on this journey. Since then we have climbed Ben Nevis many times together. We've been up via Gully Number 3, Gully Number 4, the Ledge Route and the Carn Mhor Dearg Arete. Funnily enough though, she's never suggested the Tower Ridge route again. I sometimes wonder why. But I think we both know that I'll never be a 'real mountaineer', and once in that gap was enough. Adele is the real deal. In winter, she's got her crampons on before mine are out of the bag. She knows everything you need to know about rope and knots. She's climbed many of the highest mountains in the world but she's also climbed all 282 Scottish Munros AND all 227 Tops.

My time with Adele in the Highlands, and especially on Ben Nevis, further deepened my love for Scotland, and I feel honoured that I have now earned the right to call him the Ben.

If you were going to choose a definitive love song for Scotland, you couldn't go wrong with Robert Burns' 'My Love Is Like a Red Red Rose'.[85] Nor would you be criticised for having the iconic Scots tenor Kenneth McKellar sing it for you. (Although when Kenneth was on the show himself in 1977, he asked for the equally iconic Scots folk musician Jimmy Shand to play it for him on his accordion.) It's not my favourite Robert Burns though. Mine is 'Green Grow the Rashes O', the first Burns poem set to music. It's more of a lust song than a love song – because it's about how the sweetest hours that the boys can spend are with the girls. I love it – especially the version by Michael Marra – chosen and saved from the waves by Scotland's former Makar, writer Liz Lochhead. Michael's version is sung with so much yearning that it's more lachrymal than lustful. It's become my second all-time favourite Scottish song – after 'Amazing Grace' on the bagpipes and before The Proclaimers sing about sorrow in that oh-so-rare sunshine over Leith.

Liz Lochhead gives a great episode and one of my favourite things she says is at the end when she chooses a very different sort of love song – *'Là ci darem la mano'* from Mozart's opera *Don Giovanni*.[86] After the duet finishes and Kirsty has read out the musical credits, Liz says: *'And that was the most beautiful love song, sung by the most faithless rogue ever born. And that's what we should always remember. We only know part of the story.'*

How true, Liz. I love Ben Nevis. But when I was in that gap, I hated him.

Love is only ever part of the story.

5

'I got terribly terribly drunk listening to "Buffalo Solider"
and we danced all round the garden and everything.
And it's always a happy reminder of loving my children
and having fun with them.'

–Jilly Cooper, 2016

Once, when I was up in Scotland with Adele, she conceded to a treat. Instead of heading high to rock and snow, we walked the last 25 miles of the West Highland Way – Scotland's first and most famous long distance trail which runs from just north of Glasgow up to Fort William. It was a treat because this is my favourite sort of day in the mountains – and not Adele's. I am a woman who prefers a path; she is a woman who likes it when there isn't one. It meant we were able to walk in step and chat, whereas generally when I saw Adele, I was at the bottom of a rope exclaiming: *'Why am I doing this?'*

And she was at the top saying, *'Because you want to climb Everest.'*

There's a nice path all the way to Everest base-camp, but after that you enter the Khumbu Icefall – the most difficult and dangerous part of the ascent. And when you do that you've got to put on a harness, helmet and clip onto a rope, and wear crampons (which if you don't know what they are (and I didn't) are shoes with sharp spikes for walking on ice). And when all that happens, everything gets more serious. I knew if I wanted to achieve the challenge I'd set myself I needed to learn all that stuff. But that day walking on the West Highland Way from Kingshouse up the Devil's Staircase down to Kinlochleven and then across to Fort William, we strolled side by side and chatted all the way. And that's when I got to ask Adele what her own eight discs would be if she were ever to go to a desert island.

She didn't want to play the game at first. Arts chat like this is not her natural habitat. But on pressing her, the first track she chose was from *The Sound of Music*. It seemed a perfect choice to me – a song from the ultimate mountaineer's musical.

Adele said from the age of two, she wanted to be outdoors. Her mum bought her a pair of red wellingtons to wear in the garden and she loved them so much she refused to take them off. She curled up her toes and screamed so loudly, that in the end she was allowed to wear them in bed. She remembers her mum singing: *'How do you solve a problem like Adele?'* – swapping in her name from 'Maria' in the original song.

The actual Maria von Trapp – whose real life story inspired the musical – appeared on *Desert Island Discs* in 1983. I had been kind of expecting/hoping that she would choose one of the musical's songs among her eight tracks. But she doesn't. In fact, she says she signed her contractual rights away ten years before the musical was made so she didn't make any money out of her story which, given the fact that it's the biggest grossing musical film of all time, seems a very good reason for *not* choosing one of its songs.

Maria is a great raconteur and describes how she had a religious epiphany standing on a glacier in the mountains at sunset. She says it's something she wishes that everyone could see – colours you didn't even know existed changing in front of your eyes. And it was such beauty that made her think she had to give herself to God; and with rucksack on back, rope over shoulder, ice pick in hand she immediately made her way to the nearest convent and presented herself as a postulant.

I love the word 'postulant'. I didn't actually know it before. But you can't go on an adventure like this and not become intimately acquainted with it because Julie Andrews is such a good singing one and the 'Prelude' and 'Climb Ev'ry Mountain' from Rodgers and Hammerstein's *The Sound of Music* should be a 'must listen' song on all mountain playlists. The musical also has one of the best love songs ever written – 'Something Good' – the schmaltzy number sung in a moonlit garden when Maria and Baron von Trapp finally get it together. In fact, the song was chosen by the Queen of Romance Jilly Cooper – in case proof is needed of its superlative soppiness. She says she loves it because it's a song about redemption and she believes in the idea of getting a heavenly man for doing something good in your wicked childhood. *'Don't you?'* she asks Kirsty mischievously as the song starts.

I listened to Jilly on Box Hill in Surrey – one of my favourite places of height just outside London. I found that I could take the train to Westhumble, climb up from the stepping stones on the River Mole to the National Trust café which marks the start of the eight-mile Box Hill Hike. And sometimes I could even walk it twice around before getting the train back home for pizza and beer on the sofa. It made for good training and listening.

During her episode, Jilly talks about her long marriage and her ectopic pregnancy, which meant she and her husband, Leo, were unable to have biological children together. I had an ectopic pregnancy once – only discovered at three months. It was a perfect baby but in the wrong place – not in my womb, but my stomach. The scars from the emergency operation are my only proof that I once was a mother. Jilly says she was devastated by it but felt she was very lucky to be able to adopt instead. She says she couldn't believe the wellsprings of love that poured out of her when she did. And for her sixth track she chooses Bob Marley's 'Buffalo Soldier'[87] for her two children. Jilly says one of the best things in the world is getting a bit drunk with them and that one evening they got terribly terribly drunk listening to 'Buffalo Soldier' and danced all round the garden: *It's always a happy reminder of loving my children and having fun with them,'* she adds.

Jilly Cooper got her own 'Redemption Song', I reckon.

She must have done something good in her wicked childhood.

6

'It's not a difficult choice, actually, it's an easy choice –
"Wind Beneath My Wings".'

–Bill Morris, 1998

I admit I covet the castaways who have experienced the longest love. I could write you a list of them because it always goes in my notes whenever I find it. Jilly Cooper was married to her husband, Leo, for fifty-two years before he died of Parkinson's. And one of my favourite castaways – the Labour politician Denis Healey – was married to his wife, Edna, for sixty-five years. Both occasions he was on the show (in 1978, and then again in 2009), he wanted to take Edna to the island as his luxury item. He wasn't allowed to (animate objects being against the rules), so the first time he capitulated and took some painting materials, and the second time, he settled on a box of chocolates. He tells Kirsty he likes nougats and loves soft centres and then says: *'Ooh, don't, you're making me dribble.'* In fact, he was making himself dribble. It's a delicious moment.

The architect Richard Rogers and his wife, chef Ruth Rogers both appeared on the show, but twenty-five years apart. They tried to take each other too and refused to go if they couldn't. I like to listen to husband and wife episodes back to back if I make the connection and can. There have been nearly a hundred couples in total and it's always revealing of their relationship – e.g. Neil and Glenys Kinnock (she chose Tammy Wynette's 'Stand By Your Man').[88] And Jeffrey and Mary Archer (she didn't, but my goodness, she has!). And both Maureen Lipman and Jack Rosenthal said they had an 'our song' but weren't taking it – although I can't believe they didn't slip it into their bags. But when people do choose their 'our songs' or their wedding music, I can't help myself, I feel a pang.

Of course some unions celebrated on the show haven't lasted. When the pop icon Kylie Minogue[89] asked her current boyfriend to select a piece of music for her to take as a surprise, he delivered a romantic monologue written by his father and recited by himself. Kylie saved it from the waves but a year later news hit the headlines that the couple had split up. I feel for Kylie on her desert island – looking the picture of beach chic in gold hotpants – with only that one track to listen to. Similarly, the TV presenter Davina McCall chose and saved Sarah McLachlan's 'Angel'[90] which she called her and her husband's *sexy song*. They've also separated now so it must be tricky that's the only track she's got with her too.

That's life though.

Separation and divorce happens. And I liked it a lot when the actress Joan Collins was adamant that just because she'd been married multipe times, it didn't mean she'd had a tragic love life, because each husband in their time had been terrific. But she says if you're with someone and it's no longer bringing you happiness, you need to get out because *'life is short and life is sweet and you don't want to be saddled with a man who is making you sick'.*

I try to emulate Joan Collins a lot in life. I once did the conga with her at a party at my theatre. She was in her early eighties at the time and I thought that was a pretty great way to be living a short and sweet life.

In fact, I've had the privilege of meeting a few *Desert Island Discs* castaways. Years ago – before all this started – I listened to and loved the episode with the Polar Explorer Ann Daniels and contacted her to ask if she would meet me. She agreed. I wanted to talk to her about whether motherhood makes you happy because I had been fascinated listening to her tell Kirsty about her own desperation for a child. After six years of infertility and reproductive surgery, she was given one shot at IVF and conceived triplets. And then, when her children were around two-years old, she responded to an advert seeking 'ordinary women' to be part of the first all-female team to go to the North Pole. When she was offered a place, she came under intense media criticism for leaving them. A man who was a father would never have faced the same scrutiny as a woman who was a mother. Then, after the expedition ended, her marriage broke down. She says she is often asked whether the two things were related but they're not. Her marriage was breaking down anyway; the North Pole had nothing to do with it.

People ask me whether my relationship broke down 'because of the IVF'. It's as if they want there to be one single, simple reason. But I think there are more likely to be multiple reasons for relationship breakdown. I would find it easier to list you eight than one.

After Ann and her husband separated, she went on an expedition to the South Pole. As a memory of this, she chooses Nina Simone's song 'Feeling Good'[91] which she says she sang as she crossed Antarctica. For her it signified a new start and a new life. I love Nina Simone too – she's probably my all-time favourite female singer – and I know she'll be with me on my desert island looking great in boots and a bikini and no doubt taunting me for spending too much time in the shade. But it wasn't until Ann chose it that I realised it's the ultimate song of 'Self Love'. That makes it a legitimate love song I reckon – because there isn't enough of it around.

Nevertheless, I still can't help myself coveting the most enduring love stories. Like when the actor/writer/talented-at-so-many things Hugh Laurie was cast away in 1997 and chose and saved Van Morrison's 'Brown Eyed Girl'[92] to remind him of his wife, Jo, and then returned to the desert island sixteen years later and chose and saved it again. That got me bad.

And when the businessman Digby Jones, and the trade union leader Bill Morris both chose and saved Bette Midler's 'Wind Beneath My Wings'[93] that got me really bad too. Even before the end of the show Digby tells Sue that if she's going to make him save just one, this is going to be it because he couldn't have done all that he's done without his wife, Pat. And Bill moved me even more when he spoke about his first wife, Minette, who died of cancer at an early age after supporting his career – at the expense of her own – but who didn't live long enough to see him get to the top. At the end of the show, when Sue asks him to save one record from the waves, Bill says simply: *'It's not a difficult choice, actually, it's an easy choice.'*

I had a blue-eyed boy who was the wind beneath my wings. It lasted sixteen years. Then, well, let's just keep it simple for now – the dandelion clock stopped.

7

'If I could write a love song like this, I'd be a happy man.'

*'When I did decide what tree I liked the best,
this is the song I'd put on.'*

–Tim Robbins, 2010

I was lying on the top bunk in a hut at base camp on Mount Elbrus listening to the rock musician Alice Cooper. He was a beguiling guest. I liked how he described Bob Dylan as *'ragged'* (a great word for my list of great words). How he had replaced alcohol with golf. And how he'd been married for thirty-five years despite – as Kirsty observes – rock stars and marriages not being entirely compatible. There's that long love again (noted).

Just to be clear, this was 'Base Camp', not 'Advanced Base Camp'. Sometimes mountains have two. Advanced ones are higher and often abbreviated to ABC – which is an acronym (and nothing to do with the alphabet or a Jackson 5 song).[94] Base camps might seem basic places from a distance, but they are a luxurious home compared to the higher camps on the highest mountains. The tents are bigger, there are sometimes even huts, and there are usually separate dining facilities. You can spend a lot of time resting and waiting for the weather, so take a good book if you're going to one. My own mountain 'must reads' are Jilly Cooper's *Riders* and Jackie Collins' *Hollywood Wives* (Joan's writerly sister was on *Desert Island Discs* in 1986 interviewed by Michael Parkinson – it's a masterclass in sexual chemistry). Personally, I don't want boys' adventure stories when I climb a mountain, I want page-turning romance and a good podcast . . . That is the mountaineer that is me.

At Elbrus base camp I was sleeping in a dormitory of six people and, like a child, I had bagsied the top bunk. The one in the corner, furthest away from the door. It wouldn't necessarily be everyone's top choice. It means you have further to go to the toilet in the night which was outside and round the back. But, on the plus side, it means that everyone who goes to the toilet isn't passing your bed. So you don't have to think: *'they're going to the toilet'*. I prefer not to think about toilets on mountains. They're messy. It's not good for my head.

Mount Elbrus is in Russia and is officially the highest mountain in Europe (many people think Mont Blanc in France holds the title but it doesn't). I was climbing on the north side (i.e. not the south). For mountaineers this is an important note of distinction. Often there are several different routes and many of the highest mountains are climbed from the south which is generally warmer and therefore (marginally) easier. Everest, for example, can be climbed from the south (in Nepal) or the north (in Tibet). The south – which is the side it was first summited by – is the one that most people take today. And it's the same on Elbrus where, if you wish, you can take a chair lift to base camp and a snow cat to the Pastukhov rocks which means that you then only have around 1,000 metres to climb to the summit which tops out at 5,642 metres. It's not quite like taking the train to the top of Snowdon, it's still a long, hard day on the south. But the north side is longer and harder.

A few days later we climbed to ABC which stands at 3,800 metres. In essence, this means from there you've got double the distance to get to the summit than you do on the south.

Many of my fellow climbing companions ducked out. On larger expeditions this always happens. People get sick. People get scared. By the time we got to the saddle – the bit of the mountain that dips between the Eastern and the Western summits, we were down to me and four others. All of them younger, fitter and faster. I felt like I was slowing them down and risking their chances of summitting. So I did the honourable thing and fell on my walking poles – i.e. I stopped and waited in the saddle while they went to the top without me.

Seventeen hours after we'd set out, I was back at camp in my sleeping bag, exhausted but unable to sleep. I felt like a failure for not getting to the top. I put on another episode: the actor Tim Robbins. I specifically chose him in that moment because he'd starred in *The Shawshank Redemption*, and I felt in desperate need of some myself.

Towards the end of the programme, Kirsty tries to steer him gently into personal territory, observing that he and the actress Susan Sarandon seemed, for many years, to be the iconic Hollywood couple who did the Hollywood thing, without seeming to be the Hollywood thing. Essentially, she's making the same point as she did with Alice Cooper. Except Tim and Susan had recently separated after twenty years and two children together. Tim says he's always avoided speaking about his private life in the public arena. But he does admit to having had a midlife existential crisis which he thinks is something to do with getting to fifty because it starts to become difficult to imagine doubling your age: *You go "oh wow". You know that hill, I've already been at the top of the hill . . . you start thinking how many years have I got left? And at those moments you go: what the hell am I doing here? . . . I asked myself the question: what is that will make you happy? What is it that you have not done that you will regret not doing?'*

And so, as I lay there awake – aged forty-eight at the time

– I asked myself the same question and, this time, unlike the first time on Sloane Street with Jimmy Carr, the answer was disarmingly simple . . .

The next morning, I got up and walked down from ABC to base camp. Then I arranged for a truck to take me all the way round to the south side of the mountain. It took a day to get there – it's a big mountain. I got in the chair lift. I slept at base camp (on the south there isn't an advanced one). And then very early the next morning, I got up and took the snow cat to the Pastukhov rocks. Then I walked up to the top of Europe. I took small slow steps but kept moving forward and I followed the best mountain advice I've ever been given: *'Don't look up at how far you've got to go, always look down at how far you've come.'*

When I got to the saddle and started the last 100 metres of ascent, I put Nina Simone on my headphones and just as I reached the summit, as daylight broke, she sang me her version of The Beatles' song 'Here Comes the Sun'. I started crying. But they were happy tears. Tears of self love.

Tim Robbins is a man who has asked himself the same questions as I have. I think he's also a man who understands love. Not only does he choose Nina Simone for his list of eight ('Sinnerman'), he also takes two of the very best love songs ever written. Fact. For his sixth track he chooses Joni Mitchell's 'A Case of You'.[95] He says if he could write a love song like it, he'd be a happy man. And for his eighth track, he chooses Marvin Gaye's 'Let's Get It On'[96] – which must be one of the world's sexiest songs. Tim says that when he's on the island, there are going to be moments where he needs a little romance; so he'll find a tree – he might even move from tree to tree taking a little time to find which one he wants to settle down with – but when he does, he'll put it on.

At the very end of the show when asked which of his eight tracks he wants to save from the waves, Tim says: *'It's between Marvin Gaye and Joni Mitchell and . . . erm . . . I guess I'm going to go with Joni Mitchell.'*

And Kirsty just replies: *'Mmm.'*

Mmm. I agree.

8

'The greatest thing you'll ever learn is just to love and be loved
in return, and that seems to me an unforgettable truth.'

–Robert Macfarlane, 2021

———————

Russia is a country of romance. You only have to listen to
Rachmaninov to know that. It's probably why his Piano
Concerto No. 2[97] became the theme tune to one of the most
enduring love films of all time. When the Russian pianist
Vladimir Ashkenazy was on the show he starts with
Rachmaninov because, he says, he is probably the most Russian
of all Russian composers. That's good enough testimony for
me. Russia equals Rachmaninov equals Romance – that makes
him a contender for any list of love songs. Surely?

I also couldn't end this section without mentioning Nat
King Cole.[98] His velvet voice has been chosen by many castaways
over the years for reasons of love. Take your pick among these
and more: 'When I Fall in Love' (his most chosen track),
'Let There Be Love' or just simply 'L-O-V-E'. I love them all. And
his version of 'Nature Boy', which was chosen by the writer
Robert Macfarlane, who writes and speaks more beautifully
about mountains than nearly anyone else I know, is also up
there as one of my favourites. Robert says that lyrically it is one
of the most perfect songs – about a sad boy who travels,

melancholy and bittersweet, very far over land and sea but the greatest thing he learns – what Robert describes as an unforgettable truth – is just to love and be loved in return.

I listened to Robert on the Dollis Valley Greenwalk which I discovered provided 26 miles of mainly flat and roadless walking (and listening), from my front door to Moat Mount and back again. No doubt the mainly flat is why I like it and the mainly roadless is good too (there's still a clear path to follow). I've walked it many times now. In the absence of elevation it was good training if I wore some weight. There was a time when I felt more like a 'Natural Woman' than a 'Nature Boy'. Not that I would ever sing it. I'd ask Aretha Franklin[99] or Carole King[100] to do that for me. I just took the unconditional love that was on offer. But not anymore. Now I've got Nat King Cole to provide the soundtrack as I travel alone very far over land and sea.

We're coming to the end of this section, and I guess you'll be expecting me to choose my shortlist of eight love songs. After all, that's the structure I've set up (eight being the magic number of this story and also a very auspicious number in the east which is the direction we're heading in).

The problem I have, though, is that all the love songs from my own life now seem to make me cry and I don't think that's what love should do. So instead, after much deliberation, I've decided I'm going to have to end this section with a list that is inspired by my castaway friends who have just played us some of the greatest love songs of all time. I hope that you still believe in love. One day I want to be able to say that I do too and maybe one of these will make my own list. But until that day comes, I'll conclude with these beautiful words from Robert Macfarlane:

'Mountains they melt us because they exist. They live in deep time in ways that absolutely dissolve human units of being.'

Really, how could anyone not fall in love with the mountains if they heard these words leading into Nat King Cole singing 'Nature Boy' on *Desert Island Discs*?

My (If You Still Believe in) Love Songs Shortlist

1. Nick Cave: 'Love Letter' – because as Anne-Marie Duff says: love is the answer. Or, alternatively, Nina Simone's 'Feeling Good' (because love is the answer but, as Ann Daniels infers, you have to start with self love).

2. Marlene Dietrich: 'Falling in Love Again'– but only if, like Marlene, you're frightened of nothing. Or, if you are frightened of nothing, then, alternatively, Mozart's *Don Giovanni* – the most faithless rogue ever born who knows how to sing the most beautiful love song, according to Liz Lochhead.

3. Rodgers and Hammerstein: 'Something Good' from *The Sound of Music* – because who knows better about love songs than the Queen of Romance Jilly Cooper. Or, alternatively, substitute it for 'If I Loved You' from *Carousel* (also Rodgers and Hammerstein), which the writer and actor Mark Gatiss taught me at another base camp on another mountain is a 'conditional love song'. I guess you could call this my 'conditional love song list'.

4. Rachmaninov: Piano Concerto No. 2 – because Russia equals Rachmaninov equals Romance – and thank you Vladimir Ashkenazy for playing it so beautifully.

5. Joni Mitchell: 'A Case of You' – because I agree with Tim Robbins that anyone who can write and sing a love song like Joni is a genius.

6. Marvin Gaye: 'Let's Get It On' – for when you find a tree to settle down with.

7. Bette Midler: 'Wind Beneath My Wings' – for a love like Digby Jones and Bill Morris.

8. And finally, it's got to be Carole or Cole – *King vs King*. Any of their respective love songs will do. Yet I'll always take 'Nature Boy' to the mountains.

Sad Songs
(aka Songs to Make Me Cry)

1. Johnny Cash: 'I See a Darkness'

2. Bob Dylan: 'Make You Feel My Love'

3. James Taylor: 'Don't Let Me Be Lonely Tonight'

4. Van Morrison: 'Have I Told You Lately'

5. David Baddiel, Frank Skinner and the Lightning Seeds: 'Three Lions'

6. Edward Elgar: Cello Concerto in E Minor

7. Tim Minchin: 'White Wine in the Sun'

8. Frank Sinatra: 'Moon River'

1

'I played this over and over again during a time when I was very, very sad and missed somebody. And at the end of the time I was reconciled.'

–Sue Townsend, 1991

The first time I saw Peter's face I was standing by a colleague's desk in an office on the Old Steine leading down to the seafront, which is essentially the end of the A23 but that doesn't sound as romantic. I had recently started a new job in a new city – Brighton – which looks out across the Channel although the sea meant nothing to me then – except fish and chips and ice cream. Peter worked there too and by the time I met him I'd already heard his name a lot. He was the sort of person people talked about when he wasn't there. And then I saw his face, and something sparked, although it would be several years before any lightning ran through my veins.[101]

Was he good looking? No. But I reckon you'll like him even if you don't fall in love with him. He has a presence – being six feet four helps. But it's more than that. He's one of those people who has an energy about them that makes you want to be in their company – because you know that when they leave there will be an unsatisfactory feeling of absence. Now, whenever I recall that moment, I think about Roberta Flack singing 'The First Time Ever I Saw Your Face'.[102]

It was the musician Jarvis Cocker – lead singer of the band Pulp – who told me that you need a song on your list for melancholy moods. I listened to him on the 24 bus from home into town when I was reliving my early twenties on a 'Britpop Adventure'. It was around then I discovered that although Blur[103] won the official 'Battle of Britpop' and Oasis[104] is currently winning the battle of *Desert Island Discs*, it's Pulp's 'Common People'[105] that has been chosen more times than any other single Britpop track.

Jarvis says that although he's largely selected stuff to jolly himself along on his island, he's also brought an alternative for special occasions – 'I See a Darkness' sung by Johnny Cash.[106] He says that when he played it to a friend, he (the friend) immediately burst into tears.

As soon as I heard it, I decided to put it on my grandmother Anna's playlist. She must have seen a darkness when she took her own life. Much of her poetry rails against female inequality and apparently she was envious of the success that her male writer friends enjoyed. She left a short poem as a note which ended with these words:

> *I am iced in with terror*
> *At the sheer doom*
> *Of my long pride and error.*

Even in death she was a wonderful writer.

I wish I could tell her she now has a Wikipedia page that says she was one of the most important feminist poets of the early twentieth century. I think she'd like that. So would my dad. He found the note and didn't show it to anyone for years, wanting to keep a little bit of her for himself. So I think Jarvis is right. We've all got to get through the tears of our life, and three minutes of music is an expedient way of doing it.

Roberta Flack's 'The First Time Ever I Saw Your Face' definitely has the right tenor for tears. But I'm not sure I'll choose it because although it moves me deeply it doesn't instantly make me cry and I need something that's guaranteed to deliver. Roberta didn't write the song herself – it's by the Scottish folk musician Ewan MacColl[107] but she brought a melancholy to it that's not in the original and which now feels right for the first time I ever saw Peter's face. Allegedly, Ewan never liked any of the cover versions but Roberta made the song a hit and won him a Grammy fifteen years after he'd composed it. He originally wrote it for the folk singer Peggy Seeger who became his wife.

I kind of hoped that it would make Peggy's list when she was on *Desert Island Discs*, but it doesn't. However, she does describe the first time she and Ewan saw each other. She says she doesn't think it was her face that made him fall in love with her, it was the 'House Carpenter' which she was singing and playing on the banjo. That was the thing that sparked the lightning of their love. And for me and Peter, it was a conversation in an office near the seafront on the Old Steine. Not quite as romantic, but better than the A23.

Roberta Flack also makes me think of the writer Sue Townsend, and the time we spent together on a mountain in Kyrgyzstan called Peak Lenin. Sue chose another Roberta song – 'Until It's Time For You to Go'. And although Sue doesn't disclose the full details, I think it must be her song to cry to because she says she played it over and over again during a time when she was very, very sad, until finally she became reconciled.

On that expedition, I spent many days and nights in my tent listening to *Desert Island Discs*, waiting for the weather.

It was a tough mountain which I didn't summit because of high winds and slow legs. But it was also hard because after the inevitable early attrition of other members in the team, I ended up climbing with two couples – lovely people in love – but that made me feel very alone. I watched as they tended to each others blisters, and imagined them snuggling close in their sleeping bags while I lay coffined in mine. And I turned to my castaway friends to shut their next-tent-murmurings out.

The first time ever I saw Peter's face I didn't know that we would live through sixteen years and eleven rounds of unsuccessful IVF together. You don't, do you? Peggy didn't know that she would spend the next thirty years of her life with Ewan the night she sang the 'House Carpenter'. Then it was time for Peter to go and that made me very, very sad. Until the music reconciled me. Like it did Sue Townsend, who also took to her desert island one of the best reconciliation songs ever – 'A Hundred Years From Today' sung by Jack Teagarden.[108] (But I won't say anymore about that right now because we're only on Chapter 1 of my sad song section and I'm not reconciled yet.) For now I'll just say this: I saw a darkness for a long time but ultimately this adventure saved me from the waves.

PS. The aforementioned endnote 101 is a reference to a lyric from 'our song' – Peter's and mine. For a long time, I couldn't write that because it felt too intimate. Which is nuts because it's just a song and I've shared far more personal details about our relationship in the press and my previous books. Like the demise of our sex life after we started trying for a baby under the tyranny of an ovulation stick. Like trying to bring him to ejaculation, in a pot, in a cleaner's broom cupboard in a fertility clinic – to be honest it would have been easier if I wasn't there. But that's the extraordinary thing about music, it's public but it's also very private. And even now I still can't bring myself to name the artist or the title. You'll have to check the endnote for that.

2

'I think I might cry while this is on.'
–Jill Balcon, 2007

———————

There are many women who have appeared on *Desert Island Discs* that have loved and cried. But there are two who resonated with me at an elemental level. Both of them actresses. Both of them married to writers. In fact all four husbands and wives have been on the show but it's the women I won't ever forget: Jill Balcon, who was married to poet Cecil Day-Lewis; and Patricia Neal, who was married to Roald Dahl. There were so many connections between my life and theirs – I guess we're all just acting out each other's stories with different people in the starring roles.

Sue's introduction to Patricia Neal mesmerised me immediately: '*My castaway this week is an actress whose life has been a mixture of professional success and private tragedy.*' It's a bold statement – unless you're saying it about yourself – which sometimes I do. Sometimes I say that in my thirties, publicly I had a successful career in the theatre but privately I had a secret life on a desperate mission to become a mother. Because it's true.

Publicly, Patricia was a feted actress, an Oscar winner. She had five children and a long marriage. But she lost her oldest child and nearly lost another, had three paralysing strokes and finally, after thirty years, her husband, Roald Dahl, divorced her and married her friend. Sue's first question to Patricia is whether she feels she's suffered more than her fair share of tragedies. And in her distinctive Southern drawl Patricia answers defiantly: *'I sure do!'* and then laughs kind of triumphantly, before adding, *'I've got to laugh about it because if I didn't, I'd have killed myself some years ago.'* These are the first words she's ever spoken to me and I love her for them.

Then near the halfway point of the episode, Sue pincers her again. We'd been enjoying hearing Patricia's tales of staying at The Savoy with actor-turned president Ronald Reagan, her early affair with another Hollywood movie star, Gary Cooper, and how when she first met Roald Dahl, he'd spent the whole night talking not to her but to Leonard Bernstein (composer of the ultimate lovers' musical, *Westside Story*[109] – which thinking about it should have been on my 'conditional love song list' because every song in it is a love song).

Then Sue bluntly asks why she's written about her life with Roald in such devastatingly frank detail and made such private moments public.

And Patricia fires back: *'You think I should be ashamed?'*

And then she says that a lady Abbot told her she needed to talk about it, write about it, because it was torturing her. They then start talking through the tragedies – the loss of her first child to measles, the near loss of her third child to a car accident, her first stroke when she was pregnant with her fifth child, her second and third strokes when she was in hospital. She couldn't walk or talk and wanted to die but says that Roald wouldn't let her, that she owes everything to him for that. And you can tell she means it, so when she says she doesn't blame him for the other women, I think she means that too. But she says it made her sad and when the marriage ended after thirty years she was heartbroken.

The last track she chooses is Joan Baez singing the haunting 'Black is the Colour of My True Love's Hair.'[110] And at the end Patricia saves it from the waves because, she says, it's fantastic. But it's dark. It's a track you want to cry to.

And I thought: black is the colour of *my* true love's hair, although he was blue-eyed and blond too.

I listened to Jill Balcon in the Lake District. It was on a day that I spent hours walking through the rain. Jill's been on the show twice. As has her husband, the poet Cecil Day-Lewis. Her father – Michael Balcon, the film producer and head of Ealing Studios – was cast away too. And I presume that her son – three-time Oscar-winning best actor Daniel Day-Lewis – has declined to join them on the island because I can't believe he hasn't been invited. Maybe it's just as well. With a family that successful they might start to colonise the place.

Jill says she first fell in love with Cecil when she was twelve years old. He was twenty years her senior, a successful poet already who had come to her school as guest of honour at a prize-giving. She says she thought he was the most beautiful man she'd ever seen. Then, nearly a decade later, on her twenty-third birthday she re-met him when she started working as an actress, and fell in love again. She describes him as having *'charm'* not in the superficial sense but in the magic sense of the word, and that she was *'enthralled'* – which I think is similar to that energy thing I described earlier that Peter has, but she says it better. And despite the fact Jill was young and Cecil was much older, that he was married as well as having a mistress, that he didn't have much money and her father deeply disapproved of their relationship, she says she had no qualms about getting involved with him because she loved him so much and would have done anything to spend her life with him.

Jill's track to cry to is 'La Mer'.[111] I'd already put it on my 'Sea Playlist' because it's been chosen by other castaways too. For Jill, though, it's a reminder of a country and language she loves and to be honest anyone who wants Charles Trenet to sing for them must be a romantic. But I'm not sure she knew it was going to make her cry when she chose it because she suddenly gets overwhelmed at the thought of it playing and says: '*I think I might cry while this is on*.' So if she didn't know, the good thing is she's got the right track on her island for when she needs it.

After it plays, she talks about Cecil's death when he was Poet Laureate and the work she's done to maintain his literary legacy, including the writing of his biography. She says it's been a comfort but also very painful because it's uncovered things she and her family never knew. She utters the word 'affair'. And then repeats it with an 's'. She finishes this section of the interview before choosing her next track – the Czech composer Leoš Janáček[112] who she says knocked her sideways when she first heard his music in the film *The Unbearable Lightness of Being*, which her son starred in. But just before that she says this and it floored me: '*It's very difficult being exposed and exposing him and trying to be truthful, which I have tried to be*.'

I believe her. She's so full of love and dignity. I listened to her as the rain fell on the Lake District hills and down my face. Sometimes life is unbearably light, sometimes it's unbearably heavy. Afterwards, I put on my own 'Playlist to Cry To'. And cried again.

3

'Nobody wants to put trust in someone they love who's let them down. Because love is an investment of its own.'

–Stephen King, 2006

When our relationship started to falter, Peter and I danced around the death of it for ages. Relighting the kindling. Getting burnt. Watching the embers. It took a year-and-a-half for it to finally end. But even then it hadn't ended. Not in my heart. A year-and-a-half after a year-and-a-half, and things had only got harder, darker. There had been some relief in the beginning; that a decision had been made. But the ashes of our relationship had stained me. I couldn't clean off the dirt.

That's why a year-and-a-half after the year-and-a-half it ended, I embarked on a series of investigations – which I now call my 'Crime and Truth Adventures'. With my headphones. On Hampstead Heath. I hoped it might help me understand the man and solve the puzzle of what had gone wrong because the unknowing of it was torturing me.

I would walk down to the playground and paddling pool that I'd loved as a child. I remember how I used to drag my dad down on a Saturday before it opened and we would climb over the railings and he'd push me on the swings. Then I'd walk a bit further on to the running track which I never went to as a child but did when I was training for the London Marathon because I had several sessions there with a running coach in the hope it would help me get faster. (It didn't.) Here I would turn left onto the grass and up to the top of Parliament Hill. Then I'd stride cross-country past the climbing tree (that's no longer there) and the bonfire (that isn't either). Along and up past Boudicca's grave (that is probably not her grave but it's a great local story and it *is* a tumulus – whatever that is). Then further up to the Westfield Gate entrance to Kenwood. Then I'd bear left, down a dip, and up past Springett's Wood to Spaniards Road. That would be one episode. I'd stand at the barrier there and put on another and then walk down retracing the same footsteps. I didn't have to think. I just walked, listened, learnt and thought.

First up I played a load of crime writers searching for clues. Colin Dexter, loyal to Morse, chose and saved Wagner – 'Brünnhilde's Immolation' (and I thought poor Brünnhilde, I know how you feel). James Ellroy had a maleness about him that reminded me a bit of Peter and chose five pieces of Beethoven. And Martina Cole made me laugh when she said she liked men but she wouldn't want to eat a whole one.

Then I listened to Stephen King – who I know is more of a horror writer than a crime writer, although he says he's just a writer who has an idea which becomes a book. And although I've not really read him I'm convinced he must be a good one. Surely anyone who can quip that when he was around two-years old, his dad went out to buy a pack of cigarettes *'and we're still waiting for him to show up, so I guess it must have been an obscure brand'*, well, anyone who can quip like that on the radio *must* be a good writer. He's also a best-selling one who has not just sold millions but hundreds of millions of books. And when writing success came Stephen says he fell into the abyss of alcohol and drug addiction – maybe because his father never found those cigarettes or maybe because he was invited to eat at what he describes as the 'Banquet of America' – *'Put me up there with [Jim] Morrison and Dylan Thomas,'* he says.

Stephen's wife, Tabitha, eventually staged an intervention and he went into rehab. They are still together now but he says it took a long time for them to reknit their relationship and the scars are still there. And then he says something which rebounds in my ears: *'Nobody wants to put trust in someone they love who's let them down. Because love is an investment of its own.'*

There's a beat of audible silence – his words so powerful and true – before Kirsty asks for his next track. It wasn't an answer but it was the best explanation I'd had. I had invested and been let down. My trust had been broken. But I was also the addict – put me up there with Morrison and Thomas. For me, my love was the addiction, and it had felt impossible to give up. Yet, ultimately, like any addict who has to face the decision of whether they want to live or die, I had severed our relationship and gone cold turkey. But even when I chose my sanity and survival, the pain didn't get better. In fact it got far worse. That's because if we are blessed enough to get given one person in life who truly sees us, Peter was that for me. So choosing life and losing him was the hardest thing I've ever done. Harder than what had come before; harder even than what was still to come.

I listened to Stephen all the way up to the Spaniards Road. Head down, feet and ears in motion. And then on the way back down, I listened to the crime writer Ed McBain (the pseudonym of Evan Hunter). And just as I was reaching the brow of Parliament Hill, he chooses Olivier Messiaen's *'L'Ascension'*[113] as his fifth track. Ed says he's got a taste for discordant, strident, violent music and there's a lot in Messiaen that sounds like a scream for help and that excites him when he listens to it. I'd never heard Messiaen's music. I'd never read Ed McBain. But it started playing, and it was just as Ed said: it was like a scream. After this – for his sixth track – he chooses Tony Bennett singing 'When Joanna Loved Me',[114] which is the complete antithesis – it's such easy listening. Ed acknowledges it might be considered as an adolescent choice but says: *'It sums up every girl or woman I've ever fallen in love with, and then fallen out of love with or vice-versa.'*

I thought of Peter. Love is an investment of its own. There was a time when I was Joanna but now I can only SCREAM.

4

'The consequences were so terrible that that's one of the places
where I learnt how important it is to tell the truth and
not lie for any reason.'

–Alice Walker, 2013

———————

It was the writer Alice Walker who first got me thinking deeply about the subject of truth. She describes the impact of an incident that happened in her childhood when she was shot and blinded in one eye by her brother's BB gun while they were playing. I was passing the Leg of Mutton Pond at the time on the path that leads up to the pub that is a song – 'The Old Bull and Bush.'[115] There are eighteen named ponds on the heath, including three that you can swim in, which have come to feel like home to me. The Leg of Mutton isn't one of them but I love it because it's got such a great name.

Kirsty says to Alice: *'It was an accident, I guess?'*

And Alice responds by saying that Kirsty's choice of words are *'pivotal'* because her brother was shooting directly at her, so it wasn't actually an accident at all and it was very confusing to have it passed off as such. And although Alice and her brother were both children at the time – so perhaps he didn't fully understand the consequences – she says it was very challenging to figure out how to deal with it emotionally. What made matters worse was that her other brother told her to tell their parents that she'd been hit in the eye by a piece of wire. And that's what she did because she didn't want any of them to get punished. But, she says, the consequences of it were so terrible that it taught her how important it is to tell the truth and not lie for any reason.

I thought again of Stephen King: *love is an investment of its own*. I thought of Ed McBain and screamed. And I walked with Alice Walker by the Leg of Mutton Pond and thought – yes, the truth is important. The consequences of lies are terrible. But why? What is it about them that makes them feel so violent when there's nothing intrinsically physical about them at all.

Soon after this, I took a hike along the Essex Way – starting from the high and low lighthouses at the coastal port of Harwich and wending my way through Wrabness Nature Reserve to the Mistley Towers on the banks of the Stour Estuary. It's a wonderful walk and despite the fact it was a sunny Saturday, I saw virtually nobody. Maybe that's because in the words of John Betjeman I was in 'the deepest Essex few explore' or maybe it was because a certain television programme has encouraged everyone to think that Essex is the place to go to for a vajazzle rather than a stroll.

I had several episodes of listening at the ready to help me in my search for the truth about truth. First up Phil Scraton – an academic in criminology who is particularly known for his work on the Hillsborough disaster in which nearly a hundred Liverpool football fans were crushed and killed. And the second was Doreen Lawrence, mother of Stephen, who was murdered in a racist attack in south-east London. Both castaways spent years fighting for truth and justice, Doreen finally receiving some when two men were convicted of her son's murder twenty years after it happened. And Phil when the families of the Hillsborough victims finally got confirmation that their loved ones had been unlawfully killed. Both episodes are a testament to the importance of truth to human beings.

I hope you're not thinking that I am comparing my situation to theirs. I write that, of course, in case you are thinking it. I know I'll never be able to call for a public trial or enquiry to uncover the truth of what happened in my relationship, even though I was injured deeply. I know the outcome of the crime doesn't hurt anyone but me. But there was something about listening to Phil and Doreen's search for truth that helped legitimatise how I felt. And I needed that. So I'll always be grateful to them for walking with me on the Essex Way. Phil saved from the waves 'You'll Never Walk Alone' – the Liverpool home anthem. And Doreen saved 'Fallen Soldier'[116] – Beverley Knight's tribute to Stephen. The music told me their truth too.

I still had several miles to go so after this I indulged in the American writer Norman Mailer. He'd been sitting on my 'must listen' list for a while as one of the iconic episodes of the show that is often mentioned in press articles. He's renowned for being the first person to dare to ask for *a stick of the best marijuana* as his luxury item – in 1979.

'This is illegal talk, Mr Mailer,' Roy responds.

'Well,' Norman replies. 'Here we are in trouble again.'

But he was being truthful about what he wanted. You have to give him that.

At the beginning of the episode, he says he picked his tracks pretty quickly without much deliberation. Then two days later he says he realised there was a unifying principle – he'd been married eight times and the eight records he'd chosen reminded him of the different women he'd been in love with.

Roy says with a hint of humour in his voice: *'Well now the first one is Elgar's Pomp and Circumstance March No. 1 – 'Land of Hope and Glory'. Now how does that come into it?'*

And Norman shoots back: *'Well I could say I was married to an English girl once and there was something about her that did remind me of Pomp and Circumstance . . .'*

Norman Mailer walked with me along a farmer's field, into a winding wood and then down to the estuary's edge. I like a man who's quick and funny. I also like a man who's truthful.

5

*'This is a song I just loved, it's a singular recording by a
singular artist – Glen Campbell singing "Wichita Lineman".'*

–Kelsey Grammer, 2017

———————————

It was another quick and funny American who first inspired
me to start writing a playlist for Peter which is full of songs
that make me cry, many of which are love songs.

I was walking back from a yoga class in Queens Crescent
which is on the Chalk Farm edge of Kentish Town. It's one of
London's oldest market streets – stalls handed down from
generation to generation selling fruit and veg and knockdown
household goods. It's great for a cheap pound of potatoes or a
bottle of bleach and not the sort of place you'd expect to find a
yoga shala. However, the classes are half the price of its sister
studio in Primrose Hill a few streets away. Mind you everything
in London is half the price of Primrose Hill. It's also closer to
home, and I was on the way back nearing the end of the Malden
Road just past St Dominic's Priory when the actor Kelsey Grammer
(aka Frasier) chose Glen Campbell's 'Wichita Lineman'.[117]

It was December 2017, still in the early days of this
adventure, and Kelsey had recently appeared on the show. As
the music played, I was suddenly hit by a strange wave of
emotion. This was one of Peter's songs. I hadn't recognised the

artist's name or the title of the track at first. But the sound was immediately familiar to me. That is the power of music. It can bring back the past or a person in an opening bar. And if I hadn't embarked on this adventure I might never have heard it again. Because it wasn't my song or 'our song'. It was Peter's.

After that day, the show's archive took on a newfound purpose for me. I started to mine it for music – all the artists, all the songs I'd heard in the background of our life together but hadn't fully appropriated for myself. If I were never to see him again – and I wasn't sure I could – then at least I would be able to play his music.

Glen Campbell's 'Wichita Lineman' was the inaugural song on Peter's Playlist. But gradually it grew to include all of the following and more: Arvo Pärt,[118] Bill Evans,[119] Charlie Parker,[120] Bob Dylan,[121] J.J. Cale,[122] James Taylor,[123] John Martyn,[124] Keith Jarrett,[125] Neil Young,[126] Miles Davis,[127] Nick Drake,[128] Pat Metheny,[129] Paul Simon,[130] Tom Waits[131] and, of course, 'Mr Sting'[132] and 'Van – the man – Morrison' (that's what Peter called them both out of respect).

But it's not every piece of music they've written. It's particular ones. Like with Bill Evans it's 'Lucky to Be Me', and with Pat Metheney it's 'Always and Forever' – both of which the actress Anne Reid gave me on the top of the bus that goes between Keswick and Penrith, after a long day of walking on the fells. And John Martyn's 'Couldn't Love You More' came courtesy of the director Anthony Minghella on Box Hill. And Tom Waits' 'The Piano Has Been Drinking' was from the wine writer Oz Clarke in a base camp, and Nick Drake's 'River Man' was from the gardener Dan Pearson in another. And thank you to the journalist John Simpson for J.J. Cale's 'Magnolia'. And to the model Kate Moss for Neil Young's 'Harvest Moon'. And to the singer Barbara Dickson for James Taylor's 'Don't Let Me Be Lonely Tonight', when I was walking home from Victoria after another trip to that running shop for another pair of trainers – I was now regularly walking them out.

When Barbara played me the track, it hit me so hard I had to stop and sit down on a bench for a while. Moreover, later the same day, when I got back to South End Green and popped into M&S for some supper shopping, the comedian Rory Bremner played me Van Morrison's 'Have I Told You Lately', and for quite a while I just wandered up and down the aisles in a daze.

As the list grew and grew, I realised something strange. Every artist I was putting on it was a man. Even though there were female musicians that Peter liked too, it was if I was recreating him in a playlist. I rarely listen to it though, because it makes me sad. But it's good to know I've got it if I need a song to cry to, and there's one piece in particular that is tears guaranteed. It's by Bob Dylan, who over the years has become a *Desert Island Discs* regular, although this song isn't one of his most chosen. In fact, if my research is as rigorous as I hope it is, it's only been taken once in the original by the actor Jeremy Irons, who said that Bob Dylan had been a great part of his life but that he didn't realise for a long time that he wrote it. I'm sure lots of people don't. Adele did a fabulous cover version (although castaways have proven to prefer her 'Skyfall').[133] But, for me, it's only the Bob Dylan version which makes me cry. Probably because he's a man, and because he wrote it, and because of his 'ragged' voice. *Ragged*. Such a wonderful word. And what is weird – I know – is that it's a song about loving someone, about going to the end of the earth to prove it. It shouldn't make you cry. But it does. Maybe because there was a time when I felt Peter would have gone to the end of the earth to make me feel his love but he stopped short before getting there, and went somewhere else.

One day – it was a rare day when I wasn't walking but was travelling back from something late at night on the Tube – I put on Peter's playlist in an act of masochism. Bob Dylan started singing 'Make You Feel My Love' and I immediately started crying. I tried to hide my face inside the hood of my jacket so no one could see me. The carriage was largely empty, so I let Bob sing and the tears fall. A few stops later, at Euston, a man sitting across and further down the carriage got up to leave and as he walked past me, he touched my arm supportively. The hood hadn't hidden me, and his kindness made me cry even more.

Nowadays if I ever see a person crying on the train, I wait until I'm about to leave, and then I go over and touch their arm. I did it to someone just the other day on the overground as I was getting off at West Hampstead. I hope it helped her as much as that man helped me. We all have our Bob Dylan moments.

We all need someone to make us feel their love.

6

'It's about 1982. I will say no more about it.
Let's let the listeners hear the words and I think
they will immediately understand . . .'

–Mervyn King, 2013

Actually I tell a lie. There is one female singer on Peter's playlist. In fact, I've got her opening the set before Glen Campbell. It's Marlene Dietrich singing 'Peter'. This amuses me – partly because it makes me think of her mischievous interview with Roy. And partly because it was chosen by the Russian double agent Oleg Gordievsky, and there's something about the combination of Marlene and a Russian spy that delights me as the first song on Peter's playlist. She sings in German and I don't really know what the song's about except I love the way she purrs the words: *'Peter, Peter.'* It's a private joke. Just for me. I don't think Peter would fully appreciate it. He'd be wary of Marlene and snap back at me that he always tells the truth and he's not a mole.

Peter and I did share a sense of humour though. It was one of the happiest things about our relationship – even towards the end. In the final urgent days of couples therapy, there were lies, but there was also laughter. And our therapist – a man of middle age who would write notes about us on a pad of A3 paper (we were too big a problem for something smaller) – would sometimes seem incredulous about how much we laughed, even when it was clear our relationship was falling apart. This shared humour was like our own language. We'd lie in bed in the morning following a therapy session and Peter would bring in the tea and then spill it all over the sheets and I'd say breezily: *'Ah well, accidents happen.'* And then we'd laugh and laugh and laugh because we both knew I was not the sort of person who tolerated accidents easily. There was such humour in me trying to.

Some guests on *Desert Island Discs* have taken tracks to make them laugh. Personally, I don't think it's quite as important as music to make you cry but I've created a playlist of the best of them anyway. I figured I might need to listen to it sometime and it became a base camp balm when things were going slowly or badly on a mountain. It opens with what has become my favourite Elvis track. 'Are you Lonesome Tonight?' – the laughing version.[134] I love listening to Elvis not being able to control his laughter and showing us a little of the man behind the music, his happiness in that moment infectious. After this I've got what must be the best two laughing songs ever written – 'The Laughing Policeman'[135] and 'Narcissus (The Laughing Record)'.[136] And then I move into sketches, including Bob Newhart's 'Introducing Tobacco to Civilisation'.[137] It's so funnily clever – when you think about it, how did putting a burning leaf into our mouths ever catch on as a thing? It also tickles me that the opposing prime minsters, Jim Callaghan and Margaret Thatcher, both chose it for their list of eight. Maybe they got on more than they thought they did – they shared a sense of humour at any rate.

I'd never heard of Bob Newhart before. I was the wrong generation and he wasn't a favourite of my dad's. Which is how I had heard of Tony Hancock, who was the wrong generation too but was. One day, while walking along Swain's Lane on my way to Highgate Wood as a change from the heath, the actor Leslie Grantham chose the 'Test Pilot Sketch'[138] from *Hancock's Half Hour* and I started laughing out loud. The mums sitting outside Gails with their oat lattes and high-fashion pushchairs looked across at me weirdly. They were probably thinking: who is that laughing woman who looks like she should be sitting here with us? But they're wrong: oat lattes are not coffee to me, and pushchairs are not a fashion I'll ever be able to wear. Maybe what I should have said is: *'Mine's a filter coffee in black, with no sugar, thanks.'*

But I didn't because I was having fun listening with Leslie. Tony Hancock is sitting in the cockpit as the pilot. Kenneth Williams is out on the wing as the mechanic. Both in a BBC radio studio. Tony takes the plane up into the air and starts flying at 2,400 miles an hour when a peculiar knocking can be heard on the windscreen. He opens the cockpit door and there's the mechanic: *'Good evening,'* he says, in a way that only Kenneth Williams can. It's hilarious. The studio audience roar with laughter.

After this, as I was walking up past Highgate Cemetery and into Waterloo Park – known as the toughest climb in London – Leslie talks about being cast as the legendary 'Dirty Den', in the TV soap *Eastenders* – a character that became indecipherable from the man. He says it was Anita Dobson, who played Angie, that made them the stars of the show but it was him that made the character of Den dirty. He recalls some of the classic moments, like the time Den claimed to be living in a Bed and Breakfast but was actually staying with his mistress. Angie made him some sandwiches to take back to the B&B and, as he was walking down the street, he threw them in the gutter. I couldn't get that image out of my head all day. I'm so glad that Angie/Anita found her 'Bohemian Rhapsody' in Brian May.[139]

Comedy is often a bedfellow to tragedy. It can make you cry, and I don't mean tears of laughter. So I've put something special on Peter's playlist that I know would make us both laugh but, up against the other tracks, also breaks my heart.

It's Mervyn King, the former governor of the Bank of England, who first gave me the idea. I listened to him on a walk up to the Thousand Pound Pond – another of the eighteen named ponds on the heath that's just below Kenwood House. Sometimes a castaway would provide me with inspiration for where to go walking and this felt like a good one!

He was a fascinating guest – personally and professionally – and one of the things that made him engaging is that he seemed to have a lot of different interests in addition to money – including football. Peter hates sport, especially football. He has this stereotype in his head of the sort of man who likes it that he despises. In fact I know I wouldn't even be able to persuade him to listen to the footballer Ian Wright's *Desert Island Discs*, even if I told him it's one of my top eight episodes of all time – which it is because the bit where he talks about his childhood teacher is radio platinum. But Mervyn King isn't the stereotypical football fan – even Peter would have to acknowledge that – and, frankly, we could have done with him to help us manage our debt after all the IVF.

Midway through the programme after having quite a heavy discussion about the economy, Kirsty manoeuvres onto his next track. *'We're on your . . .'* she giggles. *'Yes, well here we are, we're on your fifth tell me about this . . .'*

And Mervyn replies: *'This has never been played on radio before—'*

And Kirsty fires back: *'There may be a reason for that.'*

'—Or indeed perhaps anywhere else,' Mervyn continues. And without actually saying what it is the music starts—

SAD SONGS (AKA SONGS TO MAKE ME CRY)

'Oh we're all going to Rotterdam, each and every Villa fan.
Shout Villa. Aston Villa.
Because we're the greatest football team. We're the best you've
ever seen. We're Villa. Aston Villa.'

And, as the music fades, Mervyn explains that it's from
when they won the European Cup in 1982, and everyone he's
played it to says it will be the catchiest tune on the programme.
And it is, and I smiled. And I thought of Peter, and how he
would absolutely hate a football song on his list even if it was
catchy, and that made me smile even more. So I've put one on
his playlist to make us laugh (and our therapist would probably
be scribbling furiously on his piece of A3 paper right now).
But I couldn't find Doug O'Brien's 'Rotterdam 82'[140] so I had
to choose something else. In the end I plumped for 'Three
Lions'[141] – the European championship anthem from 1996.
It's got the right amount of football fan ladishness which Peter
would hate. And it works its tragicomic magic brilliantly after
Bob Dylan's 'Make You Feel My Love.'

7

*'It's the one instrument in the whole orchestra that makes
me cry. Because it always sounds so lonely.'*

–Betty Driver, 2011

O ne of the things this adventure has given me is an understanding of the orchestra like I've never had before. I mean I always knew the violins were on the left, the cellos on the right and the woodwind and brass were at the back, from my own days in the school orchestra. But now I feel I've got to know the instruments personally. I have my favourites and I have different requirements for different moods. If I'd thought more about this earlier in life, I'm not sure I would have ended up playing the oboe. Although 'Gabriel's Oboe'[142] by Ennio Morricone is one of my favourite tracks to end my longest walks to and always helps me get through the final mile, along with Pachelbel's Canon,[143] plus two different Adagios for Strings – Albinoni's [144] and Barber's[145] (I'm partial to an adagio, it's my favourite speed). I have all four of these pieces on my 'Peaceful Playlist' and they are perfect listening when I've walked upwards of 25 miles and am nearly home where a shower and something salty are always waiting.

If I had to choose my favourite sound in the orchestra now, I think it would be the cello. The actress Betty Driver (better known as another 'Betty' from another TV soap, *Coronation Street*) says it's a '*lonely*' instrument. So if you're looking for a sound to make you cry, the cello could be it. It could be the most soulful sound that exists. Betty chooses Brahms – the adagio(!) from his Cello Sonata No. 2 in F Major[146] played by Steven Isserlis who is one of seven cellists to appear on the show in its first eighty years. I've listened to and loved them all but there is one woman who is extra special to me.

Jacqueline du Pré was in her early thirties when she was cast away, in 1977, but had already stopped playing due to the multiple sclerosis which would precipitate her early death at the age of forty-two. And although I'm a bit ashamed to admit this, I will, because I want to be truthful: I think one of the reasons I love her as I do is because I like people in pain. And I especially like creative prodigy when it's touched by personal tragedy. (FYI, the pianist John Ogdon did a Jacqueline du Pré on me as well.) So if you're going to be cast away, and you're going to take some cello, and the cello you choose is Elgar's E Minor, then, in my opinion, there's no one else who should play it except Jacqueline – preferably with Sir John Barbirolli conducting. The cellists Yo-Yo Ma and Paul Tortelier both paid this homage, which surely says a lot.

I first listened to Jacqueline's episode straight after I listened to the writer Susan Hill – who was part of my 'Crime Adventure', although she's probably more known for her ghost stories, especially *The Woman in Black*. Susan also has the requisite level of talent and tragedy that I like. She lost her first fiancé to a sudden coronary thrombosis – a blow and shock she says she's never got over – and later went through a period of infertility and miscarriages and then had a daughter who was born prematurely and died at five-weeks old.

As I was walking along the always damp and gloomy path which runs past the Stock Pond and then the Ladies Swimming

Pond, and then the Bird Sanctuary Pond after that, Susan says she first heard the Elgar live during a rehearsal in Coventry Cathedral. She says she hid herself at the back of the church and felt as if she was watching greatness being born: Jacqueline playing her cello like a demon, her golden hair streaming and flying like an angel's, Barbirolli conducting and the orchestra making music like she'd never heard before.

I turned up Fitzroy Park – one of my favourite roads off the heath and climbed up to the Highgate Flask – one of everyone's favourite pubs. I put on Jacqueline's episode (she was my number 373). And then as I was coming down from the Flask, past the neo-Gothic houses of the estate known as Holly Village – which wouldn't look out of place in a Susan Hill novel – she chose her sixth track: Victor Borge's 'Phonetic Punctuation'[147] – as a bit of light relief. It involves Borge telling a story in which all the punctuation (full stops, commas, exclamation marks, etc.) have their own comic sounds. Jacqueline says she's heard it many times and is still unable to listen to it without getting a stomach ache from laughing. And later, of all the tracks she chose, it's this one that I decided to pick for my ever-growing playlists inspired by my castaway friends. I put it on my 'Comedy Playlist' (along with a burning leaf and a laughing Elvis). It always makes me think of her when I hear it. I like to think of her laughing.

Immediately after I listened to Jacqueline, I put on her husband – the pianist and conductor Daniel Barenboim (my Episode 374). I decided to walk a loop of ponds so I went past what people called the Dog Pond and then the Men's Swimming Pond and then The Model Boating Pond next to that – although I haven't seen any craft on it for years, just the odd coot on a raft.

When they first married, Daniel and Jacqueline were the music world's golden couple. And throughout Jacqueline's episode, she talked constantly and lovingly about *'my husband'* and many of her choices are linked to him and to them playing together with their friends. But I was immediately wary of Daniel, as it became clear during his episode that when she got ill, he had embarked on another relationship. Although he never divorced Jacqueline, by the time of her death, he had two sons with another woman. He talks slightly hesitantly about the double life he led for a while, and his gratitude to the press for the amnesty around it, something I can't believe would happen now.

Daniel's own episode was recorded on location in Jerusalem in 2006, nearly twenty years after Jacqueline's death, his second wife and the mother to his two children sitting in the same room listening. It was obviously a significant and lasting relationship and although I still felt for Jacqueline, I forgave him just a little bit – but mainly because he took her playing the Elgar Cello Concerto in E Minor, with Sir John Barbirolli conducting. He says: *'There's something completely unique about her being at one with the instrument and with the music.'* It seemed to be an expression of his continuing love for her, and I liked that. I also thought it's a bit like me: at one with *Desert Island Discs* as I'm walking. And I admit I was secretly hoping that at the end Daniel would save Jacqueline from the waves – that maybe she was the love of his life and this was how he would show it. But he doesn't. In fact, he refuses to take any of his tracks to his desert island. He says he only wants the scores.

And my heart wept a little then.

For me, and for Jacqueline.

8

'It brings tears to my eyes because in many ways it is romantic but also in other ways it takes you into this huge vacuum of the possibilities and you realise how small you are, how insignificant you are in this cosmos.'

–Wangari Maathai, 2007

———————

My dad's funeral was one of the best days of my life. I know that sounds wrong but it's true. I read a poem; Peter did the eulogy; the congregation recited 'The Owl and the Pussycat'.[148] Towards the end of his life, my dad suffered a series of strokes which took him on a slow slide downwards. Eventually he lost nearly all means of communication and could only say a couple of things. One of them was: *'Am I dead yet?'*

To which I'd reply: *'Not yet dad. Nearly!'*

And the other thing, right up until the end, was he could recite his mother's poetry and 'The Owl and the Pussycat' by Edward Lear – he got such childlike pleasure from the words.

The very last words I said to my dad when I left the hospital on the night before the day he died were: *'I love you dad'* and I don't know how he managed to reply because he could hardly speak by then but the very last words he breathed to me in a whisper, were: *'I love you too.'*

The next day, Peter and I got the result of our tenth (and penultimate) round of IVF. Everything had gone exceptionally well on that cycle. Three high-grade embryos had been made in the laboratory and returned to my womb – to be honest I was imagining triplets. We had every reason to be hopeful. Having suffered with the label of 'Unexplained Infertility' for years (which is the worst sort of diagnosis because it isn't one), we had finally got some possible answers and taken a course of treatment for it. But our pregnancy test was negative and later the same day my dad died. Life gives and it takes away, and I will always feel that on that day it took away a lot and gave me nothing back in return. 'The Circle of Life' didn't apply to me, it's just a great song by Elton John[149] from *The Lion King*. Yet, my dad's funeral was still one of the best days of my life. It was my theatrical tour de force.

I got up early and went to Covent Garden flower market with my sister. We bought armfuls of red roses and decorated his coffin. The hearse left our house – the one he was born in – and the whole family walked behind it down the hill. At the crematorium – the one on Hoop Lane in Golders Green, which is the oldest in London – I read a poem my grandmother wrote for him, entitled 'Letter to a boy at school'. Peter talked about his life, including the story of when he was a child and the writer Malcolm Lowry killed his pet rabbit – an anecdote that somehow made the *Guardian*'s diary section a month later. And the congregation all recited 'The Owl and the Pussycat', as if it were a hymn. It was a hymn to him.

For the music, I'd chosen 'Sit Down, You're Rockin' the Boat' from *Guys and Dolls* and I knew I also wanted a song from the Great American Songbook. I had imagined for years that I was going to choose Ella Fitzgerald[150] singing 'Ev'ry Time We Say Goodbye' (which, FYI, is her most chosen song on *Desert Island Discs*). But, in the end, I didn't. I chose

Frank Sinatra[151] singing 'Moon River'. It was Peter's suggestion and it felt instantly right – its beautiful combination of wistfulness and hope.

I like to imagine my dad lying there listening. He wouldn't have believed everything was arranged for him. *'Amazing,'* he would have said, in the way that he did, wide-eyed, lingering over the letters 'a' and 'z'. I think when someone dies at ninety-two, you have to make it a celebration of a long life lived. At the end of the service, they opened the doors at the back of the chapel. It was late February and the garden was flooded with crocuses heralding the end of winter and the coming spring. The abundance of white, purple and yellow against the green of the grass looked like they were decorating my dad's 'stairway to heaven'.[152] They truly did.

I didn't cry that day.

Afterwards, we had the wake in the Magdala pub at the bottom of Parliament Hill. I got very, very drunk and felt very, very happy. And then Peter took me home in a taxi and put me to bed.

Even so, 'Moon River' is on my 'Sad Songs Playlist'. Three years after my dad died, almost to the same February day, I sat in that same bed alone, early one Saturday morning, listening to it on repeat, crying. I'd lost my dad, now I was losing someone else. The problem with social media – which I already mentioned I hate – is it's not made for truth and lies. So if you tell someone you're out with a friend, then make sure they're in the same country as you before you don't come home. Make sure you've checked Twitter.

Now 'Moon River' reminds me of the two most special men in my life – one who made me very, very happy at the end, and one who made me very, very sad. And there's no better person to sing about it than Frank Sinatra.

Although the song has been chosen by various castaways in various versions, Sinatra's rendition of it has only been chosen once in eighty years – by the campaigner Wangari Maathai. She was the first African woman to receive the Nobel Prize and my episode 2,469. I listened to her walking through Regent's Park on my way into town. I didn't take the Tube or bother with the bus anymore, every outing an opportunity for training and listening.

I admired Wangari's philosophy on everything: from polygamy (her father had four wives – she says it wasn't perfect but the alternative isn't either), to colonialism (she says it gave her something as well as taking something away), and of how it felt to be marginalised as a Black woman when she was living in America, but then equally marginalised back in her home country of Kenya, for being too much like a white woman with Black skin. I loved her ability to see life from different perspectives. And then she went and chose Frank Sinatra singing 'Moon River' with these words:

'Anyone who has ever been outside when the moon is standing there almost like it is standing still, and you wonder what happens there, what will happen in the future, and for me moments like that I remember this song. It brings tears to my eyes because in many ways it is romantic but also in other ways, it takes you into this huge vacuum of the possibilities, and you realise how small you are, how insignificant you are in this cosmos.'

During my IVF struggle, I got a lot of solace from thinking of myself as a speck. In a hundred years from today, I'd tell myself, it won't matter whether or not I had a baby (and thanks again to Sue Townsend for giving me the song which put this feeling to music back in Chapter 1 of this section). It only matters to me because in my world, I am enormous. But if I think of myself as a speck – then I can get the idea of me being a mother into perspective. Its total irrelevance to the universe. And in London's Regent's Park on the Broad Walk just past the Readymoney Fountain, Wangari reminded me of this again with her words, and how the same is true of broken hearts. Of their insignificance in the cosmos.

So when you next listen to 'Moon River', maybe you'll cry like me because your own enormous heart has been broken, or maybe you'll cry like Wangari because you'll think of the mystery of the moon and the insignificance of us all. But then, after that, think of the huge vacuum of possibilities. Think of me on my mountainous musical adventure. And decide what adventure you want to undertake for yourself.

My Sad Songs (aka Songs to Make Me Cry) Shortlist

I could have chosen more, many many more . . .

1. 'I See a Darkness' – in tribute to Jarvis Cocker who made me understand the importance of having a song in your life for melancholy moods. And for my grandmother, Anna, who saw a darkness that I've sometimes seen too.

2. Bob Dylan: 'Make You Feel My Love' – hopefully, needs no explanation.

3. James Taylor: 'Don't Let Me Be Lonely Tonight' – a close second to Bob Dylan.

4. Van Morrison: 'Have I Told You Lately' – ditto – a close third.

5. David Baddiel, Frank Skinner and the Lightning Seeds: 'Three Lions' – but only when played after any one of the above three.

6. Edward Elgar: Cello Concerto in E Minor – but only when played by Jacqueline du Pré and conducted by Sir John Barbirolli.

7. Tim: Minchin: 'White Wine in the Sun' (if you've forgotten why, see Songs of Home, Chapter 7).

8. Frank Sinatra: 'Moon River'.

Happy Songs

1. Pharrell Williams: 'Happy'

2. Bobby Hebb: 'Sunny'

3. Miriam Makeba: 'Pata Pata'

4. Astrud Gilberto: 'The Girl From Ipanema'

5. Erik Satie: *Three Gymnopédies*

6. Pyotr Ilyich Tchaikovsky: 'Dance of the Sugar Plum Fairy' from *The Nutcracker*

7. The Carpenters/Imagine Dragons: '(On) Top of the World'

8. Bobby McFerrin: 'Don't Worry, Be Happy'

1

'I just heard this music. It made my burden so much lighter, my knees less aching. Whenever I feel a little bit depressed, I listen to it.'

–Edna Adan Ismail, 2017

I wasn't looking forward to writing the sad song section of this book. I put it off for ages. The thing that got me through was that afterwards I could write this part, so let's just get into it immediately – there's no better track to open with than Pharrell Williams' 'Happy'.[153]

I felt like I might be slowly getting there: to happy. The walking and listening had helped. I started on a hill in Hampstead and then radiated out. I got to know the streets of London better than I'd ever done before, as well as its parks, rivers and canals. If you're looking for a great long central London walk (or run, if you must) then I highly recommend Holland Park to St James'. It's green and flat nearly all the way and you'll be able to go past the Serpentine Lake, where I did all my London-based training for the Channel. It was my first wild water home and the geese still know me there and always try and tempt me in. Alternatively, for more water-based flat walking, head to Little Venice and go either east on the Regent's Canal to Limehouse Basin, or west on the Paddington Arm of the Grand Union Canal and down to Brentford.

I also adventured beyond the city and explored the whole of the UK. I'm still a bit sketchy on counties. Don't test me on the 'shires'. But I now know my Ben Nevis from my Box Hill, my Scafell from my Snowdon.

London was my first home, but now the whole of the UK feels part of who I am. And I never felt alone as long as my castaway companions were with me. In fact I wanted to spend time with them more than I wanted to be with real family and friends. They were teaching me so much about life and music. I started creating playlists for everything. Not just the songs of my youth, home, love and tears. But for my whole family – my grandparents, parents, Peter. I had music for wherever I went in England, Ireland, Scotland, Wales. For the sea and the mountains. For different seasons, weather and times of the day. It was endless. It was exciting. It was energising.

One day, I was walking along the River Lea in east London, accompanied by Steve Backshall. Before this adventure, I didn't even know there was a Lea in London. I thought it was all about the Thames. I didn't know Steve Backshall either. He's an explorer. In fact, he was once 'Adventurer in Residence' for *National Geographic*. But he's most known for the television programme *Deadly Sixty* in which he travels the world having close encounters with the most dangerous creatures on the planet. (And I don't mean some of the men who seem to be in charge these days; I mean animals with fangs and stings who can't help being venomous.)

Anyway, the reason I mention my walk with Steve is not just because I want his fab former job (although please tell me if you see it advertised). Or because I'm keen to meet any dangerous creatures on my own adventures. (Although when I swam the Channel I did encounter a lot of jellyfish. They congregate in the separation zone between English and French inshore waters. Thick like oil slicks, I couldn't avoid them and they stung me all over my body and face. However, after a while, I stopped feeling the pain (you do), so whenever I swam into a new smack (the apt collective noun for a crowd of jellyfish), I'd simply say: *'Hi guys, nice to see you again.'*) No, the reason I mention Steve is because he told me that he spends a lot of time on his own, in his own head and that he has become good at manipulating his mood with music. So if he's feeling lonely or sad, he can listen to certain tracks and make that feeling go away. He said the song he's used for decades to do this is 'Even After All' by Finley Quaye.[154]

And I agreed about music and feelings – adventurer to adventurer – because that's exactly why I've got my own 'Happy Playlist'. It's my guarantee to feeling good and Pharrell Williams' song 'Happy' is on it because I can't believe it could fail to lift anybody's mood. Surprisingly (to me), it's only been chosen by three castaways since its release in 2014 – all women, including the midwife-turned campaigner Edna Adan Ismail.

In the shadowy duelling ground of the Kenwood woods, Edna told me she was genitally mutilated as a child: by her mother and her grandmother. She said it was against the wishes of her father and it's important to say that because it's not only men who are dangerous, women can be too, especially where cultural custom is concerned. Edna described the experience as pain like she'd never known. And years later, when she became the wife of the first president of Somaliland after it declared its Independence, she decided to use her position of power to speak out against the practice. She said that in this and other ways she was not an ideal Somali wife: *'I think. I work. I voice my opinion. I have a brain. I try to use it. I'm a hopeless cook. I did not bear children . . .'*

In that moment we connected and I asked: *'Did she ever want them? Children?'*

And she said she did very much and that every hormone was used on her but it didn't happen. And then she said that maybe in the end it was a good thing because she would not have had so much time, resources and energy for her work if she had. And that whenever she's feeling a little bit depressed, she listens to Pharrell Williams' 'Happy'.

So, now, whenever I listen to the song myself, I think of Edna and all that she has achieved in spite of not becoming a mother. It makes me happy.

You can't go wrong with 'Happy'.

2

*'It's about work for me.
And it's glorious work.'*

–Ali Smith, 2016

———————

Our child was called Molly. She was fair and long limbed like her parents. There's nothing you can do about genetics. She was the best of both of us but also had attributes all of her own. She was arty as much as she was sporty. But then she only exists in my imagination so I can make her whoever I want her to be.

All the women I've met through *Desert Island Discs* who have shared with me their struggle to conceive have offered me solidarity. I have also been inspired by the other things they've done with their lives. It doesn't mean that I don't miss Molly. It just means that I'm not alone, and reminds me there is other important work to be done.

One thing I have done is compile a playlist for her too. It brought me a lot of joy. She's got Beethoven and The Beatles – neither of whom are instant choices for my own list – so I like the fact I've had the opportunity to compose one for her. It's given me some more bandwidth. And because she's not around and never will be, she can't dispute my choices. That's rather good too.

All I ever really knew about Beethoven before this adventure started was his 'Moonlight Sonata', which I told you I played on the piano as a child along with his popular 'Für Elise'. And of course I also knew of his Symphony No. 5 – even people who know nothing about Beethoven know about his advocation for a good beginning. But now I know so much more about the man and his music, including the fact that he never found love or had his own children. All this made Beethoven especially special to me and I was keen to learn more.

I now also know Beethoven wrote nine symphonies in total, and I have decided the last is a must for my Molly because of its final movement – 'Ode To Joy'. If you ask any parent what they want for their children, they'll usually reply all they want is for them to be happy. It's Beethoven's most selected symphony by far, and if you want to demonstrate your 'Remain' allegiance then you could have it as one of your home songs as it's also Europe's National Anthem. I want Molly to be proud of being a European as well as loving her UK home and above all, like any parent, I want her to be happy. So first up she's got Beethoven's 'Ode to Joy' on her playlist.

But there's also a second Beethoven track on Molly's list of eight. It's not *Fidelio* – his only opera – which several castaways have said is the best opera ever written. (I suspect there are a few Italians that might want to dispute that.) Nor is it his popular Piano Concerto No. 5 (also known as the 'Emperor'), selected and saved by prime ministers and press barons, poets and painters, and also taken by Roy Plomley himself when he was cast away. No, for Molly, I've chosen one of his late string quartets which were written after Beethoven had gone completely deaf. Not only is this an incredible achievement but many believe they are the finest music he ever wrote. In fact, the violinist Yehudi Menuhin went so far as to tell me that one of man's highest achievements is the string quartet and there is no higher than Beethoven's – *'written by this extraordinary deaf man who heard more beautiful music than any of us can ever imagine'*. And who's going to argue with Yehudi Menuhin about music? I'm not!

The truth is, though, the quartets are not an easy listen. And Beethoven does also have some high-profile detractors. The composer Howard Goodall told me that despite the fact he recognises that Beethoven is a genius, he doesn't much like him. We were walking on the north bank of the Thames towards Hammersmith Bridge at the time (my second favourite bridge in London after Waterloo; its prettier in design, but not quite so great a view). And another day, just starting out on a second lap of the Box Hill hike, the professor of neurology Oliver Sacks went further. He told me that he hates him and can't stand any of his music but is going to take a late quartet as *'a project'* to see if he can learn to understand why other people find it so sublime.

I love a project myself and when the poet and Nobel Prize-winner Seamus Heaney chose and saved Beethoven's String Quartet No. 13 – because he feels the need to improve himself and believes that this is the piece to do it – well, from that moment, I set out to like Beethoven's string quartets too. And I made it the second track on Molly's playlist. Because, as I said to Seamus *'How can you improve on what improves Seamus Heaney?'*

He shook his head, but I think he smiled too.

And I'm getting there. Slowly. But maybe Molly will do better. If she were here, I'd want to encourage her to do what the writer Ali Smith does, which she says is work for her *'glorious work'*. I was circling round the Whitestone Pond when she said it, which at 130 metres has to be the highest duck-friendly home in London. It must have offered a welcome drink for horses in Beethoven's day, while their owners were at nearby Jack Straw's Castle, where the likes of Charles Dickens and William Makepeace Thackeray were said to have imbibed. Until it was turned into luxury apartments with a gym. Bring back the pub I say!

Ali Smith says that for a lot of her life she was scared to go towards classical music. She thought she didn't know enough about it. But now she listens to Beethoven every day. She chooses and saves his Symphony No. 1, and I'd encourage Molly to start with that and work her way right through to Symphony No. 9 and his 'Ode to Joy' – which she'll already know, of course, because it opens her playlist. It's there to make us both happy.

3

'I chose "Blackbird" by Dad because Number 1,
I love the song.'

–Stella McCartney, 2017

I went to Liverpool for a magical mystery tour. I took a ferry across the Mersey to listen to the foghorns[155] and then a tourist bus round all the iconic Beatles song sites – 'Penny Lane', 'Strawberry Fields', 'Eleanor Rigby's grave.[156]

A woman sitting in front of me sang along to the soundtrack which was playing as the bus wound through the streets of the city. It was annoying. She had a terrible voice and didn't know all the words. But she was having such a good time, I didn't like to tell her to shut up. When we stopped for photos, I contemplated moving to a different seat. It was a Tuesday afternoon and the bus was nearly empty and then I thought: *Go with it Jessica – let her be a Beatle for an afternoon.* And after that I settled back, looked out the window and grinned. The tour guide pointed out the original barber shop on Penny Lane, where the boys used to have their hair cut. It's still a hairdressers but it turns out it's on the roundabout at the end of Penny Lane which is actually called Smithdown Place. But John Lennon and Paul McCartney were poets as much as they were musicians

– they knew what made great lyrics even if the woman in front of me can't remember them. I looked out the window and grinned again. I felt very, very happy in that moment, and when moments like that come, I savour them.

The next day, I visited John Lennon and Paul McCartney's childhood homes. Equally touristy but posher because they're now both owned by the National Trust. It was great to see where these two boys spent their youth, dreaming about girls and guitars, before going on to become the most chosen band ever on *Desert Island Discs*.

I wasn't a big Beatles' fan when I was growing up. I was too young and my parents were too old, so we missed the sixties in our house. In fact, I've realised that my dad's musical taste essentially terminated when his mother died. And my mum doesn't really have one, so I think hers must have terminated when Jesus was crucified (although thanks to my castaway friends for helping me add some other songs to her playlist like Leyla McCalla's gorgeous '*Manman*'[157] (that's 'mother' in Haitian Creole) and Maurice Chevalier's 'Louise'[158] (that's my mum's name).

But back to The Beatles. Of course I knew who they were because we sang their songs in my primary school. Along with 'Penny Lane', we did 'Yellow Submarine' and 'Maxwell's Silver Hammer' (which in retrospect feels an odd choice because it's about a misogynistic murder, but times were different and we all loved singing the '*bang, bang*' that made sure she was dead). Suffice to say The Beatles are like Beethoven. You might not know the full catalogue but everyone's heard of them.

In fact, what I find fascinating about The Beatles in terms of *Desert Island Discs* is not that they are the most chosen band. That's (nearly) obvious. But it's how many different tracks have been chosen over the years. The total tops over eighty and that doesn't include the songs they released as individual artists. Like it doesn't include John Lennon's 'Imagine'. That's what marks them out for me. It's (nearly) easy for a great artist to create one great piece of work. But to make so many different songs that resonate with so many different people: that's creative genius. It puts them up there with the likes of Beethoven. And with Frank Sinatra, of course, who is the most chosen solo artist on *Desert Island Discs* and has had over a hundred different songs selected. The difference is, though, Frank didn't write his music like The Beatles and Beethoven did. He preceded the meteoric rise of the singer–songwriter, which reached its pinnacle with artists like Ed Sheeran[159] and Amy Winehouse[160] (although for Amy the pinnacle became a precipice).

The Beatles gargantuan influence has also infiltrated the show's choice of castaways. Brian Epstein, their manager, went to the island. George Martin, their producer, went twice. They both chose Beatles tracks – *natch*. Yet Paul McCartney is the only member of the band who has been cast away – as part of the show's fortieth anniversary celebrations in 1982. However, we were together (Paul and I) in Glencoe in Scotland in the winter of 2019 for more Munro-bagging. We walked from the Ballachulish Hotel to Ballachulish village to buy some provisions – pork pies probably. I love the word 'Ballachulish' (and I've now had the chance to write it three times). And I love a pork pie, ideally with hot Ribena on a snowy Scottish mountain. And I assume Paul loves Scotland too – because his 'Mull of Kintyre' is a love song to it and is, of course, on my 'Scotland Playlist'. Which is why I took him there. And one piece of rather moving trivia that I'll share with you is that Paul chose and saved from the waves John Lennon's 'Beautiful Boy', which was also chosen and saved by Yoko Ono. In fact, they are currently the only two people to have picked it. Let's hope it stays that way – it's better poetry.

But for Molly – who is my beautiful girl even though she never existed – I would choose another Beatles' song. It's my own personal favourite, also chosen by Paul's daughter, the fashion designer Stella McCartney, when we walked together up to the Kenwood nursery garden one day, where I was also able to show her my favourite view of London's skyline from the heath. I like it even more than the top of Parliament Hill. She said I had good taste. And also told me that her biggest struggle has been choosing which of her dad's songs to pick, but she's decided on 'Blackbird' because she loves it and because she's so proud of him for writing about the civil rights struggle. (The Beatles were apparently the first band to refuse to perform in America at segregated concerts.) However, it's also just a simple song about a beautiful bird, the sound of which finishes the track. And I would want Molly to have it on her list because every child needs to know about The Beatles. It's as essential to a musical education as Beethoven. And 'Blackbird' might be a song about a sad subject yet it also makes me very, very happy whenever I hear it (although I promise not to sing it on the bus). And that seems to me to sum up one of the great conundrums of life: that things can be sad and happy at the same time.

4

'Well, it's very happy . . . Everything was just so wonderful and this reminds me of that time.'

–Penelope Wilton, 2008

It was fun composing my playlist for Molly. She's got eight tracks in total. But I'll limit myself to telling you about just one more. Then we'll walk on. After Beethoven and The Beatles, she's got Stevie Wonder.[161] Because everyone needs the wonder that is Stevie in their life.

I had started going to the Peak District fairly regularly. It was wilder than London and Box Hill but was nearer to home than the Lakes, Wales or Scotland. I discovered this great circuit on Kinder Scout which is the highest point of the peaks and the site of the mass trespass in the 1930s which did so much to ensure public rights of access to the countryside. (And which was the subject of Ewan MacColl's rambler's song.) I would get the train from London St Pancras to Edale in the early morning, then I'd walk out onto the Pennine Way, up Jacob's Ladder, right and along the top to Grindslow Knoll. It was sometimes really muddy up there but I've discovered that if you abandon yourself to mud, it can be quite a nice thing; you just have to accept there isn't a shoe on the market that is made for walking in it. I'd also recommend not being up there when it's getting dark, as it's very easy to get lost and if you're listening to Mahler's Symphony No. 9[162] on your headphones, the strange animal-shaped rocks combined with the foreboding music will totally terrify you. But when I'd learnt these important things, I loved it. After I got to Grindslow Knoll, I'd drop down into Grindsbrook Booth then I'd scramble up Grindsbrook Clough, right again across the top to 'Ringing Roger' and back down to Edale. There, I'd stay the night in The Rambler Inn and have a pint and homemade curry for supper and, after a full English breakfast the following morning, I'd do it all over again, and then get the train back home. It was a kind of bliss.

The opera singer Thomas Quasthoff was with me on one of those two day trips and it was him that persuaded me that Molly needed 'Sir Duke' on her list – Stevie Wonder's tribute to all the jazz greats that inspired him: Glenn Miller,[163] Count Basie,[164] Louis Armstrong, Ella Fitzgerald – and the king of them all, Duke Ellington.[165] If Molly's dad had been with us that day (he wasn't and if he was he would have probably wanted to turn back and head to The Rambler Inn before we got to the bottom of Jacob's Ladder), he would have no doubt argued that Molly needed Miles Davis and Charlie Parker on her list as well. As her father's daughter, there's no way she would have been able to grow up without becoming a lover of jazz. But her dad wasn't there. I was with Thomas Quasthoff and so she's getting Stevie Wonder instead.

Before we started walking together, I knew Thomas was an opera singer – because that's what it said on the first line of his bio – but I hadn't read any more. And to be honest the last few opera singers I'd walked with had been a bit boring, so I wasn't that excited. I've always wanted to like opera more than I do. I remember years ago – long before this adventure started – I was listening to *Desert Island Discs* at home one Sunday (sorting out the washing) when a guest chose Kiri Te Kanawa singing 'O Mio Babbino Caro' from Puccini's *Gianni Schicchi*.[166] I liked it instantly and was so delighted that I liked it that I went out and bought the CD of the whole thing. But then I hated the rest of it, so the fact I now know that no other castaway has ever chosen another song from this opera is some sort of validation of my taste.

But solidarity and inspiration often comes when you need it and that day it came in the form of Thomas Quasthoff. I certainly didn't know he was a thalidomide baby and despite his disability had become one of the most acclaimed opera singers of our time. 'Sir Duke' summed up his positive spirit in a song, and it lifted my heart to the hills as I walked the final descent to the pub (although my heart does generally lift on the down).

I've always liked Stevie Wonder. 'I Just Called to Say I Love You' came out when I was a teenager around about the time boys became an obsession and the thought of one ringing me to say this was the thing I wanted most in the world. Although thanks to the sculptor Antony Gormley, who sat with me on the overground to Clapham Junction, I now also know the Portuguese version by the Brazilian singer Gilberto Gil. I think I might even prefer it to the original – if you're planning on ringing me now. (And, for the record, the reason I didn't walk to Clapham that day was because I was heading onwards from there to a ramble somewhere in Surrey with the 'Long Distance Walkers Association' who I would sometimes get to put me through my paces. It was good training, although it did mean I had to make small talk with 'real people' for a day and I missed my castaway friends.)

Around six months after me and Thomas Quasthoff were in the Peak District together, the actress Penelope Wilton made me think about Molly and Stevie Wonder again. She shares with me a love of walking in England for which she wanted Elgar, so we had something in common from the beginning and I knew we were going to get on well. Then later, she told me about her first child – a little boy who died in her womb at twenty-nine weeks. And then her second – a little girl who was born at thirty weeks, weighing just two pounds and nine ounces.

'*Oh amazing, absolutely amazing,*' Penelope said, recalling how her baby, now a grown-up woman, managed to survive at that weight at that time. '*She was beautiful. In fact she wasn't really. But I thought she was beautiful,*' and then Penelope chose Stevie Wonder's 'Isn't She Lovely'. For her daughter. Which he wrote to celebrate the birth of his own.

When Penelope picked it, I felt a rush of '*melanjoy*', a word I've invented myself because there isn't one in the English language for feeling happy for someone and sad for yourself at the same time, and there should be. It's a simple fusion of the words *melancholy* and *joy* and I know it's a real emotion because it's how I always feel when I hear other people's pregnancy announcements and baby stories. I felt happy for Penelope but at the same time I felt sad that I would never be able to include this song on my own *Desert Island Disc* list for Molly. Because that would be really weird, right? And there are already too many stereotypes about infertility and insanity. So instead, she's got 'Sir Duke'.

I really liked Penelope though. I was genuinely happy for her, and for her last track she chose a song that always automatically lifts my mood, and which I've got on my own 'Happy Playlist'. It's Bobby Hebb's 'Sunny'.[167] In a way it's a bit like The Beatles' 'Blackbird' because it's a song that is inspired by a sad subject, but the music itself smiles. Hebb allegedly wrote it after his older brother was stabbed to death outside a nightclub in Nashville but said that it was a song about looking for brighter days in darker times. Penelope said when she chose it: *'Well, it's very happy and . . . eh . . . there are days, and there were days, when I was just beginning . . . where I . . . everything was just so wonderful and this reminds me of that time.'*

There's something so poignant in her words. The meaning of them almost hidden because words can play hide-and-seek just like children. But I think I know what she wanted me to find. There were days when things were very dark and then she began to feel it be might be OK and that was wonderful. And so the music came and it was 'Sunny'.

5

I had started to feel more alive. I don't know whether it was the music or the movement. But I wanted to walk the world – up, down and across – listening to all the playlists I was creating.

Travel has always been my happy place. Ever since my Diana Ross days as a seven-year old, I've dreamt of leaving home and going somewhere new. I first went to Asia when I was eighteen in my 'gap year' between school and university to teach English in Indonesia. It opened my eyes, my everything, and whenever anyone chooses the Gamelan,[168] its traditional music, I like them just because of that. I then immediately took a second 'gap year' and travelled round India for six months. I visited the Taj Mahal, bathed in the Ganges and ate so much food from a hotel buffet in Chennai (although back then it was called Madras) that I was sick in the toilet. Even that's a happy memory now and whenever anyone chooses Ravi Shankar[169] on the sitar, I like them just because of that.

I first went to Africa during the long summer holidays of my university years – with my dear friends, Tara and Beth. We went on safari and climbed Mount Kenya – the second highest mountain in Africa. Not because we were into mountaineering but because that's the sort of stuff you do when you're young. It was my first and only experience of high altitude until this adventure started. I remember feeling terrified as we traversed across a steep snowy section near the summit. We didn't have the right equipment; we'd picked up a cheap guide in town. And although we managed to get to the top and were triumphant, I also remember thinking – 'Should we be here right now?' We hadn't assessed the risks or aquired the requisite skills. We just did it because when you're young you think you're invincible. It doesn't mean it's not possible when you're older. It just requires more courage, more knowledge and much more work in the gym.

The soundtrack of that trip all those years ago was the Kenyan hotel pop song 'Jambo Bwana' – which has not been chosen on *Desert Island Discs* (yet) despite its earworm quality. But since then my 'African Playlist' has expanded, thanks to all my castaway friends. The first track I added was Ismaël Lô's 'Tadieu Bone',[170] given to me by Tidjane Thiam – the first Ivorian businessman and the first Black man to lead a FTSE 100 company. It wasn't just his sexy French accent that got me. Or his remarkable life and success. He chose songs of struggle and the soul, and one of the most moving and memorable things he said to me was what makes the difference in life between people is not how far they can rise, but how low they can go.

And I said: 'Yes Tidjane, I know low.'

I am also indebted to the writer Bernardine Evaristo and the musician Bono[171] for introducing me to Beninese singer–songwriter Angélique Kidjo.[172] And no African playlist would be complete without the sound of freedom – 'Nkosi Sikelel' iAfrika'[173] – South Africa's national anthem.

But my own personal favourite South African song was given to me by Inga Beale – the first woman to become the CEO of Lloyds of London in the insurance company's 300+ year history. I was at the junction of Old Street and the Goswell Road – in fact not too far from where Inga worked in the City – when she played me Miriam Makeba's 'Pata Pata'.[174] From the opening word '*Saguquka*', I felt happy. I have no idea what it means in Xhosa, but I don't need to. That's what I love about music from faraway places. The best of it conveys its meaning without needing you to understand the language of the lyrics.

Peter and I travelled a lot when we were together. Going on holiday became compensation for an unsuccessful round of IVF. My little list book of all the countries in the world I've been to grew rapidly for a while (we did a lot of IVF . . .). Some of the favourite days of my life were when we took a tour round Normandy in France, during which we visited the composer Erik Satie's[175] house in Honfleur. I adore Satie – his music manages to blend spiky energy with tranquil calm, and there's something about that which makes me feel happy.

On another trip, we went to Venezuela. We woke up to gunfire in Caracas and visited the Angel Falls (high but a trickle). Our soundtrack was the Buena Vista Social Club[176] (I know it's Cuban but my life wasn't as musically nuanced then), and all the Gilbertos. You can't go to South America and not listen to Astrud, Bebel and João. You can't go to South America and not listen to 'The Girl From Ipanema'.[177] It's sun in a song. Half in Portuguese, half in English, I don't understand the Brazilian bits (but from the opening '*olha*' I feel joy). And although I accept there's a hint of melancholy in the English, i.e. the singer's adoration of 'the girl' is unrequited; the girl herself is tall, tanned, defiant. That's what I like about it.

When we went to Venezuela, I also managed to persuade Peter to climb Mount Roraima which to give it its proper title is a *'tepui'* – a table top mountain. Remembering this now makes me think I must have always had some sort of call to the hills but it was a big deal at the time. It wasn't technical or particularly hard. It was more like a high hike. But, Peter doesn't like hills. He doesn't even do stairs. Allegedly, though, it was the inspiration for Arthur Conan Doyle's *Lost World*. And Peter does Arthur Conan Doyle. That's how I managed to persuade him.

He thinks he's Sherlock Holmes. I think he's Moriarty.

(Does that sound harsh? Don't worry, I think it will make him laugh.)

The hike up took us two days, we camped at the base and then on the summit, and Peter didn't stop complaining until we got to the plateau, which is like a lost world of pre-historic rock formations. He lay down in our tent exhausted until our guide brought out a homemade bottle of Margerita at which point he miraculously revived. Funny that. I smile about it now.

Several years later, I found myself hiking the hills of Hampstead Heath with the actress Betsy Blair, who said that she'd have to have a bit of music that goes with *'everybody, and happiness and love'* and that would be 'The Girl From Ipanema'. She was seventeen when she married the Hollywood icon Gene Kelly; he was twenty-nine. They divorced but she said the song was in part for him because Gene brought her – and the world – a lot of joy, and that she had felt so sad the last time she saw him a year before he died.

I imagine that the last time I see Peter will be like the last time Betsy saw Gene. I hope there will be one, even though the absence of him can now be counted in years and feels like a death-in-life. Betsy said the last time she saw Gene, she kissed him on the cheek. And I'll kiss Peter and tell him: *'I'll never forget Normandy and Erik Satie; and Roraima and the Margerita.'* I'll give it my best Whitney Houston and say: *'I will always love you.'* [178]

Then I'll follow that with some Franz Lehár, maybe *The Land of Smiles* or *The Merry Widow*.[179]

A while later, I went to Camden Town with the adventure broadcaster Simon Reeve. Not a very exotic trip – the bank followed by Boots. Simon was great, though. He talked about his struggle to conceive his son. It's rare for men to come out about stuff like that in public and I admired him. He chose Stormzy's 'Wiley Flow'[180] – which namechecks Everest. I immediately thought: I'm adding that to my 'Mountain Playlist'. And after it played, Simon started extolling the virtues of saying 'Yes!' to going on adventures in life.

Do you want to go out at night and see bears in the forest? Say: *'Yes!'*

Do you want to go and meet an endangered tribe in western Burma. Say: *'Yes!'*

'Think about the risks. Mitigate them of course. But, embrace life and take chances on planet Earth because it's the way to feel alive . . .'

I went to Africa and climbed Kilimanjaro, the continent's highest mountain which stands at 5,895 metres and Miriam Makeba sang: *'Saguquka'!*

Then I went to Argentina and climbed Aconcagua, the highest mountain in the Americas at 6,961 metres. I listened to 'The Girl From Ipanema' and imagined Peter going *'ah'.*

I felt alive.

6

'And in the morning when I open my eyes and I look,
I think "oooo". I say "thank you dear God, I'm still here".'

–Alicia Markova, 2002

———————

I also went to Russia – as I already told you – and climbed Mount Elbrus – the highest mountain in Europe at 5,642 metres. There, just as Simon Reeve advised, I assessed the risks: *I was slower than everyone else.* I couldn't mitigate them: *they were younger and fitter than me.* So I came down, circled round the mountain and climbed from the other (easier) side instead.

The other reason I'm mentioning Elbrus again is that Russia is not only home to the music of romance, it's also the music of dance. And I have to have at least one thing I can dance to on my 'Happy Playlist' – not least because when you get down from a mountain summit after a shower and something scrumptious, I defy anyone not to feel like dancing then.

To be honest, when this adventure started I hadn't danced in a long time. I gave it up in my mid-thirties at the confluence of becoming a Chief Executive and trying to become a mother. Earlier, in my twenties – when I wasn't the boss nor feeling like a failure as a woman – then I could always be relied upon to kick off my heels at a party. But power and pain had immobilised me. And dancing is like technology. If you don't keep doing it regularly – you're lost.

So I admire all the castaways who still shake their stuff and have taken a track to dance to on their island. I know that the glitterball should probably go to ABBA's 'Dancing Queen'.[181] But for my own dance track, I'll be taking the Russian composer Tchaikovsky[182] – inspired by the 'Ballet Adventure' I went on with some of my castaway friends.

Now I realise this might seem odd. If you can no longer hit the dance floor drunk at a disco, then ballet? Really? But I've always had an affection for it because of my mum. When she was a little girl, she wanted to be a ballerina. In fact, it was probably my grandmother, Mima, who wanted it more than my mum did. I suspect Mima saw it as a route out of the stigma of illegitimacy. And my mum would have wanted it for her. She tried really hard. She even got accepted into the Royal Ballet School. But then she broke a tiny bone in her foot and couldn't stand on point anymore for which she was expelled. And what is remarkable about my mum is she never pushed me to fulfil her failed dreams. She didn't dress me in a tutu or take me to the ballet. Occasionally, though, when she wanted my dad to notice her – which was sometimes difficult with my dad because he was quite solipsistic – she would do a pirouette or arabesque in our sitting room. He'd like that, which was good because my dad was at his best when he was happy, and my mum was happy if she could make him happy. She's never wanted happiness for herself.

My own 'Ballet Adventure' started with Alicia Markova – the first British prima ballerina. She was cast away twice, the second time aged ninety-one. She chose two pieces of Tchaikovsky to take with her. And I know what I'm about to say will reveal my utter ignorance, and I know you might be flabbergasted, but it's only because of *Desert Island Discs* that I now know that Tchaikovsky is 'the man' when it comes to ballet. He composed *Swan Lake*, *The Nutcracker* AND *Sleeping Beauty*, which are basically ballet's bees' knees. And I know that disclosing this as someone who worked in the theatre probably sounds weird and wrong but I've decided to do it in case I'm not the only one. Because if I'm prepared to say it and look stupid, who knows, other people might feel able to own up as well. There might be widespread common consent, which is exactly what I experienced when I first came out about my infertility and unsuccessful IVF.

At the time, I thought I was one of only a tiny number of women in the world who had struggled to conceive or experienced miscarriage because very few people talked about it – privately or publicly. And the stories that did seem to exist always delivered miracle babies at the end. It was also a time before social media communities had really taken off. There was Facebook but, in my thirties, it was increasingly full of my friends posting their three-month scan and new baby photos. Alongside the melanjoy, it made me feel inadequate. And then I wrote a book about what I'd been going through and everything changed. I realised I wasn't alone, I was part of a silent epidemic. So maybe there's also a silent epidemic of people like me who want to know more about music. I'm writing this for them. Maybe my honesty will encourage them to go on their own *Desert Island Discs* adventure.

I loved Alicia Markova. I loved the stories about her career, and how she never married or had children – '*the music got me too soon*' – and I absolutely adored the moment when she told me how supple she still is and started fluttering her arms and twisting her neck. And then she said: '*And in the morning when I open my eyes and I look, I think "oooo". I say "thank you, dear God, I'm still here."*'

It was Alicia who started me off on my 'Ballet Adventure'. After her, I listened to all the ballet dancers and choreographers that had ever been cast away. I developed a special walk for this. From our front door, I would head up, over and down into Golders Hill Park, which is officially still part of the heath but has gates and opening hours and even a tiny zoo. And I'd head to the far north-western corner to Swan Pond and when I got there I'd play a blast of the 'Dance of the Sugar Plum Fairy'. Then I'd say 'hi' to the wallabies who live next door and would show me their *sautés* and then I'd head home smiling.

I adored those days.

Just like Alicia they made me think: *thank you, dear God, I'm still here.*

7

*'I used to find it really one of the most exciting things
I'd ever heard.'*

–Edmund Hillary, 1979

In early March 2020, I walked the whole of London's Capital Ring. It's a 78-mile loop around the city which takes in a lot of green spaces. I completed it in three days, returning home each evening to eat (crisps) and sleep. Since my mountainous musical adventure started I had been saving two special castaways for when I was nearly on my way to the top of the world. I didn't know then that occasion would be the Capital Ring. I didn't know what the Capital Ring was then. And it turns out I still wasn't anywhere near the top of the world when I listened to them. But I didn't know that then either.

These two special castaways became my Capital Ring bookends. The first at the start of Day 1 on the section from Highgate to Stoke Newington; and the second at the end of Day 3 from Hendon back to Highgate.

Day 1, bookend one: Kazuo Ishiguro – one of my favourite wordsmiths. I've chosen this description because he became this before I'd read any of his books. (I now have and love them, so he's also one of my favourite writers.) But towards the end of my IVF years, I discovered something he'd said in an interview with a journalist that has become an aphorism I live my life by. In a world littered with inspirational quotes that are read and instantly forgotten, it stayed with me. He was talking about the fact that he left his home in Japan when he was a small child and grew up in England where he still lives. And because of this, he has always carried a feeling of an alternative person he might have become if he'd never left his country of origin. He said: *'There is another life I might have had, but I am having this one.'*

And you'll find these words on 'Wikiquote' and in pretty pictures on Google Images. They've gained traction because they're exactly how I and others must feel too. In my case, if I hadn't struggled to conceive or the IVF hadn't failed, I'd be living a different life. For one thing, I'd have a legitimate reason to sing 'Wheels on the Bus'[183] (yes, even on the bus).

I describe the feeling of being childless as 'the pain of never' – a phrase that has gained it's own small traction in the world because other women feel it too. I will never feel my child's first kick of life; I will never be able to say hello as they're placed on my chest for the first time; I will never witness their first steps, first words, first day at school. And perhaps the hardest pain of all, I will never hear anyone call me 'Mum'.

Instead, here I was walking London's Capital Ring with my favourite wordsmith and writer – Kazuo Ishiguro. It's a different life from the one I'd wanted and planned. But it's not at all bad. And Kazuo didn't disappoint. For starters, he confessed he has a problem with orchestras. He said he didn't really understand them. I told him about me and Tchaikovsky, and also that I much prefer a single instrument to a symphony too. I love a solo piano and share Kazuo's taste in Chopin and Keith Jarrett. And then he went and chose a love song which turns out is the only love song in a complete canon that still makes me happy not sad. Not only that, he asked for it to be sung by the slinky singer Stacey Kent[184] ('*slinky*' is his word, and it's a fabulous one).

There was a period in my thirties when Stacey Kent was my favourite jazz singer although, until that walk with Kazuo, I'd all but forgotten her. She's not a desert island staple. But back when I was in my thirties, we would go and see her playing live in the jazz clubs of Soho and I had this dream that I was going to ask her to perform at my wedding. I've never felt that strongly about getting married (my small stand against the patriarchy) but during that period I started yearning for conventional things – a diamond ring, a house and garden, 2.4 babies – and Stacey Kent was part of that dream. If I had got those things, she would probably be on my final *Desert Island Discs* list. Instead, I'd forgotten she was even a contender, until she started singing my favourite Gershwin and Gershwin number.

I say Gershwin *and* Gershwin because there are two of them – Gershwins – in case you didn't know. I hadn't fully registered it when all this started. Nor did I know there are two Engelbert Humperdincks[185] (weird, but true). And there are two Strausses (actually there are more than two but there are two main ones – I prefer the one who wrote the music to dance to (Johann)[186] but castaways have historically preferred the other (Richard).[187] And there's a Samuel Taylor Coleridge[188] and a Samuel Coleridge-Taylor[189] (one a white British poet, one a Black British composer, and both are men we should all know).

The two Gershwins were brothers. George was the composer, Ira the lyricist. Together they wrote some of the greatest songs of the Great American Songbook, including my London Marathon song 'A Foggy Day' and the only love song that still makes me smile: 'They Can't Take That Away From Me'. It doesn't matter who 'they' are. Indefinable others who aren't entirely malevolent. The point that matters in the song is that when you have had a love so full of happy memories, nobody can take that away. And the great thing about your best castaway friends is not only do they articulate what you feel for you, they choose your music too.

Other highlights from the Ring Cycle (mine, not Wagner's), included the artist Paula Rego down by the Royal Albert Docks, choosing Ike and Tina Turner's 'River Deep, Mountain High'[190] for memories of dancing a little drunk after dinner. Rivers, mountains, drink, dinner – all things I like. And TV Presenter Bamber Gascoigne – in the Wandsworth area – getting his wife to choose all his discs for him. (Consider this love, bravery or not caring enough about your list.) And, finally, I just have to mention the Victorian dinosaurs in Crystal Palace Park in the deep south of London, not somewhere I'd visited before. They've got nothing to do with my castaway friends or their music but I was so fascinated by them that I had to turn everyone off for a while and sit and watch them while I ate my lunch.

After three days and nearly 80 miles back home across Hendon Park, and then through sweet little Northway Gardens and finally into Highgate Wood, it was time for my second bookend: Edmund Hillary, the first man (along with Sherpa Tenzing Norgay) to summit Mount Everest, as part of the British expedition led by John Hunt. I felt an immediate affinity with him because he says that as a child he didn't do a lot of sport. It was only later that he got into mountaineering.

He starts with a musical memory from his youth – the folk song 'Red River Valley.'[191] And says that when he was a child he would to go to the movie theatre in Tuakau – the town where he lived in New Zealand – and they'd play this before the film began and it was one of the most exciting things he had ever heard. The song opens with the words: *'From this valley they say you are going, we will miss your bright eyes and sweet smile.* It felt significant to me that the song was about leaving, given that Edmund himself would ultimately leave home to undertake one of the most legendary adventures of all time. In fact, several of the tracks he chooses are about going away – he also picks 'Leaving on a Jet Plane'[192] and Vera Lynn singing 'Now is the Hour',[193] a song about saying goodbye.

I guess for some people these choices would seem poignant but they feel exciting to me. Saying goodbye, leaving home and getting on a plane make me think of going on an adventure. Like Edmund, I was headed to the Himalayas. And the thought of that made me slightly scared. But it also made my heart sing.

8

'*This song came out right at the time when my brother was diagnosed . . . We'd sing it and it would put a smile on his face.*'

–Winnie Byanyima, 2022

A few months after I turned forty (more than a decade ago now), I attended an intense therapeutic residential course called 'The Hoffman Process'. At the time I was hoping it might identify whether there was a psychological reason I couldn't get pregnant. By far the worst part of infertility and IVF for me was nothing to do with my broken body, it was how it messed with my head. And although I don't think positive thinking gets you pregnant, I do believe in the mind–body connection. The therapeutic process I went on didn't result in a child but it was transformational nonetheless. It led to me stopping fertility treatment and start doing other things, like writing books and swimming the English Channel instead.

On the last night of the process, I danced for the first time in years. And the song that I will always associate with that evening is Bobby McFerrin's 'Don't Worry, Be Happy'.[194] In fact, it's the one song I've known from the beginning of this adventure will definitely make my ultimate list of eight. The other seven tracks, I still need to make a decision about.

I might know the artist but need to decide on the song. Or I might know the theme (childhood, home, love, something sad to cry to) but not have decided on the track yet. Some options are still wide open. But this song will be on my island for definite because it makes me very, very happy whenever I hear it.

What's a little weird about this – and I know this because I've been recently reading about music psychology – is that this key musical memory happened when I was forty. Research shows that generally people's most intense musical memories come from the very recent past or their youth. The latter is known as the 'reminiscence bump'. Any academic working in this field would probably surmise that's why this story started with my songs of childhood. Our most potent musical memories are mainly formed when we are young, generally always before the age of thirty. But 'Don't Worry, Be Happy' came into my life with significance beyond that bump. And it isn't a recent musical memory either. It's the first song I put on my playlist of Happy Songs – some of which are there because I already knew and liked them, others of which have been introduced to me for the first time during the course of this adventure. Such as Miriam Makeba's 'Pata Pata'. And Manu Chau's 'Bongo Bong'[195] – shout out to the former editor of *Vogue* Alexandra Shulman for giving me that one on the Regent's Canal near the City Road Basin. And to Henry Marsh for giving me B.B. King's 'Don't Look Down'[196] on the Docklands Light Railway – and he's a neurosurgeon so must know what's good for the brain.

I suspect the reason I remember 'Don't Worry, Be Happy' is because it represents a transformational moment in my life. And I think I'll remain devoted to all the new songs I've discovered because this adventure has also been life-changing. I'll need to wait another ten years before I can confirm it for definite but during the course of it something shifted.

I was sad. I didn't know what I wanted from life anymore. I started listening to the back catalogue of *Desert Island Discs* on my headphones. I needed a context for the listening, so I started walking.

I walked all over London, and then across the UK and abroad. The show's castaways became my companions. Their lives helped me make sense of my own, and their music became my music. This adventure of ears, legs and heart changed my life and that was before I had even started on the final stretch of the journey when, I hoped, that any dues I owed *'to the dirt'*[197] would be paid and I might get to look *'down on creation'*[198] from 8,848 metres '(On) Top of the World' – with The Carpenters and the Imagine Dragons who wrote the definitive tracks for that location.

I had listened to and written up 2,979 episodes on my spreadsheets and had around 300 to go. I was secretly pleased that so far no one had chosen Bobby McFerrin's 'Don't Worry, Be Happy'. In fact, I'll admit that I did dream that maybe one day I would be the first person to do so . . . And then that dream was dashed by the Charity Campaigner Winnie Byanyima when I was at the airport on my way to Nepal. But I'm used to my dreams being dashed, and if it was going to go to anyone, I'm glad it was her.

Winnie had all the character ingredients I love in a castaway. She was a refugee and a revolutionary; and had tragically lost her brother to HIV. It was a loss that motivated her to become executive director of UNAIDs and dedicate her life to eradicating the disease. She told me her brother didn't actually die of it; he died of the stigma. And I said I understood because infertility and childlessness can be stigmatising too. And then Winnie described how Bobby McFerrin's song came out right at the time her brother was diagnosed and she'd put it on in the car as she drove him to clinics and treatment. And they'd sing it together and it would put a smile on his face. And that the work she does now is honouring her promise to him that one day there'll be a cure.

We've all lost people that we love. I'm not the only one. And we all have broken dreams. I'm not alone in that too. That's why I'm writing this story. For all the people who have hurt and are still hurting. If that's you, I want you to know that Bobby McFerrin puts a smile on my face – as it did for Winnie and her brother. I want you to know that I believe being happy *is* possible when you're on the right adventure and you've got the right music.

As for my happy shortlist, I just have to acknowledge here that Beethoven, The Beatles and Stevie Wonder aren't on it, but that's because they're really songs for Molly and as I can only include eight I've had to omit them. And 'They Can't Take That Away From Me' isn't on it either, although that is my song and it does make me happy. But it's really a love song and I've already written that list and, like I said, it's only a 'conditional love song' list, so if necessary I can change it.

It turns out there are just too many happy songs I wanted to include. That's what happy music does. It breeds.

My Happy Songs Shortlist

You know the one that will make my ultimate list – but they all make me very, very happy.

1. Pharrell Williams: 'Happy' – because you can't go wrong with 'Happy'.

2. Bobby Hebb: 'Sunny' – because the music came and it was.

3. Miriam Makeba: 'Pata Pata' – for the *Saguquka!*

4. Astrud Gilberto: 'The Girl From Ipanema' – for the ah!

5. Satie: *Three Gymnopédies* – for happy memories.

6. Tchaikovsky: 'Dance of the Sugar Plum Fairy' from *The Nutcracker* – for my pliés and my sautés.

7. The Carpenters: 'Top of the World' / Imagine Dragons: 'On Top of the World' – because if you're writing a list of songs for being on top of the world when you're on top of the world, it must be OK for two-to-become-one.

8. Bobby McFerrin: 'Don't Worry, Be Happy' – I'm getting there, I am.

The Interlude –
Songs for a Wonderful World

1. Louis Armstrong: 'What A Wonderful World'

1

*'It's very good wake-up music,
it's kind of a like a third cup of coffee.'*

–Dave Brubeck, 1959

---

*'It's the music I love to wake up to in the morning
if I want to be happy.'*

–Dave Brubeck, 1999

We'll be heading to Nepal soon. In the 'Overture', I promised you danger and derring-do and that's all coming up. But, first, a little Interlude. I'm still in my happy place and I can't go anywhere without my 'Songs for a Wonderful World'. So let me be 'The Happy Wanderer'[199] for a while.

I took the train from London Paddington to Kemble in Gloucestershire. I felt a frisson of excitement as I started walking down the road towards the Thames Head Inn. The beginning of a new adventure has the effect of alarming all my nerve endings. I had originally been planning to do this last year to celebrate a special birthday. But a new national lockdown which came into force in November 2020 had prevented me. Like so many 1970 babies, all my fiftieth birthday plans were scuppered. But no matter. The Thames path wasn't going anywhere. So there I was – exactly a year later – plan resurrected. I was intending to walk the whole of it in seven days – from the source of the river to the barrier – a distance of 185 miles – culminating on Sunday 21 November 2021 – my fifty-first birthday.

The Thames Path is one of England's National Trails and I guess it should (and maybe does) go all the way to the sea but the official route stops at the barrier – a series of monolithic tent-shaped silver gates that span the width of the river and are designed to stop central London from flooding. Any 'real mountaineer' would probably disdain my suggestion that this was 'training' for Everest. And, yes, it's true, the River Thames doesn't have much in the way of elevation. But covering 185 miles in 7 days essentially breaks down as 26.4 miles per day – and walking (just over) 7 marathons in 7 days is not nothing. Besides, it was my birthday. We've all got to have a little pleasure from time to time.

I reached the aptly named Thames Head Inn where I was staying for the night before setting off early the following morning. I called this Day Zero – I had a Sunday roast in the pub and watched something good on Netflix and then chatted to the couple sitting next to me who were very impressed with my proposed undertaking. The next day (Day 1), I had 23.3 miles to cover. But to do that I had to find the source of the river first – not as easy as you might think because there isn't actually any water there, just a stone marker.

It was a bright and crisp November morning – a frost-on-the-ground-type-of-day – and as I set out the sun started coming up and, I don't know how the science works, but mist was rising off the grass in that glorious way it does when the conditions are just right. I put on my 'Morning Playlist'. I think everyone needs songs to start the day. And for me and for many of my castaway friends, there is no one who does it better than Bach.[200] As the pianist András Schiff once old me: *'He's a cleansing procedure, like taking a bath or a shower.'*

I've loved Bach for years. I used to play him on the piano and the oboe and I have a hunch he was a list lover like me. And, if pressed to choose, I'd probably say that his *Goldberg Variations* are my best Bach – especially when played by the Canadian pianist Glenn Gould. In fact, if I meet a new castaway friend and we hit it off immediately, then oftentimes they've gone and chosen Glenn and his Goldbergs. And I nod and think: *'Ah, yes, of course.'*

But for the beginning of the day, it's got to be Bach and his Brandenburgs. There are six of them in total – the *Brandenburg Concertos*. I've got them all downloaded but I've chosen No. 2 for my morning compilation – and that's because of Dave Brubeck – the American jazz pianist whose track 'Take Five'[201] is one of the highest selling jazz singles of all time. However, Dave didn't take five to his island (despite the fact it's the most selected of Bach's six *Brandenburgs*). Both times, he was on the show (in 1959 and 1999), Dave took No. 2. He told me it's like a third cup of coffee and the music he loves to wake up to in the morning if he wants to be happy. I liked Dave a lot – he's a man who was loyal to the music he loved for forty years – in fact he only changed two tracks across his two lists over all that time. He also shares my taste in morning happiness.

Other songs on my 'Morning Playlist' include my darling Nina Simone singing The Beatles' track 'Here Comes the Sun' (I've always loved Nina's version more than the original, even before Elbrus (If You Still Believe in) Love songs, Chapter 7). As do chef Yotam Ottolenghi and the singer songwriter John Legend[202] who both chose and saved Nina's version from the waves. I told Yotam he can come and cook me and John breakfast to it any time.

I've also got 'Oh What A Beautiful Morning', from the Rodgers and Hammerstein musical *Oklahoma*. And 'Good Morning', from the film *Singin' in the Rain*.[203] And Cat Stevens' classic 'Morning Has Broken'.[204] But my playlist will always start with Bach's Brandenburg Concerto No. 2 – my and Dave Brubeck's musical coffee.

I found the source of the Thames – a tombstone looking thing below the branches of an old ash tree – and then turned back on myself and headed towards Cricklade – the river just a stream at the beginning. I had brunch on the high street in the November sun, at a little café with tables outside covered in red and white checked cloths. The locals seeing me smiling, all stopped to chat. And I felt possibly the happiest I've ever felt.

2

'When you sit out in your garden, and you hear this little chap on the chimney top, you know that all's right with the world.'

–Alan Titchmarsh, 2002

———————

'Somehow it gives me hope that whatever human beings do, nature will try and respond and do its absolute utmost to see it through and to bounce back.'

–Isabella Tree, 2019

———————

From Cricklade I walked onto Lechlade where I had a room pre-booked at a place called Vera's Kitchen. I didn't get to meet Vera or see her kitchen but it was a lovely little place. I'd choose a B&B with an ensuite bathroom over a tent and a pee bottle any day.

A pee bottle, in case you've never heard of or used one, is exactly what it sounds like. At the highest camps on the highest mountains, you have one because during the night you need to go to the toilet more often than usual on account of the altitude; and it's too cold and too much of a phaff to leave your tent to do so. Therefore, if you're a woman you need to get proficient at squatting over a bottle or purchase a Shewee, a funnel-shaped contraption that basically means you can pee like a man – standing up without taking your trousers down. I never got into the Shewee myself – I guess because it was another piece of technical equipment to master and I was already struggling with crampons and carabiners. In the early days, I would spend many hours lying awake in my tent just thinking about needing to go to the toilet. That's because going felt too much of an effort. Eventually, though, I got over this and the moment I thought it, I would get up and go and then I'd be able to get back to sleep. It's the best piece of mountaineering pee-ing advice I can give you. Better still, stay in a B&B with an en-suite.

Day 2 and I set off from Lechlade, starting the day with my 'Morning Playlist', and I was then joined by the writer A.N. Wilson who I blame for getting me lost. Yes, I know: how can anyone get lost on the Thames Path with a whacking great river to guide you? But when he asked for Barbara Cartland singing her version of 'A Nightingale Sang in Berkeley Square',[205] a hint of amusement in his voice, I was so gobsmacked by her rendition of it that I took a wrong turning and headed into Buscot village and lost my way for the next half an hour. In my defence there's a confusing criss-crossing of paths and water at the lock there, so maybe others have made this mistake too. And I wouldn't change it because it was a memorable moment – I knew immediately that Barbara and her nightingale would have to go on my 'Birdsong Playlist'. I'll never forget where I first heard them.

You'll find all sorts of avian lovers on the BBC's desert island. There are a lots of songs about birds. From Delius' Cuckoo[206] to Fleetwood Mac's 'Albatross' (or 'Songbird' if you want to go pretty).[207] One of my most favourite songs about birds is 'Skylark', which is one of my most favourite of Ella Fitzgerald's songs too – which is quite an achievement because Ella basically nailed everything she sang. As the poet John Cooper Clark said when he played it to me: *That's what Ella*

Fitzgerald does. She sings beautiful songs beautifully.' What a wordsmith. To me that sentence is beautiful poetry.

But lots of people have asked for real birdsong too.[208] The conservationist Isabella Tree wanted the 1942 recording of a nightingale in the English countryside which is gradually counterpointed with the thrum of another kind of bird – a Lancaster bomber – on its way to a Second World War bombing raid in Germany. The two sounds together each form their own kind of music which Isabella says somehow gives her hope that whatever human beings do nature will try and respond and do its absolute utmost to bounce back.

My own favourite real birdsong, though, is the sound of the blackbird. Not just because of Molly and her Beatles' track. But also because I've adored so many of the castaways who have chosen it – it's the most selected birdsong on the show. And now whenever I hear this little chap as I'm waking up or walking, I think of the words of the gardener Alan Titchmarsh – like him it makes me feel that all's right with this wonderful world. But on the BBC's island alongside blackbirds and nightingales, you'll also find real skylarks, curlews, pink footed geese, a mistle thrush, a burchell's coucal, a laughing kookaburra and even Sparkie Williams' 1958 champion-talking budgerigar. You will also be delighted with the plethora of dawn choruses to wake up to.

In the past, castaways frequently asked for recordings by Ludwig Koch who, in 1889, as a boy of eight-years old, made the first ever known recording of a bird. It was a white -rumped shama and it must have been his pet because he grew up in Germany and the shama didn't. In the 1930s, Koch – a Jew – fled to the UK where he published the first ever recorded songbook of British birds. Sadly, it's not available on either Apple or Spotify but you can listen to it at the British Library. Koch is referred to as the father of wildlife sound recording

– predating David Attenborough, who is such an undisputed legend that he's been cast away four times. Koch himself was cast away just once. He didn't ask to take any wildlife recordings himself, although he did take Haydn's 'Song of the Quail'.[209]

After I'd retraced my footsteps to the river, I said goodbye to A.N. Wilson, and put on my 'Bird Playlist'. It ends with Pablo Casals playing the Catalan song 'El Cant dels Ocells' ('The Song of the Birds')[210] on the cello (my instrument to cry to). The Spanish opera singer Placido Domingo told me that Casals finished all his concerts playing this piece. He says you can hear the sadness of a man in exile in the music. Casals had left his beloved Spain and vowed not to return until the dictator Franco had been deposed. He died before that happened but his ashes have now been returned and interred in his beloved home of Catalonia. It's the perfect end to my 'Bird Playlist'.

As the music played, I smiled and waved at the two Thames swans – mated for life – that were gliding by. I didn't feel a pang at all.

3

*'And all of a sudden the courtiers brought the corgis . . .
and so for twenty minutes the Queen and I, during this
lunch, just fed the dogs.'*

–David Nott, 2016

---

*'I had a small kitten in my battle dress . . . and for the last
three or four days of our retreat I had this kitten with
me all the time.'*

–Richard Doll, 2001

I walked for six hours before stopping for lunch. I defy anyone
to walk for that long with more mileage to come and not
feel that a fish finger sandwich with chips is manna with a
Michelin star. Well, maybe not if you're a vegan, but I'm sure
you get what I mean.

I had originally been planning to push on to Oxford and
thankfully I hadn't yet booked a room for the night because I
realised that this was over ambitious. So I used it as an excuse
to have a second cup of coffee while I found somewhere to stay.

Now, here's a pointer. I love Britain's national trails. I want
to walk all of them – across England, Ireland, Scotland, Wales.
But – top tip – make sure your accommodation is not too far
off the route (even if you're not walking marathons like me).

Because if it is, I guarantee you'll grow to resent the unnecessary distance at the start and end of each day. And the problem I had on Day 2 is that Oxford was too far to go but all the suitable accommodation en route was already full, so I had no choice but to divert a mile off trail into Eynsham, a fab little town but a road-roaring schlepp from the river.

But before I even got to the road, I had more river walking to do. Down to Bablock Hythe caravan park where the path briefly turns away from the water and then across a field that was full of sheep. The light was starting to fade, I had walked upwards of 24 miles, and I was deeply regretting that second cup of coffee . . .

For the record, I have no problem peeing outdoors. All I need is a rock or a tree. It's better than peeing in a bottle in a tent – although there's still the risk of trouser trickle. But pooing is another matter. I don't like going in public toilets and the whole 'Number 2' situation on mountains is something I've had to manage with grit and grimace. But to have to go in an open field, just off the Thames Path, well, I'd only do that if I was desperate. Which I was. And those sweet sheep, with their gentle black velvet faces, who were clearly already bemused by this weird woman walking in the twilight, just watched me intently. Not with any malice or disgust, just with intrigued interest and I loved them for it.

A few days later, I walked with the lovely Lucinda Lambton who is also an animal lover. It was on one of my favourite bits of the trail where the track leaves the path past Goring & Streatley and curls up into a wood. I know it's weird to say that my favourite section of the Thames path is the bit where you can't see the river. But then I am an eccentric (I presume you've got that by now), which Lucinda is as well – although don't call her that because she hates the word. She chose 'Four Legged Friend'[211] as one of her tracks – she says she loves dogs as much as she loves people – and afterwards it inspired me to listen to my 'Animal Playlist' for a while.

During the course of this adventure, I've encountered a lot of dogs. There are so many out and about these days – sporting their latest jackets just like the many mountaineers I know. I have noticed, however, that good dog songs seem to be fairly limited. Noel Coward's 'Mad Dogs and Englishmen' and Elvis' 'Hound Dog' are the most chosen canine tracks on *Desert Island Discs* (although – fun fact – 'I Wanna Be Your Dog'[212] was chosen once, by David Byrne). And I also have a favourite dog story courtesy of the surgeon David Nott which involves him, the late Queen Elizabeth II and her corgis. I also have a favourite cat story which involves the scientist Richard Doll and a kitten during the war. Both tales are very moving. Sadly I haven't got time to tell you them here because we need to get to the Thames Barrier, but do go on a walk with your headphones and have a listen. Good cat tracks are more plentiful in number. Andrew Lloyd Webber's *Cats*[213] offers a whole musical of feline fun. But I think my favourite is Rossini's cat duet[214] – not to be confused with Ravel's.[215] I've got both on my 'Animal Playlist' but I prefer Italian meowing to French.

We've always been a feline family. My dad loved cats and they loved him in a way that made me envious. Cats have avoid-antennae for rambunctious children – and I was. But they were drawn to the gentle vulnerability of my dad. After I moved back to our house in Hampstead I got two kittens – you could call them fur babies. But as my life became increasingly nomadic, I relied on my mum to look after them. Really, they're hers now but they've become a bit like our children and us the odd couple. We argue about how much they should be fed – I'm more generous where food is concerned than she is. And if I get a bit too forceful – which a grown-up rambunctious child can be – my mum implies that I don't have a right to an opinion because she's the one who looks after them most of the time. The cats look at us intently and wonder if there's going to be a divorce.

I've met a lot of birds and animals while walking the world with my castaway companions. I haven't met a yeti yet but I know a Sherpa who has seen the footprints . . . In fact, I'd like to write much more about my 'Animal Playlist'. I'd like to tell you about an Archbishop of Canterbury who chose a song about hedgehogs,[216] and a Hollywood heartthrob who took a tale of a flopsy bunnies,[217] and an acerbic satirist who chose 'The Hippopotamus Song'[218] – and it wasn't a joke, his voice cracked with emotion as he asked for it. And I'd also like to play you 'Simon Smith and His Amazing Dancing Bear'[219] because I love that dancing bear even though the RSPCA wouldn't approve.

But I can't, there isn't time.

We've got to walk 185 miles of the Thames Path and then head to Nepal. So suffice to say, the animals in our lives, and their music, are my constant reminder that this is a wonderful wild world. (And one day I hope to see a Yeti!)

4

'Eine Kleine Nachtmusik'.
–Ruth Westheimer, 1990

_____

'*Morgan the Moon.*'
–Ruth Jones, 2019

_____

One of the things I've learnt during the course of this adventure is that there's a massive difference between walking 10 miles, compared to 20 miles compared to 30 miles, just like there's a massive difference between climbing 100 metres of ascent compared to 500 compared to 1,000. And what I quickly realised on my Thames Path Challenge is that the daily mileage I'd set myself was a huge deal, especially in November with limited daylight hours. On Day 3, I walked from Eynsham to Wallingford (29.1 miles) and on Day 5, I walked from Sonning to Windsor (28.7 miles) and on Day 4 – the one in-between them – I did only 21.2 miles, and that was marvellous because it meant three hours less walking and I could allow myself the luxury of a little lie-in. But as I wanted the walk to culminate on my birthday, I had no choice but to keep going. This meant on several days I ended up walking in darkness. I don't mind the dark but it's more disconcerting than daylight, especially if you don't know where you're going. I was annoyed with myself for not planning things better and for the fact my head torch wasn't working. (I did have one but had I checked the batteries?) And then a couple of my castaway friends gave me a brilliant idea – maybe this would be an excellent opportunity to listen to one of my playlists that doesn't generally get a lot of hearing.

If the world can be divided into morning and night people, I am definitely the former (i.e. I am a morning arty person, rather than a night-time sporty one). I don't have curtains on my bedroom window so I can wake up with the light and as the day progresses my energy wanes. When life has felt especially troublesome, I've had to forbid myself from even looking at my bed before 7 p.m., just in case I get tempted. Sleep is oblivion and there are times when I've needed that. But it also means that my night-time playlist doesn't get much of an airing. I've experimented with giving it a more romantic name like 'A Little Night Music' (after Mozart and Sondheim).[220] I also tried 'Moonlight Music' and 'Songs for Stargazing' (because I love a bit of alliteration). And it's a great playlist – with tracks that range from Mercury Rev's 'The Dark is Rising'[221] to Maria Muldaur's 'Midnight at the Oasis'[222] to Toploader's 'Dancing in the Moonlight'[223] to Spiritualized's 'Ladies and Gentlemen We Are Floating in Space'.[224] It's got the theme tunes from *Star Wars*[225] and *2001: A Space Odyssey*, as well as several tracks from Pink Floyd's album *The Dark Side of the Moon*[226] and lots of David Bowie ('Life on Mars', 'Starman', 'Space Oddity'). And just recently I added John Holt's 'Help Me Make It Through the Night'[227] in order to do precisely that. See what I mean? It's a great playlist!

It was the two Ruths who gave me the idea about playing it on the path when it got dark. The first Ruth – the sex therapist Ruth Westheimer – was a wonderful walking companion who told me all about her life – her heart-breaking, heart-healing life – as we walked together near the delightfully named Tadpole Bridge.

As a Jewish child in 1930s Germany, she watched her father taken away on a truck by the Nazis. He waved and smiled at her, and she never saw him again. Later she was part of the *Kindertransport*, the effort to evacuate children from Nazi-controlled Europe. Her mother and grandmother ran down the platform to get a final glimpse of her as the train moved away. She never saw them again. She said she believes these experiences gave her tremendous empathy for the suffering of other people – and the American population started to share their most intimate problems with her. But she's never been depressed because in the early years of her life, her family bestowed a sense of *joie-de-vivre* that has never left her. She chose Mozart's 'Eine Kleine Nachtmusik' as her first track, saying that despite the fact that she was so betrayed by the Nazis and orphaned, there is still something in the culture that persecuted her which is deep-rooted. And she'll always love Mozart.

After Ruth W, I walked with the writer and comedian Ruth Jones. I would often do stuff like this on days of long walking and listening. I'd find a connection from one companion to the next. Sometimes it was quite obscure – sometimes it was something as simple as the sharing of a name. And Ruth J gave me a brand new song for my night-time playlist – Max Boyce's 'The Ballad of Morgan the Moon'.[228] She told me that her dad would always buy his latest album and they would sit around as a family listening to it. And this song was a particular favourite because it was so funny. She also remembers singing it in school when she was seven, the whole class dressed up as Welsh rugby supporters in red-and-white hats with rosettes. She said she was furious when she didn't get to carry the giant leek but the song will always make her smile and all these glorious memories carry a special place in her heart. I guess the two Ruths might put Mozart and Max Boyce on their 'Family Playlists' but, for me, they are night music for a wonderful world.

So, inspired by the two Ruths, when the light started to fade, I put my playlist on. It worked well: for a bit the music energised me – a blast of 'Eine Kleine Nachtmusik' will always wake you up. But then I got spooked by the strangers in the shadows – probably only a bush or a tree – and had to turn it off and walk in vigilant silence – defeated in hearing my great night-time playlist again.

Then at the end of a long fifth day – on the outskirts of Windsor – I was moving along the path with soundless speed when I became aware of a group of people ahead. Teenage boys. There must have been about five or six of them. A couple on bikes. Their cigarettes (or more probably vapes) glowing in the dark. I was pretty sure there were cans and bottles too. They were lairy – laughing and shouting across the river at something on the other side. I felt a thrumming in my chest. The river was on my right, there were fences to my left (i.e. no sideways retreat). I became convinced I was walking to my comeuppance. It was a dark and deserted place. I was a woman walking on her own, wearing a backpack with stuff in it that might be interesting or valuable. And they were a group of lads, possibly open to an evening's entertainment. I picked up my pace. I kept my eyes facing forward. I started walking into the clearing where they had stationed themselves. I felt them noticing me – for a second I was a sudden surprise. And then I felt them watching me as I tried to quickly pass by silently, smoothly, without incurring any fuss. And just in the second before I managed it, one of the boys – one sitting on a bike – said: 'It's OK. You're alright.'

Just four words which said everything about what I was feeling, and the power that those boys had.

I carried on walking. Reducing my speed with gratitude. I looked up at the moon and heard a little night music. And then a floodlit Windsor Castle came into view, and I thought: *Boys are not bad. In fact, most of the time I quite like them.*

5

I spent the night at the George Pub in Eton – just a bridge away from Windsor – and the following morning I got up and crossed over from the north to the south bank where the path continues for a while before crossing south to north again. I had covered this part of the route before, so most of the rest of the way I was on familiar ground. The previous November – when I turned 50 and had originally planned to do this walk until the second Covid lockdown happened – I had walked 50 miles for 50 years in one day instead.

I started in Windsor at 12 midnight on 21 November (as the clock struck birthday) and walked all the way to Tower Bridge. I was joined by a tag team of solo companions – because those were the days when you were limited to how many people you could walk or congregate with outside. It took me 19 hours straight to complete the full 50 miles and my sister and nieces were my welcome party at the end. I was so tired by then I could hardly walk and the only thing that got me to where the car was parked was singing 'Show Me the Way to Go Home'[229] over and over again. We drove to my sister's for a Chinese takeaway and birthday cake – and I fell asleep on the sofa while everyone else around me ate. I think I only opened my eyes to blow out the candles.

I like being a November baby. Admittedly, when I was a child it felt like a close shave away from Christmas and the risk of only one set of presents – but as an adult who has become obsessed with seasons I think autumn suits me.

One of the most beautiful things about walking the Thames Path in November are the 'Autumn Leaves'.[230] Who knew there was so many shades of green? Actually, the horse racing commentator Peter O'Sullevan did because he once told me there are twenty in total and distinguishing between them as racing colours is one of the challenges of his job. He listed them (and Sue giggled) – almond, apple, bottle, dark, emerald, grass, Irish, jade, leaf, light, lime, lincoln, moss, myrtle, olive, pale, pea, rifle, sage and sea-green. I reckon you can see them all on the Thames Path in November, plus yellow, red, orange and brown.

I've never understood why the British, who are famously obsessed with the weather, are not *more* obsessed with the seasons. We're so lucky to have four of them. Some countries only have two (wet and dry) and if you live near to the equator – like on a desert island – there's hardly any seasonal change at all. The composer who has defined the music of the four seasons in the northern hemisphere more than any other is probably Vivaldi.[231] 'Spring' is the most selected movement from his *Four Seasons* concertos, 'Autumn' the least.

It must be hard being autumn, always having to follow in the favoured footsteps of spring and summer, especially where music is concerned. Imagine having to go head to head with Stravinksy's 'Rite of Spring'.[232] Or even worse, the Gershwins' 'Summertime' – which is apparently the most covered song in history, some estimates reckon there have been over 25,000 renditions of it. And, on the other side, imagine what it must be like to be followed by winter, which has probably inspired more music than any other season of the year. This is partly down to the fact that for many people winter is synomous with snow and Christmas. And Christmas and snow are musical gold.

Numerous castaway friends of mine have chosen festive songs for their island. Some say it's their favourite time of year so they'll need something to celebrate with. Others want music that feels cold to temper the heat of the South Pacific (most people imagine they're going to a tropical island). Bing Crosby's 'White Christmas'[233] is the most chosen festive song, which is not a surprise really as it's the world's best-selling single ever. But carols are also popular – my all-time favourite is 'In The Bleak Midwinter'.[234] But I also love the *Carol Symphony*,[235] which is great if you've had enough of Crosby and choirs and want to go instrumental with a festive flair. It was first introduced to me by Rod Hull and Emu – a *Desert Island Discs* comedy classic matched only when Miss Piggy visited the island. In fact, Frank Oz – her creator and companion there – also took a carol for memories of his *'family-minded family'* who insisted on singing them before opening presents (which drove him crazy at the time). But isn't it funny that he now wants a carol with him on his island? Because ultimately family trumps presents.

I adored Christmas when I was little. It was a time when the whole of our family were together. My aunt was a great cook (my mum wasn't) and it was my favourite lunch of the year. We also had a tradition that you couldn't open your presents until after lunch but that was OK because I love lunch almost more than I love presents. Afterwards, bellies stuffed and parcels opened, we'd all go out and romp over the heath before coming back for tea and cake. And then I'd sing the 'Twelve Days of Christmas'[236] with all the actions and everyone would laugh at the partridge in a pear tree for some reason.

When I became an adult, I started to abhor December. Throughout my thirties, Molly – or the lack of her – made it hard. Christmas is also synonymous with children, which can be painful if you haven't got the family you long for. For quite a few years, we would go away somewhere hot. Somewhere we weren't reminded of the children we hadn't got.

But since I embarked on this adventure, I've noticed that things feel different. It's helped reclaim my love of winter. Now, when the clocks go back I don't think short days, cold nights or I've got to get through blooming Christmas. I think frost on the ground, snow on the tops and it's time to head to the Highlands.

I think *what* a wonderful world.

6

'It's "Rainbow Connection" sung by Kermit.
I defy anyone not to fall in love with this song.'

–David Mitchell, 2009

———————

'It's a song of great hope that there is something better
over the rainbow . . .'

–Ruthie Henshall, 2008

———————

I spent the last night on my Thames Path walk at the Red Cow in Richmond. I do love a pub with rooms. I think it's because I can pass through relatively unnoticed – the bar being more important than the beds. I like it when the place I'm staying has another life. The Red Cow is a live music venue too, so I got into bed to the sound of boozers below belting out 'American Pie'.[237] It didn't bother me. I liked it.

And the next morning – my fifty-first birthday – I got up and started on the final leg to the Thames Barrier. For most of the rest of the way I was on ground that I had covered many times before – including my training for the Marathon but also all the different lives I've led over fifty or so years – the Thames being the aorta of any life-long Londoner. It was only the very final stretch from Greenwich to the barrier that I had never walked before – a rather desolate section that skirts round the O2 arena and feels like it goes on forever. But maybe that was because it was my final few miles of 185 in total. It was also the first time in the whole seven days that it started to rain. But rain felt right – it matched my mood. Because although I was really looking forward to finishing and seeing my family who would be waiting for me; and although I was delighted to have successfully completed the challenge, I was sad. It had been such an amazing adventure and it was coming to an end – that curious case of the anti-climax.

So what I did was I put on my 'Stormy Weather'[238] playlist for the final few miles in the rain. I like the British obsession with weather but only to a point because it seems too rooted in always wanting the weather to be something that it's not. As far as I'm concerned, weather is as weather does and given that you can't do anything about it, you might as well get on with enjoying whatever it's doing. Nowadays I say there's no such thing as bad weather, there's only bad clothing. I admit I haven't always heeded my own wisdom. But I do know now that a waterproof jacket and trousers are always worth their weight; and that more than one pair of gloves is essential in the mountains if you don't want to get frostbite and lose your fingers (which I almost have). But most importantly of all, I know what music you need in your ears.

For the sun you've got to have Morecambe and Wise's 'Bring Me Sunshine'[239] (which is also one of my happy songs), Paul Simon's 'Was a Sunny Day' (which is one of Peter's) and The Beatles' 'Good Day Sunshine' (for Molly's further education). And for all ambulatory adventures, you need Eddy Grant and Katrina and the Waves' 'Walking on Sunshine' (same title, different tune and lyrics).[240] Plus, if the sun is shining, then the likelihood is that the sky is blue, so the Electric Light Orchestra[241] and Willie Nelson[242] will be needed

too. When the wind comes, you definitely need Kathleen
Ferrier blowing it southerly[243] and Bob Dylan blowin' it all
over the place (even the 'g' has gone in a gust). And Ann
Peebles might not be able to stand the rain[244] but I can when
I've got Gene Kelly and Debbie Reynolds singing in it (and if
it's raining in the morning, they'll sing to you twice). I've got
Randy Newman and Scott Walker for crying in it. [245] If I need a
different colour, I've got Prince-like purple.[246] And if you like
your rain with added testosterone, then the Weather Girls are
a must.[247]

I have seen more rain in my life than rainbows, but because
of this adventure I have now experienced a brocken spectre
(I can't remember which mountain exactly but I know I did
because how else would I know what it is?) And Kermit the
frog was right – why are there so many songs about
rainbows?[248] However, there can be little argument that
Harold Arlen and Yip Harburg wrote the definitive track[249] –
although you probably didn't know they wrote it. (Did you?
Do you even know which one I'm talking about?) Whether
you want 'Over The Rainbow' sung by Judy Garland or Israel
Kamakawiwo'ole – the Hawaiian Elvis – or someone else
entirely, it's a must for all rainbowed ramblings.

The musical actress Ruthie Henshall told me she wanted
Eva Cassidy to sing it for her. She said it's a song of great hope
that there is something better over the rainbow. I then learnt
that she's someone who has needed hope, as well as something
better. She was sexually abused from the age of four by a family
friend, lost one of her sisters to suicide and also went through
severe depression herself. She said she's prepared to talk about
these things publicly because she wants to break the myth that
once you find fame and fortune everything's fixed because:
'Everybody has their stuff. Everybody goes through the rollercoaster
that is called life.' But she found love, got married and became

a mother of two daughters and said she believes there is a wonderful place over the rainbow and that she's almost over it, which is why she's saving Eva Cassidy from the waves: it sums up her life.

In that moment I didn't even feel any 'melanjoy'. My heart was just happy for Ruthie. But later when I checked out her Wikipedia page – jumping straight to 'personal life' as I always do – I saw that she and her husband separated a year after she appeared on *Desert Island Discs*, and divorced a year after that. And in that moment I surprised myself by not feeling any schadenfreude either. I just felt sad that Ruthie had probably had to go through the rollercoaster of life again. I hope she still believes in what's over the rainbow. I think I do. At the very least, I know I'm going in the right direction if I've got Israel Kamakawiwo'ole's medley of 'Somewhere Over The Rainbow'/ 'What A Wonderful World' on my playlist.

7

'And this is about journeys that connect people. We all have
them. We all take them. And for me the notion of knowing
rivers, rivers which kind of flow through the world that are
really connected and that take you places, I think that's
really really excellent . . . And I think sometimes in life's
journeys you need a little bit of rapids, a little bit of
unsettling. Too much smooth is not a good thing.'

–Sonita Alleyne, 2020

———————

One of the things I loved about my solo birthday walk is
that after a few days the River Thames became like a
friend. Every morning, as I set out on the path, I'd greet him.
At the source, he's not even there, then he becomes a stream
hidden in the reeds and then he gradually grows – the water
becoming wide and winding and wonderful. The Thames is
masculine to me (like Ben Nevis). Probably influenced by the
fact that the river has historically been called 'Old Father
Thames' and because of Paul Robeson's 'Ol' Man River'[250] –
the king of river songs.

The English Channel, on the other hand, has always been
feminine to me. And during the two years it took me to train
to cross her we became intimately acquainted. I know her first
bite of cold is something I'll never get used to or enjoy. I know
that she isn't blue or green or even mud brown – as she often

is in Dover Harbour. She's all the colours that have never been given a name. I know that the weather changes her in a gust of wind and swimming in the rain is one of the most glorious things. I've swum in her for the equivalent of weeks – not just the 17 hours and 44 minutes and 30 seconds that it took me to cross from England to France (I know I didn't mention the 30 seconds before but that was my official time).

And yet at the beginning of our relationship, I also made a devastating discovery. If I'd known it before I met her, I probably wouldn't have given her a chance. I discovered that swimming the Channel is just like going through IVF. That's because it doesn't matter how good a swimmer you are or how hard you train or even how much you want to get across, in the end you might not make it because something bigger and more powerful than you is in charge: Her. (Or 'She' – as Charles Aznavour might sing).[251] And that's just like going through fertility treatment because there's nothing you, nor a doctor, nor even the latest science and technology can do to guarantee that you will be able to conceive and carry a baby. Maybe one day that will change. Maybe one day we'll be able to control the sea and the mountains too but for now, at least, nature is still in control of the outcome of all these things.

This revelation was shocking. After eleven rounds of unsuccessful IVF, I became terrified that I was undertaking something where there was a very real chance I might fail again. But ultimately that was what made it such a journey of discovery, and recovery.

I once went on a walk with one of my castaway friends along the Thames Path who seemed to understand exactly what I felt. It wasn't my birthday walk – it was the summer, a few years before that, when I was heading west for a swim in Shepperton Lake. I had invited the fellow swimmer (and writer and comedian) David Walliams to join me. He's swum both the Channel and the full length of the Thames. He agreed with me how hard it is, that it was mainly the cold that got him down and he didn't think he was going to make it. And then he disclosed to me that he had started to think he wasn't a good person and putting himself through something so incredibly painful and difficult was because he was *'looking for some sort of redemption'*. And I said I understood entirely because when 'She' let me swim 21 miles, I stopped feeling that my infertility was some sort of retribution and started to believe that nature did love me. But then I lost the person whose love I had taken for granted and that reopened the old wounds and added new ones, which is what had led me to the mountains.

The writer and naturalist Helen Macdonald talked beautifully about the power of the natural world. She wasn't with me on my Thames Path birthday walk either – we weren't able to meet until a few weeks later in December, just after I'd finished it. My family greeted me at the Thames Barrier, as planned, with flowers followed by pizza. After which I curled up in my bed and slept for hours. But a few weeks later – on the morning of Friday 10 December 2021 (which would have been my dad's 102nd birthday) – over breakfast, on the sofa, a rare occasion with *Desert Island Discs* in realtime on the radio, I met Helen Macdonald.

She was so eloquent when she said that when we encounter the natural world we bring an extraordinary amount of human meaning to it, but that sometimes you can look past that and see what's really there. She described an experience she'd recently had with an albatross. She said she was looking at it, thinking about poetry and the sea and then, *'it looked right down its squid cutting beak at me with these amazing dark Madonna-like eyes and the entire world was just made new in that moment'*. She says experiences like this can feel almost religious. I guess in some ways I have brought a lot of human meaning to my journey from sea to summit. And maybe it's not a meaning that's really there. But it does feel almost religious. I'll always credit the London Marathon for being part of this adventure. It taught me a lot. It's a good first step if you want to walk seven marathons in seven days along the Thames Path. But ultimately I think I was called to the highest mountain in the world for the same reason as I was called to the sea. Because after loss on loss (sorrow x 4), I needed to know if nature truly loved me.

For her fourth track, Helen chose Velvet Underground's 'Ocean'[252] which I added to my 'Sea Playlist'. In my early twenties, I once spent an afternoon with Lou Reed without knowing who he was (what's even more embarrassing is it was just me, him and Laurie Anderson).[253] I feel that wouldn't happen now – not after this adventure. And after I had added the song, I decided it was time to create another water-based playlist. One with REM's 'Find the River'.[254] And Jimmy Cliff's 'Many Rivers to Cross'.[255] And Paul Robeson, of course. I've called it 'I've Known Rivers',[256] which is a great song by Gary Bartz and NTU Troop based on a poem by Langston Hughes which the Master of Jesus College Cambridge, Sonita Alleyne, first played me. Because I do now know a river that flows through this wonderful world. Happy birthday to me!

8

'Like I always say: it's a wonderful world.
And everybody's saying the same.
So I think you ought to give me a little spin of that one.'

–Louis Armstrong, 1968

Louis Armstrong's 'What a Wonderful World'[257] isn't currently the most chosen song on *Desert Island Discs* but when we get to the end of time it probably will be. Louis asked Roy for a spin of it himself, although he didn't save it from the waves. He saved him and his All-Stars band playing 'Blueberry Hill'.

When journalists write about the history of the show they rarely mention that Louis chose five of his own tracks. Instead, when it comes to self-selection they prefer to namecheck the singer Elisabeth Schwarzkopf and/or the pianist Moura Lympany. They say that both women chose eight of their own recordings – the inference being that this is the ultimate act of narcissim. It's not correct though. Moura appeared on the show twice – the first time she took her favourite music and the second time she took her musical memories. And Elisabeth did something similar. She said she's never listened to her own recordings so she sees this as a chance to relive her life and remember friends. In fact, for her last track – Richard

Strauss' *Der Rosenkavalier* – she only wants the overture and specifically asks not to hear herself singing.

So now that I'm an aficionado of the show, I'd like to mount a defence for all the castaways who have taken themselves to their island. To my mind, it's rarely an act of self-obsession and promotion and much more likely to be an evocation of a happy memory. And I don't think there's anything wrong with that. If you can't sit on your desert island and sing 'thanks for the memory',[258] when can you?

I love Louis Armstrong. Who doesn't love Satch? I love that he took five of his own records, his own autobiography as his book and his horn as his luxury. And I also love Elisabeth and Moura, in fact every castaway who wants to take a musical memory of when the world was wonderful to them. Because the truth is that the world isn't always wonderful. We don't get the things we want; we sometimes lose the things we have. You need grit to thrive. Sometimes just to survive.

Grit – like the writer Malorie Blackman has. She told me on a walk from Battersea Park to Clapham Common once that her manuscripts were turned down eighty-two times before she got a publishing offer.

Grit – like the agony aunt Denise Robertson has. She told me on a walk in Northumberland about losing her sister to a sudden heart attack (aged only forty-two) and after that being widowed (twice). Her first husband died of cancer; her second of a stroke. And then she lost her son to cancer too.

Grit – like the journalist Alex Crawford has. She told me in a base camp far away that the worst experience of her life was while working as a war correspondent in Libya. She was trapped in a mosque watching civilians all around her getting killed and I could still hear the fear in her voice as she described the cacophony of noise from machine guns and AK-47s; and the smell of people bleeding. It was a reminder that not all journalists are bad. Some make sure they listen to an episode of *Desert Island Discs* before writing about it, and some even risk their own lives to tell the stories of others. Like Alex.

And if these three wonderful women who have experienced so much rejection, bereavement, even murder can all choose and save from the waves 'What a Wonderful World' , well, who can argue? I can't. What a wonderful world it *must* be. And thank you Pops – for singing about it so marvellously.

So, I know I usually end each section with a shortlist of eight songs but this one's impossible. These days I need music for all weathers – sun, wind, rain and rainbows – and for all seasons, plus Christmas, which is its own season and I love again. I also need my music for the morning and the night, in fact every time of day. And for my animal and bird friends, as well as insects and fish. I didn't even mention those before but I've got playlists for them too. And I can't write a shortlist for a wonderful world without including my mountain music or my songs for the sea, and now rivers too. No. Compiling a shortlist of only eight is impossible so one song will have to stand in for them all – just give me a little spin of this one:

Louis Armstrong: 'What A Wonderful World'.

Songs of Faith & Survival

1. Gavin Bryars: 'Jesus' Blood Never Failed Me Yet'

2. Miley Cyrus: 'The Climb'

3. Gloria Gaynor: 'I Will Survive'

4. Labi Siffre: 'Something Inside So Strong'

5. Keala Settle: 'This Is Me'

6. Elton John: 'I'm Still Standing'

7. The The: 'This Is the Day'

8. Dire Straits: 'Brothers in Arms'

1

I now find it hard to untangle what came first: my decision to listen to every episode of *Desert Island Discs* or my dream to walk to the top of the world. They have become so inextricably linked in my mind. And while the majority of this journey has been about walking and listening, occasionally I've had to put my headphones away to focus on the technical stuff. It's not the part of this adventure I've most enjoyed. I've never been someone who is good with anything remotely machine-like. At the beginning of this story I didn't even really do headphones. So the interface of high mountains and all the equipment and skills you need to climb them was not in my comfort or fun zone. Maybe I should have just put on my favourite podcast and walked the world. But once 'I dreamed a dream'[259] of what this journey was, I couldn't *un*dream it.

So over a period of several years, I learnt what I needed to learn (about knots and stuff) and everything I did and everywhere I went became training – from the streets of London to country trails to ascending a vertical piece of ice. I climbed the highest mountains in the UK as well as other continents around the world. And I went to the Himalayas numerous times – home to the highest hills on the planet.

The first time I went to Nepal after the embryo of my dream to walk to the top of the world had implanted, I climbed Island Peak – a 6,000-metre mountain in the Khumbu Valley, which is Everest's hood. We flew in a tiny plane to Lukla – known universally as the town with the most dangerous airport in the world because the runway is basically the size of a rug. And then we trekked all the way up the valley to Pheriche, which feels like you're walking onto the set of a Western. After this point don't expect much vegetation, it's all rock and then as you go higher, snow and ice.

From Pheriche the Everest base camp trekkers head straight on and the Island Peak climbers veer right. The mountain got its name because it looks like an island in a sea of white and it was the most technical climb I had ever attempted at that point. It was the first time I crossed a steel ladder over a crevasse, ascended a rope on a jumar, abseiled down on a figure of eight. Not only were these experiences I'd never had but they were full of words I didn't even know. It was terrifying. But there I was in the fire of the ice and I somehow managed to summit.

On expeditions like this one when the climbing was hard and high, I carried my headphones and castaway friends in my rucksack; in the main they only came out when I got to my tent. But climbing the highest mountains in the world involves a lot of tent time. The two challenges were still inextricably linked.

To date, all the Everest Summiteers who have been on *Desert Island Discs* have been men who are 'real mountaineers' – boys who were essentially born in a base camp. And some 'real mountaineers' (not necessarily my castaway friends but some others who I've met on this journey) scoff at the idea of climbing Everest. They think that these days it's too obvious, too tame. But walking to the top of the world is not easy and I resent it when anyone follows that line of thought. There may be harder mountains to climb in the world and it's true, that more and more people are attempting it (including unlikely athletes like me). But it's still difficult and dangerous, and it's not a challenge to be undertaken lightly by anyone.

When I met them (those 'real mountaineers' in my 'real life') and they asked me why I wanted to do it, I'd say I was a middle-aged woman with a dream. Or sometimes if I was being cheeky I'd just say: *'a lot of pain'* – that would shut them up. I didn't tell them that my dream was specifically to walk 8,848 metres while listening to eighty years of my favourite radio show in order to choose eight discs to take to a desert island, where I'd be 'a stranger on the shore'[260] at first but then they'd find me 'sittin' on the dock of the bay',[261] happily wasting time away. I didn't tell them this all started because it was the only thing I wanted from life anymore. I was already an anomaly in the mountains. I feared this would just make things worse.

In fact, I probably think of myself more as a Brian Blessed-type of mountaineer – the larger than life, booming voiced actor who attempted Everest three times. He was actually more gentle than I expected when he joined me at the end of a 24-mile walk around London. Sue – who was also with us that day – asked Brian when he first fell in love with it/her/him? And Brian laughed and said that, yes, Everest is a woman. Even though she was named after a man – the British geographer George Everest who never even saw the mountain that bears his name. Her real name is *Chomolungma* – it means 'Mother Goddess of the World' in Tibetan. And yes, *Chomolungma*'s a woman. That's the name I call her by now.

Although Brian got very close to the top of *Chomolungma* on his three attempts, he never stood on her summit. He said that he knows that the people he climbed with probably thought he was mad. He didn't want to use oxygen which is the purist and hardest way to summit any mountain over 8,000 metres. The few that attempt it are impressive individuals and I'm not one of them. In the 'Os' versus 'No Os' mountaineering debate I am an O and not a NO. Sue asked whether Brian was on some kind of spiritual endeavour and he replied: '*I thought the mountain loved me.*'

She seemed bemused by this answer but I told him I understood exactly.

When the highly impressive 'real mountaineer' Conrad Anker was cast away, he also talked of the spiritual side of climbing mountains. He said he's not religious but they are his cathedral and that, in 1999, he felt as if he was experiencing '*some sort of cosmic, karmic retribution*'. That year Conrad led an expedition to find the bodies of the legendary climbers George Mallory and Andrew Irvine in order to try and uncover the perennial mystery of whether they had been the first men to summit *Chomolungma* in the 1920s before they tragically died on the mountain. When they discovered Mallory's dead body, photos of it were somehow sold to the tabloid press which then went viral. Many mountaineers blamed Conrad for this, considering it deeply disrespectful. Then later that same year, his best friend and climbing partner was killed in a massive avalanche when they were together on Shishapangma, another 8,000-metre mountain in the Himalayas. He only just survived himself.

I understand what Conrad means by the mountain's cosmic karmic retribution and what Brian means by her love – because my own relationship with the mountains and *Chomolungma* gradually became similarly profound. Just as it had with the sea and the Channel. And my castaway companions provided me with so much insight into human experience and endeavour, and their music fuelled my movement. When Conrad Anker chose 'Can't Find My Way Home' by Blind Faith[262] as his seventh disc, saying that it is for everyone he's lost out there, his voice cracking ever so slightly, I thought to myself: I have faith that the mountain and the music will help me find my way home. And they did.

2

'This song really reflects that moment of me being awakened to the power of imperfection.'

–Akram Khan, 2012

It was 12 March 2020. Three years to the month the trajectory of my life was changed by Jimmy Carr on Sloane Street. And two weeks before I was due to leave for Nepal to climb *Chomolungma* – what I now call 'Attempt Number 1'. I was in the Lake District. A regular visitor by then. I had started coming not just to pay homage to my grandfather but to chase the Penrith Ramblers up the fells. They were much faster than me and despite their mean age of sixty-five – always won. It was excellent training for bigger hills. I'd spend one day walking and talking with them and one day out on my own listening to *Desert Island Discs*. Then the next day I'd get the train home. The 12th of March was a day after a Rambler-led lashing. I had been planning to climb Skiddaw – one of the Lakes highest fells – but there was a lot of wind and rain forecast and I knew it was a bad idea to venture onto the highest tops alone. However, I needed all the elevation I could get, so instead I walked from Keswick up Latrigg – one of the Lakes lowest fells. Then down. And up. And down. And up. And down again.

I had chosen an eclectic selection of castaways to join me that day. It included Bill Gates (who gave me the aforementioned Willie Nelson's 'Blue Skies' for my 'Weather Playlist', although there was no sign of one that day. And the comedian Norman Wisdom, who gave me a song for my 'Insect Playlist' – 'Flight of the Bumble Bee'[263] – I didn't see any of those either, they don't like rain). And I also listened to the contemporary dancer Akram Khan who gave me Gavin Bryar's 'Jesus' Blood Never Failed Me Yet'.[264]

Obviously I hope that you're going to listen to all the music in this story (listed for easy reference in my endnote algorithm). I assume that some artists and tracks that I've mentioned you'll already know, but some you might not and maybe you'll be encouraged to want to hear them. I'd love that. And if you haven't heard of this one then do give it a try because it's a profound piece of music. The composer Gavin Bryars – who created it – told me about how it was made when I serendipitously bumped into him in the BBC archive a few weeks later. I asked whether he fancied a walk and that's when he told me the piece came about because a friend of his had been filming a documentary about rough sleepers and gave him the outtakes of the footage to record over. And on these discarded reels he found the sound of a homeless man repeating a fragment of a song – 'Jesus' Blood Never Failed Me Yet'. Gavin said he didn't know the song and if he had, it might not have had the same effect. The man's voice was rough and lived-in but musical and tender. And over the top Gavin painted in layers of orchestration to accompany him. The result is something extraordinary, almost ethereal. But before Gavin told me all that, Akram Khan had chosen it – on Latrigg in the Lakes – and he said that the piece is very important to him because in the classical dance world they are always trying to achieve perfection and this song reflects the moment he was awakened to the power of imperfection.

Later that evening, showered and warm again, I was sitting in the Star of Siam on Keswick's Main Street. I was just starting on the paradise of a pint and prawn crackers when a message from an old colleague suddenly popped into my inbox:

I've just seen the news that they are cancelling this season's climbing on Everest . . . I'm so sorry.

I didn't believe it at first. Her message discombobulated me but I continued on eating and drinking and thinking it couldn't be true. However, within the next 24 hours her words were confirmed. This thing called Corona/Covid – I hadn't even fully registered what it was called at that point – had clearly decided no one was taking enough notice of it and that needed to change. The Chinese government shut the north side of *Chomolungma*. The Nepalese government shut the south. And ten days later the UK entered its first lockdown. I went home and didn't leave home. But there is always power in imperfection . . . I created a new playlist – my 'Faith Playlist'. And put 'Jesus' Blood Never Failed Me Yet' on it.

Chomolungma is not like other mountains. There's essentially only one month a year when people can climb her: May. That's not to say that other brilliant and brave climbers haven't tried to summit her in other months of the year and a teeny tiny number have. It's just that there's a reason that Hillary and Norgay planted their flag on her summit on 29 May 1953. It's because May is *Chomolungma*'s most clement climbable time of the year. She is also not like other mountains, in that you have to allow two whole months for an expedition to her slopes, which was why I was leaving the UK for Nepal at the end of March. You have to get to base camp; you have to acclimatise yourself to the altitude. All this takes weeks before you can even begin a summit bid. I tell you this in case you don't know, and you're interested. I tell you this because once the mountain was closed for the 2020 season, I knew I would have to wait at least another year before I could contemplate a chance to climb her again. I call 2020 my 'Attempt Number 1'. Although it was really a non attempt.

During the year that followed, the *Desert Island Discs* part of this adventure saved me. As everyone's life was turned upside down, I had the focus of my listening challenge. And I still had a lot of listening to do . . . for the first few weeks when we were confined to our homes, I had nothing in the diary (because I thought I was going to be on a mountain) so I wrote up all the early episodes of the show on my spreadsheets instead. Despite the fact that in the beginning, the shows were unrecorded or the tapes were discarded, the guests are still listed on the BBC website with their song choices. My grid of every track taken – which has now reached nearly 27,000 entries – grew and grew.

For our allotted daily exercise, I would walk on Hampstead Heath with a heavy pack to try and maintain my hill legs, with my headphones on listening to all the episodes I had remaining. I became known locally as the Hampstead Heath Mountaineer. And when the novelist David Mitchell appeared on the show during the latter part of that year, he made me smile because he became the first person to ask for the complete archive of *Desert Island Discs* as his luxury item. He said that he was worried that being cast away is going to be *'a bit like lockdown but worse, lockdown without Zoom'* and as the show is like a library of babel of human stories and experience, it will assuage his hunger for company. I nodded and said: *'You will be assuaged, David, you will.'*

When the first restrictions loosened, I ventured a bit further afield. It was in the Peak District in early October 2020 – just before the second lockdown that scuppered all my original fiftieth birthday plans was announced – that I walked with the nun Sister Frances Dominica. Her story of founding Helen House – the world's first hospice for dying children – is incredible. She then also became 'a nun with a son' when she adopted a severely malnourished little boy from Ghana who it was assumed would die but miraculously didn't. On an average day of long walking I can easily get through ten episodes – once I managed thirteen – but sometimes an episode just gets to me so much that it has to become a full stop for the day. And Sister Frances Dominica was one of those. The episode finished just as I was about to start a final descent down Jacob's Ladder (I'd been doing my usual Peak District Circuit but had decided to go the opposite direction that day) and I could have managed another one before getting back to The Rambler Inn. But instead I put on my new 'Faith Playlist' and when I got to the bottom and started across the fields to Edale, even though it was a grey afternoon in October and the light was getting lower, a massive shaft of sun suddenly shone through the hills just at the moment that 'Jesus' Blood Never Failed Me Yet' played.

There is power in imperfection. Akram Kahn knows it. I think Sister Frances Dominica knows it, too. And in moments like that one, I knew there was power in not going to *Chomolungma* in 2020. There was perfection in the imperfection. Jesus' blood hadn't failed me. Yet.

3

'That is a faith that will never die.'
–A.H. Halsey, 2003

―――――――――

I am not religious in a conventional sense although I would echo the words of the postulant turned religious writer Karen Armstrong who told me in my tent when I did finally get to *Chomolungma's* base camp that all religions are the same in their teachings of compassion. The tragedy is when they are used for political and violent ends. She told me this when I made my first actual attempt to get to the top of the world. However, I will always think of it as my second attempt. I've not just been through multiple attempts of IVF. I've had multiple attempts at multiple things. And I may not be religious in a conventional sense but I admit I've done my fair share of praying for my luck to change. I asked the Gods of Goth to 'Please Please Let Me Get What I Want'.[265] But the Gods of Rock 'n' Roll said: 'No – 'You Can't Always Get What You Want' – Sorry!'[266]

I went through a period on this adventure when I met a string of biologists whose thoughts about religion were compelling. I smiled when Richard Dawkins told me on a walk to Brent Reservoir that God is akin to Father Christmas and the Tooth Fairy. And straight afterwards I walked with

Lewis Wolpert, who told me that when human beings first became conscious, the people who survived and thrived were those who could explain the unexplainable and God was a good answer. But now that science has debunked that, the people who are more likely to prosper today are those who acknowledge that God isn't the answer. Like him, Lewis said, and laughed.

I enjoyed my walk to the reservoir with Richard and Lewis (it's a far better reason for going anywhere near the north circular than IKEA). However, I have equally enjoyed my time with all the religious leaders and teachers I've met too. I adored Archbishop Desmond Tutu (who saved 'We Are the World'[267] from the waves and took an ice cream maker as his luxury – his favourite flavour rum and raisin). I told him: *mine too*. We were walking near the Kenwood dairy on Hampstead Heath at the time – the three, small, cube-shaped outbuildings that provided the main house with milk and cream from the Kenwood cows back in the nineteeth century. I'd never given these buildings any thought before – until Desmond and his ice cream.

I also adored Rabbi Lionel Blue, who accepted gracefully he couldn't take a dog as his luxury because it was against island rules. We were walking from Preachers Hill up East Heath Road to The Pound, which I never knew was called that until I started taking an interest in maps in order to plan my castaway walks. Lionel said he'd leave his dog there and take a toilet bag as his luxury instead so he could look and feel his best when chatting to the dolphins.

But dog or no dog, God or no God, one thing is as true for me as it is for the scientist James Lovelock: *'I like religious music.'* James (he of the Gaia Theory) told me that although he's an agnostic there's something about the atmosphere of the music of churches and cathedrals that he finds moving.

And I agreed. That's why I've made my 'Faith Playlist' which opens with Handel's *Messiah*[268] (the most chosen single piece of music in the whole history of *Desert Island Discs*), and after that Gavin Bryars. But because I am agnostic in my musical taste, it also includes the Muezzin's 'Call to Prayer',[269] Kanye West[270] and Nirinjan Kaur's 'Triple Mantra'.[271]

In what was to become the final year of this adventure, on the overground to Highbury and Islington and then walking down Upper Street to the 'Breakfast Club', which is a good destination when I wake up feeling 'pancakes', I took a stroll with the sociologist A.H. Halsey. I don't know why it took so long for me to meet him. Sociology has always quite interested me as a subject – despite the fact it never had the status as the other 'ologies' at school. But then again we met when I needed to meet him, which has happened so often with my castaway friends. First, he told me that *'male sinfulness'* has been a pretty constant force in human society. I needed to hear that – from a man. And second, he said that although he was a Christian, the gradual revelation of Darwinian and genetic forces had made him rather disbelieving of the historicity of his religion. Except, he said, in one important fact: *'We have a purpose. All of us have a purpose. You have a purpose. I have a purpose in life which can't be explained in those terms. You just know that it is so. That is a faith that will never die as far as I'm concerned.'*

I don't remember there ever being a time when I believed in Father Christmas or the Tooth Fairy. Not even when I was little. I've always been suspicious of those types of stories. I'm much more interested in fact than fairytale. But, at the same time, I've also always wondered why I am me and not someone else. That is a question that puzzled me from a very young age when I started to wonder whether my family and friends actually existed when I wasn't with them. (I've never found out the answer.) But I definitely agree with A.H. (Chelly to his friends) that I feel as if I have a purpose that can't be defined in Darwinian terms. I just know that it is so. And I think perhaps it is something to do with taking on exceptionally hard physical and mental challenges and sharing them with the world. And I can now say with more surety than I've ever known before that my 'Faith Playlist' has helped me fulfil that purpose, and Nature's archangel *Chomolungma* is my God.

4

'I believe that God knows who I am. He knows my name.'

–Amanda Khozi Mukwashi, 2021

_____

On 31 March 2021 – a year after I was first due to go to *Chomolungma* – I landed in Kathmandu. After a couple of nights we flew to Lukla and then walked up to Namche Bazaar – the capital and beating heart of the Khumbu Valley. It's from here that you can first see her and what will surprise you is that she actually looks quite modest standing next to all her mountain sisters. You imagine she's going to tower over everything but she doesn't. She's just a little taller than the rest of her family, but not by very much.

I will always remember the first time I came to the Khumbu – not just because of the beauty of the mountains and the achievement of climbing Island Peak but because of memories made with my castaway friends. Like the composer James MacMillan who played me Gregorian chant[272] in a teahouse, which is the most perfect music for morning in the Himalayan mountains. And the perfumer Jo Malone who walked with me across swinging bridges of fluttering prayer flags and gave me my signature song for this whole adventure: Miley Cyrus' 'The Climb'.[273] Jo – a woman who built an international brand from three plastic jugs in a tiny kitchen – said the song is the voice of every entrepreneur she knows – because every entrepreneur knows what it is to climb a mountain: *'There are moments where you want to quit and give in. But my advice is stand still, the storm will pass. Carry on, and get to your destination.'* I loved this and had no idea then how much I was going to need Jo's words and Miley's song as this adventure moved up, down and along.

After spending a couple of nights in Namche, we moved onwards towards base camp, stopping en route to climb another mountain – Lobuche. She's about the same height as Island Peak. But you turn left when you get to the Wild West of Pheriche, not right. This is all part of the essential acclimatisation process required when you're walking at altitude and intend to go as high as it gets.

It's difficult to explain the difference between walking and climbing. Like it's difficult to distinguish between a mountain and a hill. The words can be interchangeable, especially among 'real mountaineers'. But for the record after I leave a base camp (wherever that base camp is), I'm climbing not walking. And, to me, *Chomolungma* is a mountain not a hill. Anything else feels disrespectful to the 'Mother Goddess of the World'.

Sadly my second attempt to climb *Chomolungma* in 2021 was like my first, in that it wasn't to be. The Nepalese government reopened the mountain, I got there and did all the required acclimatisation, but I didn't get to the top of her – what 'real mountaineers' would call a 'non-summit'. This is an alternative word for 'failure' but I don't mind it as a substitution. Failure suggests its opposite: success. And what I've realised is that summitting or not summiting high mountains should never be thought of in these terms. It's a much more complex equation and I know that now because I've failed, *and* I've succeeded.

The year of my 'non-summit' (which I think of as my second attempt, even though my first was a 'non-attempt') has already entered the history books as one of the worst seasons ever on *Chomolungma*. A combination of what I call 'The Three Cs' (Cyclones, Covid and a Chest Infection) were the official reason I didn't get there. I got the Chest Infection. Our Sherpa support team got the Covid. Everyone got the Cyclones. But when our expedition had to be shut down (due to the C that was Covid) I was also secretly relieved. Because if I'm to be totally truthful – which I want to be – I wasn't sure I could do it. While I did get dangerously ill with the Chest Infection (putting me at risk of pulmonary odema, which if you don't know what that is, is not a good thing), I felt that I wasn't fit enough. I wasn't fast enough. So when the expedition was pulled and no one could summit, it was actually a relief and a reprieve. I came home knowing that the Hampstead Heath Mountaineer wasn't ready for the Himalayas – even though, during Covid 2020, she'd listened to a lot of episodes of *Desert Island Discs*.

I returned to London – via eleven days of quarantine at a hotel near Heathrow. Nepal had been put on the 'Red List' between my going away and coming home. Many people wrote to me while I was confined, consoling me with a cliché. They said: *life is about the journey not the destination*. But I don't agree. I'm with Jo Malone and Miley Cyrus. I think life is about journeys *and* about destinations. We all need both. And I'm not saying that a 'non-summit' can't be a destination because I believe that it can be, it's just I felt I hadn't got to my destination yet – wherever it was. I was still on my journey.

Once a day, we were allowed outside to exercise for an hour. I was escorted to a car park next to the hotel and walked round and round its perimeter for the allotted time, catching up with all the castaways I'd missed while I was away. It was there in that car park that I met the CEO of Christian Aid: Amanda Khozi Mukwashi. She was number 2,821 on my list and her first song was Miriam Makeba's 'Pata Pata' – evoking happy memories for us both.

But it was Amanda's fifth disc that changed my mood that day. She told me as we looped round the tarmac that in her early days of working in the UK she was *'broken'*, that she had nothing and nobody to rely on but God. But she believes that God allowed it to happen because he wanted to remove any sense of entitlement or arrogance and it was from this that she took strength. In fact, she describes herself as being *'gracefully broken'* and Tasha Cobbs Leonard's song 'You Know My Name'[274] speaks to that period of her life. She said: *'I believe that God knows who I am. He knows my name.'*

A non-summit is not a failure. But it was hard. I can't pretend that it wasn't. I'd lost the hope of my Molly. I'd lost the love of 'my man'.[275] I was broken. I had also endured the disappointment of not being able to go to the mountain in 2020. And then in 2021, I was walking round a car park in Heathrow and whenever people enquired where I'd come from, the next thing they asked was: 'Did you summit?' And I had to say 'no.'

But maybe like Amanda I was meant to be *'gracefully broken'*. All sense of arrogance and entitlement taken away. Maybe from this I drew strength for what was still to come. And, in that moment, I did know this: Miley Cyrus is right – life is a climb and *Chomolungma*, well, at least now she knew my name.

5

'It's very overblown, but it's completely fabulous.'
–Helen Fielding, 2020

'It speaks to me about the crosses that we experience in life.'
–Rose Hudson-Wilkin, 2014

'Because this is me. And also it will lift my spirit when I'm there.'
–Nick Webborn, 2022

So would it be third time lucky? Three times' a charm? Well, three is my favourite number even though I generally prefer even to odd. Like, I'd rather eat two doughnuts than one. Or six olives than seven (in fact I'd rather eat twelve than eleven). And, obviously, even numbered eight is the theme of this book – eight tracks; eighty years, 8,848 metres (in fact, 8,848 metres and 86 centimetres high). But above all I love a list of three. Maybe you've noticed that already; if not you will now.

But before I tell you my summit story, I need to tell you about my 'Survival Playlist', which is the conjoined cousin of my 'Faith Playlist' – because sometimes surviving is an act of faith. I'd like to tell you about every song on it because they're all important. But there are lots and it would take too long, so I've had to pick just three to step forward to represent the full list.

First, there has to be a female anthem. The obvious contemporary choice would be a Beyoncé track.[276] I love Queen Bee. I would happily be a worker in her hive. And I predict that in twenty years time (because *Desert Island Discs will* still be around for its centenary I'm sure), she'll be up there with one of the most chosen artists on the show (even more so than her husband).[277] But if I've got to pick just one song to represent all female anthems, then it can only be Gloria Gaynor's 'I Will Survive'.[278] Every woman who has been hurt by a man needs this on her headphones. They needed it when it was first released in 1978; they need it now and they'll still need it in twenty years time. *'It's very overblown,'* the writer Helen Fielding admitted. *'But it's completely fabulous.'* And there's no need for me to say anything else when you're in the company of the creator of one of the world's most enduring female icons of all time – Bridget Jones.

Second, is Labi Siffre's 'Something Inside So Strong'[279] which was actually the inaugural track on my 'Survival Playlist' and still opens it today. The first person I heard choose it was Nicola Sturgeon, first minister of Scotland at the time. Nicola said that when she's feeling down a blast of this cheers her up. I listened to her episode on the sleeper from Fort William home to London. One of my greatest pleasures of the last few years has been coming down from a hard day on Scotland's Munros and boarding the train. I'd go to the restaurant car and have a gin and tonic and cashew nuts (an aperitif is never as good without a canapé). I'd follow it with Haggis, Neeps and Tatties and a mini bottle of red wine and maybe a cheeseboard with another. Then I'd head back to my berth slightly squiffy and climb into the narrow little bed and listen to *Desert Island Discs* as the train rattled south.

After Nicola had got off the train at the Borders, I downloaded Labi Siffre's song and played it on repeat. Apparently, he was inspired to write it both by South Africa's struggle against apartheid but also his own life experience as a gay man. But it's a song that works in the context of any fight for justice and survival. It was also chosen by Rose Hudson-Wilkin – the first Black woman to become a Church of England bishop. I'm figuring I don't need to go into any detail on what a struggle that must have been. She said it's a song that speaks to her about the crosses we all experience in life.

The third and final song is 'This Is Me': the theme tune of the film *The Greatest Showman*, sung by Keala Settle.[280]

When I came back from *Chomolungma* in 2021, I knew there were some things I needed to do. First up, I listened to the brilliant Baz Luhrmann 'Sunscreen Song', based on the Mary Schmich essay. Because 'Everybody's Free (To Wear Sunscreen)'[281] and I definitely hadn't worn enough of it and by the end of the expedition looked like a lizard. I also vowed to get on better with buffs – which help prevent the notorious 'Khumbu Cough' which, in turn, prevents chest infections and summit terminations. Crucially, I knew I also needed to get fitter and faster. Age may be an explanation for my slow speed on the mountains. As is the fact I only started doing any of this in my mid-forties. But it's not an excuse. I knew I had been relying on my aptitude for endurance in which I'm a world expert. And I know that sounds boastful but if you look at the dictionary definition of the word – *the ability to withstand an unpleasant or difficult process or situation* – who'd want to be a world expert in that? But I also knew it wasn't enough and it was fuelling my doubters. I needed to do something about it.

So I joined a high-altitude gym in the City of London and in the six months before I returned to *Chomolungma*, I exercised in a chamber with limited air. I cycled. I treadmilled. And, most heinous of all, I did hundreds of step ups onto a box with a pack on my back filled with 10 kilos of weight. I felt like I had one more chance to reach the destination of my dreams. So I stepped up and gave it my all.

I've heard many people say that any endurance challenge is 80% mental and 20% physical and I don't agree. For me you need both skills in equal measure, and you need to work on the bit you're weakest at because when the going gets tough you're going to need that more than the other. I'm probably mentally stronger than nearly anyone I know. If there were an Olympics for it, I'd give it a go. But if you're doing a challenge that requires both mental *and* physical toughness, then one skill cannot substitute the other. What I realised is that I had been relying too much on what I was already good at and that wasn't enough. If I really wanted to climb to the top of the world, I needed to ditch my arty side and get sporty.

This meant there was less time to listen to *Desert Island Discs*. I all but abandoned the ten-episode 25-mile walks I'd so much enjoyed. I'd sneak in a show on the 214 bus to the gym. I'd sometimes listen while walking on the treadmill but the bike and the box required too much energy for any listening other than the sound of small yelps of puff. However, one day in the gym on the treadmill, I was joined by the doctor and chair of the British Paralympic Association Nick Webborn and he gave me this third and last song.

Nick's life story is just one of the many inspirational life stories I've heard on *Desert Island Discs* but it's an amazing one. As a young man, he was injured in a rugby match which left him severely disabled and his experience of having to apply for more than 120 jobs before finally getting his first position as a doctor is one of ultimate faith and survival. (And by the way he's now a professor.) Such spirit and persistence astonishes and galvanises me more than anything. Nick said that he was choosing Keala Settle's 'This Is Me' because it's a great anthem for disabled people but also for anyone who feels discriminated against, as it's about accepting who you are and saying to the world *take me as I am*. At the end, he saved it from the waves and said: '*Because this is me. And also, it will lift my spirit when I'm there.*'

This story – my story – whatever sort of story it is – *is me*. And whenever I listen to Keala Settle, I think of Nick and of me in the Altitude Centre. It lifts my spirit. It lifts my spirit as high as the top of the world.

6

'This is the ultimate resilience song.'

–Sheryl Sandberg, 2017

———————————

I know I'll be processing my *Chomolungma* summit story for the rest of my life. Some aspects will recede. Some will come to the fore and take on new meaning. Life stories are like that, always shifting in shape. It's hard to understand them fully until you get to the end. So this isn't a definitive version. It's one version. Told in three parts through three songs. And it isn't the truth. But it is my truth.

Summit Story: Part 1
Song 1: Elton John's 'I'm Still Standing'

On 1 April 2022, I landed in Kathmandu. I should have landed on the day before but my plane got cancelled (twice) and then on top of that one of my kit bags got lost in transit. It wasn't a good start. But it did mean I had an extra day to finish things at home, and then another extra day in Kathmandu to relax and pray my bag would arrive, which it did. Small blessings which are listed in my 'Blessings Book'.

I then flew to Lukla at the foot of the Khumbu Valley – I listened to my 'Mountain Playlist' all the way there. We trekked to base camp which stands at 5,300 metres and becomes a temporary town during the climbing season. I was faster getting there than I'd ever been before. Everyone was impressed. It was a nice feeling. My work in the altitude gym had delivered a new 'me'. And all these 'good vibrations'[282] continued right up until my summit bid which started in the early morning of Sunday 8 May.

To digress for a moment, in case you're reading this and don't know the logistics of climbing *Chomolungma* (and I didn't before this adventure started so I'm not going to assume you do). In total, an expedition takes up to two months, which involves the trek to base camp and several acclimatisation climbs to adjust to the altitude. But once you're ready to set out to the summit, you're looking at an average of approximately six days. Four to the top. Two back down again. On the way up you rest for a few hours at four different camps on the mountain (Camp 1 at 6,100 metres; Camp 2 at 6,500 metres; Camp 3 at 7,300 metres; and Camp 4 at 7,900 metres and then you climb to the top – 8,848.86 metres high. And a successful climb is not a summit. A successful climb is a summit and then getting back down to base camp safely.

Also, before we begin, I just want to say a few words about 'queues' – that much beloved British subject. One of the things I've realised over the last few years is that everyone has an opinion about 'Everest' – good and bad – that's what happens when you're the most famous mountain in the world. And one of the most prolific opinions seems to be that she's some sort of bus stop. One morning, I was out walking with my pack on the heath, when I encountered a woman down near the Parliament Hill Bowling Club. She stopped to ask me what

I was training for and when I took off my headphones and told her, she said: *'Ughhh. How horrible. Why do you want to do that? It's full of queues.'* She'd obviously seen the photo that went viral of a queue of people along the summit ridge.

I shot back: *'Have you been? You should go before you denigrate her – she's magnificent.'*

After that episode, I became reluctant to tell strangers what I was training for in case of their reaction, and mine. Contrary to what the press might have you believe, there are still only a few hundred people who climb *Chomolungma* each year (it's nothing compared to the 150,000 people that climb Ben Nevis, or even the 40,000 people who climb Kilimanjaro). And sometimes inclement weather (wind is a villain) does mean there are only one or two days in 365 when it's safe enough for anyone to summit. When that happens, it can get busy up there, which can be a problem. There's definitely work to be done to make things safer. But she's not a bus stop. She's a magnificent mountain. It's an honour to get to know her. To get anywhere near.

But 2022 was a wonderful weather season (unlike the cyclones in 2021) and when a good summit window opened, we set off on our bid from base camp. Base camp is home, and the first thing you have to do when you climb *Chomolungma* is leave your tent bedroom in the middle of the night and go through the Khumbu Icefall – the most difficult and dangerous part of the ascent. It's like the portcullis of the mountain and in some ways it's a good thing it's there because if it wasn't many more people would probably want to climb to her top turret without the requisite experience. This giant tumbling cascade of ice is moving and melting all the time, which means that any moment you could be obliterated by it. This is why you leave at night when the temperature is at its lowest, the ice is frozen and at its most stable. You climb in crampons, in harness on rope with your jumar (part moving handle, part locking device). And you cross its cavernous crevasses on lightweight wobbly metal ladders. This is basically like walking a tightrope in stilettos with hundreds of metres of blackness underneath. If you have a fear of heights, or a fear of death, then my guess is you won't go near it. That's why the Icefall is a portcullis and my own personal nemesis. I'll never forget crossing my first ever ladder on Island Peak – standing on the edge, my heart heaving, trying not to look down or even think about looking down but still having to place each crampon carefully on the rungs to maintain my balance. Since then there's been one song, and only one song that I've needed . . . 'I'm Still Standing' by Elton John.

On my summit bid, the Icefall didn't go well. I projectile vomited before I even got to the bottom of it, which is half an hour out of base camp where you put your crampons on. My only explanation for this now is nerves. I think because I was about to face what felt like six of the most important days of my whole life starting here, with my nadir. All the speed I'd shown earlier in the expedition had gone. I continued to be sick all the way up it – streaks of bright yellow bile painting the white snow because there was nothing left in my stomach. I couldn't eat. I couldn't drink. My pace was so slow that I was a life-threatening liability – huge blocks of ice melting above us as the day heated up. But, still we kept going and eventually after eleven intensely challenging hours finally reached Camp 1.

The next day, we climbed up through the Western Cwm. In many ways this is the easiest part of the ascent – if it were lower in altitude it would be a nice valley stroll. *Chomolungma* is to your left looking down, in fact it's the first time you get a proper look at her, as from base camp she's largely obscured by her high mountain sisters. Nuptse is standing to her right. Lhotse is standing at the head of the valley. To me they are the original Three Sisters. The main hazard of the Cwm is the sun – it's not as dangerous as the Icefall so you don't have to leave at night but it can become a snow desert and at the end there's a scorpion's tail: the climb up to the top of Camp 2 is a killer.

Very early the next morning when we were getting ready to leave for Camp 3, I vomited violently again. Things weren't going well. My expedition had ended at Camp 2 the previous year and I feared history repeating itself. A decision was made to rest up and wait, so I lay in my tent listening to my expedition companions leaving without me. It was hard and humbling after being so strong earlier in the expedition, and although it was the right decision, I knew I was throwing the dice – the benefit of rest and recovery on one side, the detriment of prolonged time at high altitude on the other. Heading on up was a risk. Staying where we were was risk. Everything's a risk on high mountains.

We spent three nights at Camp 2. I tried to rest, eat, drink and not think. And during that time something else happened. It was confusing, unsolicited and uncomfortable and occurred several subsequent times on the ascent. I won't pause to write anything more about it here but it would later become a significant part of my summit story.

After three nights, we pressed on – over the bergschrund at the base of the legendary Lhotse Face, which is a vertical ice wall at the base of *Chomolungma*'s mountain sister at the end of the Western Cwm. We reached Camp 3 – with its tents literally clinging to the side of the mountain and spent a few hours resting. I was sick again before leaving but this time we couldn't wait, we had to continue or go down. It would be too dangerous to prolong our time further at such high altitude and we were now using oxygen, which was limited. We continued. Up through the Yellow Band (a distinctive ribbon of sandy coloured rock) and the Geneva Spur (a mountain in itself).

These were places on the route I'd only heard of and imagined before then and one of the things I want the world to know about *Chomolungma* is that she's far more than her summit. She's the Icefall, the Western Cwm, the Lhotse Face, the Yellow Band and the Geneva Spur; and then she's the South Col – the saddle between her and Lhotse's peaks – where we rested again for a few hours before setting out in the early evening for the final leg of the journey to the top of the world.

We left the Col at around 6 p.m in a dusk orange light and started up the Triangular Face. At the beginning of the final ascent I was hovering outside myself thinking: *'You're finally here. Or are you not here? I think you're here. But maybe you're not?'* The climbing isn't particularly hard at this point – just a slow slog but even on oxygen the height messes with your head. We then veered right across to the Balcony which is the last place on the route you can properly rest, reaching it about midnight.

Here in the dark something bewildering happened – I got separated from my guide – but I carried on with others to the summit ridge. Which is horrendous – thin as a thread with a verticle drop, rocky and slippery in parts, people passing each other as close as lovers. No queues, thankfully. But I did have to cross a dead body at the foot of the Hillary Step – the final scarily steep rocky pitch before the summit – named after one of my dear *Desert Island Discs* friends. The body's been there a couple of years apparently, perfectly preserved in the ice so much so that he looks like he's only just died. My crampons kept slipping on the rock just above his corpse. For too long, I stumbled and skidded, terrified of knocking him off the mountain. That was horrific and, honestly, I did think in that moment: *What the hell am I doing up here? What sort of obscene dream is this?*

*

When Facebook's former COO Sheryl Sandberg was on *Desert Island Discs* in 2017, she took Elton John's 'I'm Still Standing' as her seventh disc, describing it as the *'ultimate resilience song'*. Sheryl seems to be an embodiment of resilience herself, not least because she had lost her husband two years before being cast away to a sudden unexpected heart attack when he was forty-seven years old. When she chose 'I'm Still Standing', as I was walking past my favourite beech tree on Hampstead Heath which has stood in the same spot for over a hundred years, I started singing the song out loud. A runner passed and smiled at me. I'll never forget that moment, nor will I ever forget the moment after six days and a final thirteen long hours through the night, I reached my destination, and stood on top of the world.

7

'In those long and strange days in Peru, lots of fairly weird things happened to my head, some of it delirious, some of it sensory deprivation. And at one point I got this song going through my head.'

–Joe Simpson, 2004

Summit Story: Part 2
Song 2: The The's 'This is the Day'

In fact, I didn't stand for very long. As soon as I arrived I sat down. I got the customary summit photo, but I didn't remove my oxygen mask to smile. I didn't feel how I thought I'd feel. I'd never expected to be modelling by the prayer flags or punching the air in triumph, as other people around me were. But I had imagined there might be tears of relief that after so many years dreaming of this moment, I'd finally got there. Instead, I just felt numb. Metaphorically though, I was still standing and I could have stood up, literally, if I wanted to. It just felt better to sit down and have a look around. And it is beautiful up there but then it's beautiful on the top of all mountains. When I climb to the top of Parliament Hill and it's crowded with people, I get why they're there. Summits are special. They offer the best views you can get, inside and out.

After twenty minutes, we started the descent. It was hot and hard-going. Every limb in my body was yelling. And then after five, maybe six hours of going down, suddenly I wasn't standing any more – literally or metaphorically. Something falling from above hit me hard in the leg, knocking me over into the snow. On the triangular face above Camp 4, still in the Death Zone where there is no helicopter rescue because it's too high. The sudden unexpected smack stunned me: *'What the fuck was that?'* The answer came quickly: an oxygen bottle tumbling down at speed had struck me on the side of my left leg just below the knee and then continued on down without a care in the world.

Now, writing this from the comfort of my bed at home in London, I could conjecture what happened even though I'll never know. Oxygen bottles are heavy – with or without air. On the way up I had witnessed the terrible sight of Sherpas hurling empty tanks off the mountain into the void. Another practice was to fasten them in the snow with an anchor and collect them on the way down. But in the end, whether the oxygen bottle had been discarded, or dislodged or whether it had simply detached and escaped from the back of someone's bag doesn't matter. It was a freak accident. It happened. But the result was I could barely stand. That's not a good thing when you're still at 8,000 metres and your own oxygen is running out. If you were going to choose anywhere in the world to injure your leg, this isn't it. I knew it. The people I was with at the time knew it too. And as much as they tried to help me, I could only manage to move a few steps bent over double before I needed to rest. The weather was good – that was one thing – but everyone was exhausted and stressed. *'Just leave me here to die,'* I said.

What I realise now is that I didn't think I would die. Not at that point anyway. I just thought: *'My best chance is me.'* I knew where Camp 4 was, the terrain wasn't difficult, the weather was clement – my mountain had not been able to divert the human-made injury but she had given me that at least. I thought they should look after themselves and that I would save me.

They didn't leave me though and eventually after what felt like hours but was probably less, a couple of Sherpas came up from below to help. Young and strapping, they became a human crutch. And together, me facing backwards (because that was less painful), and them facing forwards, I counted ten steps aloud before requiring a rest. We moved slowly downwards and eventually after twenty-four hours on the mountain, reached Camp 4 on the saddle of the South Col in the orange light again.

I drank half a cup of hot liquid and passed out.

But I was far from being safe yet.

When I woke up, I couldn't see. I kept blinking and rubbing my eyes trying to focus. There was light and darkness but nothing else. I started to feel a mounting sense of unease. With no emergency rescue possible at Camp 4, descending the mountain with an injured leg was already a terrible prospect. But getting down injured and blind, surely that was impossible? I didn't dare say anything to anyone. I felt too ashamed of so much disability; I felt too ashamed for ever wanting to climb to the top of the world and putting myself and others at so much risk. Like the oxygen bottle incident, I don't suppose I'll ever know what happened to my sight either. It could have been snow blindness. I had taken off my googles when I got injured because I was hot and struggling to move with stuff all over my face. I knew it was a bad idea but I still did it. Or it could have been altitude blindness. While comatose in the tent, my oxygen mask had slipped off. But whatever it was when I woke up and couldn't see, that was the moment I first truly caught sight of death. He stared for a little while, just to terrify me.

But something – was it my mountain? – looked after me again. I reattached my oxygen mask and after a while I must have fallen back to sleep and when I woke up somehow my vision had returned. And on the miracle that is Ibuprofen, I slowly set off on the descent to Camp 2. Uninjured it might take a couple of hours to get there. It took me nine, and of all the weeks and days I had spent on *Chomolungma,* they were by far the worst. Hours that I want to convey the horror of but can't bring myself to write about in detail except to say that every step was hard and hurt and felt like a game of Russian Roulette – one movement away from another accident, injury, even tragedy. Of everything that happened up there this was the most grievous part of my summit story. Not just because it came after the accident and the resulting pain and struggle that ensued from that. But because of something else. Someone else. Someone who in those dark and difficult nine hours let me down badly. But that was also the day I became the closest I'll ever be to becoming a real mountaineer. I wanted to live, and my best chance was still me.

Eventually, I reached the relative safety of Camp 2, where I collapsed in a tent, twisting my head to vomit to the left and – I'm sorry for the squalor of what I'm about to write – shitting myself from the other end. But I was alive. At least I was alive, and nearly safe.

The next day, a helicopter came and took me to base camp. It was touch and go that it would be able to pick me up because the weather had turned bad. But suddenly the clouds parted, it was on its way and I struggled to the landing point in a blur of Sherpa, ice and pain. But it wasn't possible to reach Kathmandu, so after just a couple of minutes in the air it dropped me at base camp and I was carried to a tent near the helipad to wait while the weather improved. My left leg now completely covered with a blossom of bruises.

The following morning, I was flown out. In the hospital the consultant looked sorry, he even apologised, when he gave me the results of my X-ray. I had fractured my fibula and, in that moment, we both knew that, somehow, I had managed to climb down *Chomolungma* with a broken leg. I didn't need any music to cry to then. The tears finally came.

I was on Parliament Hill when I listened to Joe Simpson's episode of *Desert Island Discs* from 2004. His best-selling book, turned award-winning film, *Touching the Void*, recounts the story of his terrifying summit of the mountain Siula Grande in Peru where he broke his leg and then fell 24 metres into a crevasse, coming as near to certain death as anyone can. All mountaineering fans know about Joe and his climbing partner Simon Yates who famously 'cut the rope' that caused the fall – it's one of the most famous survival stories of all time. As young men Joe and Simon were both excellent climbers interested in new routes and first ascents rather than the comparatively well-trodden trail up the south side of Everest – happy to leave that for amateurs like me. And I know my limits. I'll never be a member of the Alpine club like Joe or Simon. I'll never be like the superhero mountaineers Messner or Nims and climb the fourteen highest peaks in the world. But, please don't underestimate how hard I worked to get there or how tough it is for those who do. The view might be comparable. But never confuse climbing *Chomolungma* with climbing Parliament Hill.

I devoured Joe's episode like I have all the male 'real mountaineers' who have been on the show. The story of how he got himself out of the crevasse and then crawled on his own (because Simon had assumed he must be dead) for three days and three nights back to base camp is beyond extraordinary. And he says that although he was very religious as a child – so much so that he had once wanted to be a priest – in those long three days and nights, he found there was no one and nothing there. Only a void. And it was realising that which confirmed his lack of faith and strengthened his own ability to survive. Then he says: *'In those long and strange days in Peru, lots of fairly weird things happened to my head, some of it delirious, some of it sensory deprivation. And at one point I got this song going through my head.'*

Joe's song is 'This Is the Day' by The The.[283] He says it was a band he'd listened to in the eighties but didn't realise until when he was crawling for his life that he knew every single lyric. I had put the song on my 'Mountain Playlist' after he chose it. I listened to it on the tiny plane flying to Lukla at the start of the expedition and now it's become the song of Part 2 of my summit story.

I had my very own *Touching the Void* moment up there. I would never say it was as traumatic as Joe's. I'll never know because I'm me, not him. All I know is that I looked at the void just as he did. However, unlike Joe, I didn't lose my faith: it confirmed that *Chomolungma* is my Goddess of the World. And I'll always believe that it was she who saved me.

8

*'I hope to become a better human being. A kinder, wiser,
funnier, more courageous human being. For me.'*

–Maya Angelou, 1987

Summit Story: Part 3
Song 3: Dire Straits' 'Brothers in Arms'

For three days in Kathmandu, I spoke to hardly anyone. Everything that had happened playing in my head on repeat. I wrote to a few family and friends that I had summitted. I put the obligatory post on social media (which probably isn't obligatory but I did it anyway). However, I didn't mention that I'd broken my leg or disclose to anyone the full story. I was in shellshock.

My sister picked me up from Heathrow Airport and some of it started to ooze out like puss. It felt messy. I didn't like it. Over the next few days, my dear friend Beth kept calling me and gradually I said more. But only because she kept calling. I'm grateful though, it had to come out before it had any chance of healing. However, I made no attempt to speak to anyone else. I hardly left the house. I had a good excuse – my leg was broken. But the injury was nothing compared to the emotional pain I was in. I had summitted and then survived

267

a horrific accident but the paradox is that it felt more like a failure than either of my two 'non-summits' had been.

It wasn't until two weeks after my return that I spoke to my dear friend, Tara, and for the first time relayed the whole story from beginning to end in one go, exactly as it happened. This is the story that I now call: Part 1, Part 2 and Part 3.

Tara has experienced more trauma than anyone I know. Her father's severe mental illness, her mother's death from cancer when she was thirteen, her brother's suicide when she was seventeen and on top of all that the inappropriate behaviour and betrayal of her adored and trusted youth athletics coach. And because she's experienced and dealt with all this, she's wise and wonderful. She was the first person who helped me to understand that I had incurred two separate injuries on my mountain. A physical injury – breaking my leg – but also a psychological injury – a transgression by someone on my support team who I myself had adored and trusted and, who if things had been different, would have been part of this story, but instead is only conspicuous in absence. And it was the combination of these two injuries that broke me.

I now call the psychological injury Part 3 of my summit story. In fact, it was more than psychological. But all the other words I could choose to describe it feel disgusting and dangerous.

So how do I tell you this part of the story without giving the detail which I'm not ready to do, whilst conveying the magnitude of what happened, and showing my solidarity with anyone in the world who might say 'me too'. I turn to a castaway, of course. I turn to the writer Maya Angelou, inter-viewed by Michael Parkinson on *Desert Island Discs* in 1987.

Let me say this first though. Mine and Maya's stories are *not* the same. She is a Black American woman from the deep South who was raped by her mother's boyfriend when she was a child of seven-and-a half-years old. When this came out in public, the man was kicked to death. Maya's belief that *'my voice had killed him'* made her mute for years until she says that *'poetry'* rescued her.

And I am a fifty-something white English woman from north London who subjugated and silenced herself to summit and survive on *Chomolungma*. First, on my way up the mountain at Camp 2 and again at Camp 3 – when I was sick and struggling and was subjected to behaviour that was unsolicited and uncomfortable, which I couldn't extricate myself from because I was in a tent clinging to the highest mountain in the world. But nor did I confront it because I wanted so much to summit. And then coming down from Camp 4 when my leg was broken and I was at my weakest and most vulnerable – when I was subjected to behaviour that was much darker and more difficult to deal with. I had no choice then but to endure its cruelty in order to survive. And finally, when I'd reached safety and was heralded by all as a hero for breaking my leg in the death zone and climbing down, there was a last disappointing, concluding blow.

Furthermore, I felt unable to disclose the full horror of all that had happened to anyone on my expedition team for a complex combination of reasons including shame. I couldn't stop thinking: what was an unlikely athlete doing trying to climb *Chomolungma* anyway? There are far more appropriate ways to mend a broken heart. It was my sister, and my dear childhood friends Beth and Tara who became my first witnesses. I will always cherish them for making me realise that the psychological injury I had incurred was deep and real and rightfully painful.

Let me say it again. Mine and Maya's stories are *not* the same. What happened to me on *Chomolungma* is *my* story. But I am mute like Maya. Partly because I don't think I'll ever fully understand why it happened and am fearful of saying something that might be wrong or misinterpreted. Partly because I want to protect the person involved who, yes, mistreated me but was also instrumental in helping me to achieve my dream to climb *Chomolungma*. And partly because what happened occurred on the highest mountain in the world where nothing and nobody behaves normally, because you're closer than you'll ever get to the extremities of life and death. However, if my injuries had been caused by my mountain, I might be able to feel *'gracefully broken'*. But they were not – they were all human-made, in fact I'll go further and say they were all *man*-made. And I felt betrayed.

Two-thirds of the way through Michael's episode with Maya, he asks her whether she's ever wished that she was six feet, white and male. I know what he's implying, because if I had been six feet, white and male myself, the transgressions that happened on *Chomolungma* wouldn't have happened to me. I'm sure of that. In fact, I don't think they would have happened to me anywhere else. Certainly not in my arty London life where I am the strong and sassy product of my feminist poet grandmother and my suffragette-founded secondary school. If they had happened there I would have confronted them. I wouldn't have stood for them. I think they only happened on my mountain because I was in a place and position where I was at my most vulnerable. It has given me a newfound insight and empathy for what other women might have been through professionally and privately in other contexts where they were vulnerable too.

When Michael asks Maya the question, she simply laughs and says that she wouldn't want all those *'unfortunate, unachieveable expectations'* (of being six feet, white and male). And then she says this: *'My expectations are just beyond my reach and they have to do with me. Not with the world. I hope to become a better human being. A kinder, wiser, funnier, more courageous human being. For me.'*

Why write anything else, when you have a best castaway friend who can say what you feel for you. All I want from the world now for myself is to become a better human being. That's why I embarked on this adventure. That's why I'm trying to write it. Maya says poetry rescued her. Music rescued me.

Throughout my summit bid, there was one song that played over and over in my head – just like 'This Is the Day' did for Joe Simpson. For me it was Dire Straits' 'Brothers in Arms'.[284] It's not my favourite mountain song or even the signature song of this adventure – that will always go to Miley Cyrus' 'The Climb'. Nor did I love Dire Straits in my youth, although I did have the album the song was on – mainly because Tara's first boyfriend was a fan so, until she dumped him, we listened to it a lot. (He was rather nice, he didn't deserve the dumping but that's teenagers for you.)

So far in the eighty-year history of *Desert Island Discs*, the original track has only been chosen once – by the conservative politician David Davis. And, no, I didn't think I'd be ending my three-part summit story with a Tory politician. But I'm an honest person and sometimes incongruity can make for the best lyrics. I had listened to his episode at *Chomolungma*'s base camp the year before, in 2021 – the year of the three Cs – so the spirit of him must have still been around. And although the song has several themes that can be applied to my story, it's the opening lines that bubble up from its mystical musical melody which played over and over in my head.

> *These mist covered mountains*
> *Are a home now for me*
> *But my home is the lowlands*
> *And always will be—*

One of the things that moves me most about these lyrics is the double use of the word 'home'. I'm one of those lucky people who've got multiple homes, although only one that is made of bricks and mortar which stands on Parliament Hill, in London, and was bought by my grandparents in 1919. I've hung up my mountaineering boots at the door along with the Pegasi – in fact, I gave them away to a Sherpa in Nepal – and I've returned from my home in the mountains to my home in the lowlands I love.

Chomolungma will forever be a home to me, but I'm now back home on the streets of London with my eight songs of Faith & Survival.

My Songs of Faith & Survival Shortlist

1. Gavin Bryars: 'Jesus' Blood Has Never Failed Me Yet' – because there is always perfection in imperfection.

2. Miley Cyrus: 'The Climb' – because it's the signature song of this whole adventure. And because life is about journeys *and* destinations, and you won't achieve either without a climb.

3. Gloria Gaynor: 'I Will Survive' – because every woman needs a female anthem on her playlist.

4. Labi Siffre: 'Something Inside So Strong' – because every *one* needs something strong inside.

5. Keala Settle: 'This Is Me' – because I can only live and tell this story my way.

6. Elton John: 'I'm Still Standing' – because I am.

7. The The: 'This Is the Day' – because it is.

8. Dire Straits: 'Brothers in Arms' – because it will always remind me of my home(s).

And now you know why Dire Straits is the hidden track on my 'Songs of Home Shortlist' (Songs of Home, Chapter 8).

Songs to Die To

1. Dylan Thomas: 'Do Not Go Gentle Into That Good Night'

2. Henry Purcell: 'When I Am Laid in Earth', from *Dido and Aeneas*

3. Wolfgang Amadeus Mozart: Various

4. Monty Python: 'Always Look On the Bright Side of Life'.

5. Leonard Cohen: 'Anthem'

6. Sandy Denny / Nina Simone: 'Who Knows Where the Time Goes'

7. Giuseppe Verdi: 'Chorus of the Hebrew Slaves', from *Nabucco*

8. Franz Schubert: String Quintet in C

   Bonus Track!

1

Dylan Thomas:
'Do Not Go Gentle Into That Good Night'

I don't want to die on a mountain. Not even the highest mountain in the world which is as close to heaven as you can probably get. Before I left for Nepal, I had to complete and sign a form stating what to do with my body if I did. Die, that is. Should they try and get me down, and repatriate my remains? Or leave me up there in the snow? I signed that I was happy to stay. I wouldn't want to cause any bother – which is, I guess, what that guy lying at the foot of the Hillary Step felt too. But a mountain – however magnificent – would be the bleakest of deathbeds. I know that now. So when I got injured and said, 'Leave me here', I was lying. I was just asking for mercy.

No, I don't want to die on a mountain. But if I had done, then Modest Mussorgsky's 'Night on the Bare Mountain'[285] (or 'bald' mountain depending on how you translate your Russian) would set the right tone. It's a frenzied piece of music which opens with violins at their most violent, accompanied by the timpani and more trombones than are necessary. It's only at the end, when the woodwind section takes over, that it achieves any calm. Now, when I listen to it, I feel that Mussorgsky knew what it would be like if you got hit by an oxygen bottle above 8,000 metres on *Chomolungma*'s triangular face and you were terrified you might never get down.

I wouldn't choose to die to that track but if I had done, it would have been the right one.

But it has made me think about the music I do want to die to. Not least because it might help to manifest the circumstances of my death. And the first track on my list is Dylan Thomas: 'Do Not Go Gentle Into That Good Night'. I've chosen it because I think you have to start to die by doing everything you can to defeat mortality – which is essentially what the poem's about. This is a wonderful world and none of us know what's on the other side, so try and resist death for as long as you can. And of course Dylan Thomas is also on the list because he's a link to my family. I think of him partying downstairs in our house. And now I also always think of my friend Alan Plater who chose this poem as his 'Damascus Road' choice. Remember? (Songs of Home, Chapter 2), where he says there's a sense of destiny in everyone that tells them who they are – but you have to have the courage to respond when you hear it call. And I think I know what mine is and I've responded: I'm an Adventure Activist – I believe in the power of adventure to change your life and the world, and want others to know it too.

But when death does come – and it will. It has for Alan and so many of my castaway friends – ideally I'd like to be comfortable. At 'home, sweet home'[286] in my bed, with a super soft mattress and freshly washed sheets in the highest of thread counts. I'd like it to be early summer. Late May or the beginning of June. But maybe that's just because I am thinking and writing this now as I sit in my own bed, looking out over London after my return from *Chomolungma*. The window's half open, letting in a small breeze and the smell of green leaves. Their chlorophyll is dazzling me after months of living where no vegetation grows. I'd like to die first thing in the morning – my favourite time of day. And now let's think what other final tracks shall we play?

2

Henry Purcell:
'When I Am Laid in Earth',
from *Dido and Aeneas*

When I returned to *Chomolungma* for my third and final summit attempt, I left a lightly hidden piece of paper listing everything I wanted playing at my funeral – if I were to die on the mountain. I requested that the congregation arrived to Jacqueline du Pré playing Elgar, and left to Glenn Gould playing Bach. As the taxi drove away to take me to Heathrow, I wound down the window and shouted: *'And Mum, if I die, look behind the picture on my mantlepiece.'* A man walking past with his dog who was wearing a bright red jacket (the dog not the man) couldn't stop himself from looking at me aghast. But my mum understood as she waved me goodbye.

When I got back home – because I lived and didn't die but almost did – I became even more obsessed with death music. That's when I first realised that there's a distinct difference between the tracks you want to die to, and the ones you want played at your funeral. Your funeral music is how you want to be remembered – not necessarily the same thing as what you want to hear as you take your last breath.

The English Baroque composer Henry Purcell's 'When I Am Laid in Earth' from his opera *Dido and Aeneas*[287] proves my point perfectly on this. It's got superb 'To Die To' credentials – not least because Dido's dying as she sings it – but the repetition of the words *'Remember Me, Remember Me'* probably feel a bit too egoistic for a funeral for most people. I went to my spreadsheets to remind myself who had chosen it. It's a castaway favourite but in the first eighty years has only been saved once from the waves: by the feminist Gloria Steinem.

Gloria was my episode 309 in a hotel bath in Manchester. I looked at my notes – the ones I've kept on every episode and are now the word count of an overly long novel – and read: *'Not feeling great today. Needed some strong female inspiration and Gloria was it. She spoke beautifully on living our parents' unlived lives; and on not having children; and how her husband taught her to die. So much great wisdom. Must listen to it again one day.'*

So, I did.

This was not helpful in completing the listening part of this adventure which I was trying to draw to a close. I still had about 10% of the archive to get through when I returned from Nepal, not assisted by the fact that the BBC had uncovered ninety episodes which had previously been thought lost and released them in celebration of the show's eightieth anniversary in 2022. They were already written up on my spreadsheets but now I had to listen to them as well. However, sometimes you want to see an old friend rather than make a new one. So Gloria (and Kirsty) came with me and my fractured fibula, as we hobbled to the post office to send a birthday card to a real friend. And it was as if the universe – or maybe it was *Chomolungma* – had instigated our reunion because there was so much that was good to hear again.

At the end of the show, when Kirsty expresses surprise that Gloria got married for the first time in her sixties, Gloria says that she was surprised too.

And I thought: *'So much is still possible, Jessica.'*

Sadly, though, after just three short years of marriage, Gloria's husband was diagnosed with a brain lymphoma. She says he taught her about dying: *'I never understood when people said about very painful things, "it was meant to be" or "I wouldn't change it". But I kind of feel that way. Somehow. Yes, I would have changed it but as it was, I think it was important to both of us.'*

For her eighth and final track, Gloria Steinem chooses Purcell's 'When I Am Laid in Earth'. She saves it from the waves. And I'm glad she did because I like Dido. I think she was treated badly by Aeneas. There have been times when my heart has hurt as much as hers. The hardest thing about my (successful) summit was feeling betrayed by a man, and what made it harder still is that I had already felt betrayed by another man, in fact that was the reason I was there. These two betrayals became the bookends to this story. But then there are many things in my life that have been very painful. I know I'll never get 'everything I wanted'[288] and my bucket list-list will always be uncompleted. Yes, like Gloria, I would have changed it, but as it was I think it was important too.

3

Wolfgang Amadeus Mozart:
Various

Mozart is probably *Desert Island Discs'* top man to die to. He also happens to be the most chosen composer on the show – beating Beethoven and The Beatles. I think it's because of his versatility. Concertos, Operas, Masses, Symphonies – Mozart mastered them all. And his Requiem in D Minor is the most gorgeous of goodbyes. He wrote it right at the end of his life. In fact, he passed away before he could finish it.

The 'Lacrimosa' is my favourite section of the Mass. Two minutes of mournful musical bliss as a final gift to the world don't get much better than this. In fact, many of my castaway friends have taken it to die to. As the comedian Jennifer Saunders said when she chose it: *'I think I'd like to take one majorly sad thing for the time when you think there isn't a boat coming and you can just put it on and imagine you might be about to die.'* Then she giggled, which I liked too.

But although Mozart's *Requiem* might be the most obvious choice, he offers a wealth of obituary opportunity. His Clarinet Concerto in A – also written just before he died – would be a pure and peaceful way to go, and could definitely double as a funeral song if you're looking for two for the price of one. And then there's also the supreme 'Soave sia il Vento' from his opera *Cosi Fan Tutte*. It's one of his most selected pieces which has been chosen for both deaths and funerals. In fact it's been saved from the waves more than his *Requiem Mass* or Clarinet Concerto (but not more than his *Marriage of Figaro*). As the writer Alexander McCall Smith said when he chose it: *'It's so peaceful and has such a wonderful message in it – if you're going on a journey, may your journey be an easy one, may the winds that take you off be gentle ones.'* I remember thinking at the time that it was a perfect song not just to die to but for my journey to the top of the world. I hoped the winds would be gentle up there and thankfully when it really mattered, my mountain made sure they were.

4

Monty Python:
'Always Look On the Bright Side of Life'

So here's a question. Are you more Mozart or Monty Python when it comes to death? Because I reckon 'Always Look On the Bright Side of Life'[289] has got to be one of the funniest songs ever written about death, if you want to die laughing (even though Mozart's 'Soave sia il Vento' is technically a joke goodbye from a comic opera – sung to two people who aren't actually going anywhere). Ideally, I don't want to have to choose between them – Mozart and Monty Python – I'd like them both. So, yes, I want a quick painless death like most people but not too quick because my 'To Die To Playlist' is running at 1 hour and 47 minutes at the moment and I'll feel cheated if I don't get through it all.

The designer Cath Kidston chose and saved Monty Python's 'Always Look On the Bright Side of Life' for her list. I've found so much solace from my walking companions over the last few years and Cath was *'breathtakingly honest'* about her own experience of not having had children when we walked together on Hampstead Heath in the early days of this adventure. *Breathtakingly honest* are Kirsty's words, not mine, but I thought that would give you the flavour. Cath was diagnosed with breast cancer in her thirties and advised by doctors not to conceive. She said it's still hard when she thinks about it but she probably wouldn't have had her business (which became a big one) if she'd brought up children. She acknowledged that in a way it had been a bit like her replacement child. And then she said: *'And if you said to me now what would you have rather done, I would, of course, as a woman, said I'd rather have children. I don't know what experience I'm missing out on luckily, but anyone I talk to says they wouldn't exchange it for anything so I believe them. But I think I've been able to fill that gap by running a business and having this sort of . . . in a sense . . . an extended family within the business.'* And right after she said all that, she chose Monty Python's 'Always Look On the Bright Side of Life'.

If I'd had children, I know I could never have embarked on this adventure. I would never have seen the view from the top of the world or become a Sea, Street, Summit Record Breaker. And when I was injured – in body and mind – and thought I might be facing the end, I didn't think for a moment about whether or not I was a mother, I just wanted to stay alive. But if you ask me now, back home safe in London, what I'd rather, then, like Cath, of course I'd rather have had Molly. Nothing will ever negate that loss. But instead I have an extended family of castaway friends. They travelled with me overseas to base camps and slopes across the globe. They taught me more about music than I've ever known. And, ultimately, it was their solidarity that helped me get to the top of the world (and down again as well). Along with *Chomolungma* herself of course. Always look on the bright side of life, right? And the bright side of death too.

5

Leonard Cohen:
'Anthem'

When I think of the fact that I have become the first ever woman to swim the Channel, run the London Marathon and climb *Chomolungma*, it feels incredible, almost unbelievable, to me. How did a middle-aged unlikely athlete ever achieve it? It certainly wasn't because I enjoyed it. I'm still more arty than I am sporty. I'd rather listen to *Desert Island Discs* than dig a snow hole, that's for sure.

In fact, I think of these huge physical challenges as a bit like my own version of self-harm. Putting myself through the physical terror of them somehow relieved my emotional pain. But what is also true is that my sadness gave me strength. So I now tell people, whatever your 'shit' is, carry it gently because, however heavy, you can use it to achieve amazing things.

And everyone has it – shit. *Desert Island Discs* is my corroboration. We all experience loss, injustice and struggle. It's what it means to be human. We all experience illness and ultimately death. Our own, our grandparents, parents, siblings, partners, friends – sometimes sooner than seems right. Perhaps most tragic of all is that some people lose their children. I say that tentatively because tragedy has no hierarchy. But somehow it seems against the right order of things. If you're a parent, think about it: wouldn't the hardest thing about having your children be losing them? Or – and I know this is more difficult for people to understand – losing the children you've never been able to have at all.

Most days I still think about that other life I might have lived. About Peter. About Molly. About the three of us. The pace of my grief is slow. It's been as slow as it takes to climb to 8,848 metres and listen to eighty years of my favourite radio show. But this adventure became *'the sun'* next to *'the black hole'* (as my castaway friend, the theatre Director Barrie Rutter, so beautifully described the birth of his daughter after the death of his son). And no one sings about this feeling better than Leonard Cohen.

One Sunday, at the end of October 2021, before I returned to *Chomolungma* for the final time, I went to visit Roy Plomley's grave, which is in Putney Vale Cemetery in west London. I wanted to thank him for all that he'd done for me in creating *Desert Island Discs*. I took the overground to Richmond and had planned a route round the full circumference of Richmond Park with a diversion across the A3 to Roy's grave. It was about 10 miles in total and I had a pack on my back – everything was about training then. As I started out through the park, kicking my way through the fallen leaves and saying 'hi' to the deer who were hanging out, I listened to the philosopher Michael Sandel live on the radio. For his sixth track, Michael asked for the Leonard Cohen song 'Anthem'.[290] He said: *'It's a song of darkness but with hope. And it's also a song against the striving for perfection. He tells us there is a crack in everything. That's how the light gets in.'*

My life cracked when I lost the hope of Molly. The crack widened when I lost Peter after that. And now I have a visible crack – in my leg – and an invisible wound that I know will take the longest time to heal. But I also know that my shit is my superpower and just occasionally, when I looked up from my feet at the view from the top of a mountain or wherever it was I was walking and a piece of music hit my heart, well, then the light did get in. And on an autumn Sunday in Richmond Park, the sun shone through the trees onto the fallen leaves and they seemed translucent. I would never have had that moment without all the shit.

6

Sandy Denny / Nina Simone:
'Who Knows Where The Time Goes'

In June 2020 there was a special edition of *Desert Island Discs*. It featured members of the general public talking about the music that had been important to them during the pandemic. The computer programmer Hugh Mullally was one of the guests. He had ended up in intensive care after contracting Covid and had been given ten minutes to talk to his family before being put into an induced coma. He said he knew that there was a chance he might die and wanted to give them something to remember him by if he did. And the thing he chose in those precious final minutes was Sandy Denny singing: 'Who Knows Where the Time Goes?'[291] It's a poignantly profound song that she wrote when she was just nineteen years old. A reminder of how precious the people we love are and to make the most of the time we have with them on this planet. But Hugh didn't die. He came back from Covid and the coma to give me another track for my 'To Die To Playlist'.

A year after my first expedition to *Chomolungma* was cancelled and ten months after I'd heard Hugh, I was lying in my tent alone at Camp 2 listening to episode upon episode of *Desert Island Discs*. A cyclone had made it dangerous for us to continue up the mountain and while there my cough had turned into a chest infection and made me a pariah. I was seeking some sort of sign from my castaway companions about what to do. I knew that even if the cyclone cleared I should probably go down because I might be risking mine and others lives if I didn't. But my worst fear at the time was failure to summit and I wanted to achieve my dream at any cost. So I'll always be grateful to the writer Paulo Coelho for telling me as I lay there not to hate myself for wanting to take the risk. He said: *'From the moment you have dreams you can at least start fighting for your dreams. And from the moment you fight for your dream, everything is meaningful.'* I thought back to the beginning of this adventure when I didn't know what I wanted from life anymore – my dream of getting to the top of the world had changed everything.

Then after Paulo's counsel, the actor John Malkovich played me 'Who Knows Where the Time Goes' – but not the Sandy Denny original, the Nina Simone version. It was recorded live on a night when she was very tired and starts with her speaking into the microphone in full doom mode about getting older and time running out. (When Nina felt like being a tragedian no one was in her league.) But for some reason rather than pushing me onwards and upwards, these two episodes became like a sign that sealed my decision to come down from the mountain. And my descent the next morning through the Icefall was one of the best days I ever spent on *Chomolungma* – she showed me her most gorgeous grin and it felt as if she was telling me that I'd made the right decision. And in the end I wouldn't have summited anyway because everyone was evacuated from the expedition shortly afterwards due to our Sherpa team contracting Covid. But I became more determined than ever to return and fight for my dream in the limited and precious time I have on this planet.

*

Paulo Coelho believes in signs. He can't write a new book until he's seen a white feather and says that when you see a sign you know it. And just the other day when I was writing about Leonard Cohen – you know the bit about the crack which lets the light in – well, I saw a laminated poster strapped to the railings of the community 'Peace Garden' at the bottom of our street – Parliament Hill – with that line from his song on it. As I hobbled up the hill with my shopping I thought: 'Hah! – it's a sign.' And I needed one that day because I was starting to feel that no one's going to want to read an alternative adventure story about music and mountains. But it's my dream that they might, so that was my equivalent of Paul's white feather and – to borrow the title of a great song – 'Everyday I Write the Book'.[292]

Sandy Denny tragically died when she was just thirty-one years old. 'Who Knows Where the Time Goes' was the last song she sang publicly. Nina Simone died at home in her sleep aged seventy. I'm glad she seems to have had a peaceful death because life for her was also a struggle. Nina will always be my singing solidarity, and her music will be one of the eight tracks in my suitcase when I head to my desert island for sure. She helps me to struggle well. I just need to decide whether I'm taking 'Who Knows Where the Time Goes'. Or 'Feeling Good' – her celebration of 'self-love'. Or 'Here Comes the Sun' for my morning joy. Or even 'Mississippi Goddam' for her activism, which inspires me to be an activist as well.

Nina's last studio album was called *A Single Woman*. It opens with the track of the same name which hasn't been picked by anyone on *Desert Island Discs* yet. When I listen to it, I know that Nina's singing for us both. It's like she's sending me a sign. I might take that. Who knows?

7

Giuseppe Verdi:
'Chorus of the Hebrew Slaves',
from *Nabucco*

Four months after I returned from Nepal, I went to Italy to visit various friends. After years of only going abroad to climb high mountains, it felt novel to take a trip that was about bimbling between one glass of prosecco and another. My leg had nearly made a full recovery. It still twinged below the knee and occasionally I felt a weird throbbing along the outside of my foot but in a way I liked it. It was like a tattoo – a reminder of what we'd been through together. People kept telling me to do some physio but I didn't feel the need. I could walk. I was grateful to be alive. I don't think I'll ever stop feeling that. I now live like I'm going to die.

My friend, Caroline, was based in Naples at the time. Her husband is in the British Army and had been posted to the NATO base there. They'd had a steady stream of visitors. I was one, and when I first arrived I asked for a night off talking about what had happened. I'd already spent the previous evening in Rome telling it all to another friend and I needed a break from the emotion of it.

Then the following day when Caroline asked what I wanted to do, I surprised even myself by suggesting we climb Mount Vesuvius together. It was my first time back on a hill and it was here that I told her my summit story. I started it at the bottom where we parked the car and finished it just as we got to the crater's edge – a very agreeable elevation of 1,281 metres. And she listened and didn't interrupt me once as we strolled slowly side by side all the way up. I told her the story in three parts – just as I have written it for you – except I added a little pre-amble at the start. I asked her to bear in mind that there is always '*my* truth, *your* truth and *the* truth' and what I was about to describe happened at 7,000 metres higher than we were that day where death is always pulling on the rope behind.

I had heard this phrase about truth for the first time in Rome two nights previously – from my friend, Cristina, who is half-English, half-Italian. We were in her favourite restaurant in a cobbled backstreet drinking wine and eating plates of cheese pasta served in their own edible cheese baskets. I had no problem with all the cheese but I was struggling to tell her my summit story. Even though several months had passed, it never felt good when I spoke it aloud. In fact, I rarely did. I had only disclosed it to a very few people. I deflected the detail with the headline – I broke my leg in the death zone – it was generally all that was needed to articulate the ambivalent emotions I had about my achievement of reaching the top of the world. And I could have done that again, but the occasion felt like it called for more honesty – eating out on a balmy evening in Rome does that. And sensing my discomfort Cristina simply said that the Italians are different from the English in that they accept that there are always multiple truths in any story – '*mine*', '*yours*' and '*the*'. And when I said this to Caroline on Vesuvius a few days later, she concurred. She'd been reading a book about the culture – John Hooper's *The Italians* – which says that their word for truth – '*verita*' – also means 'version'. In addition, it's the same word in the singular and the plural, so truth always means truths.

A few days later, I relayed all this for a third time in Puglia where I was staying with my Italian friend, Sofia, who is a linguist and a language teacher. It was in a square over coffee – the Italian's favourite drug – which we stopped and inhaled regularly while touring the Trulli. Sofia thought about the word for a while – her kind, dark Italian eyes narrowing gently – and then nodded and agreed.

For a long time, I couldn't make any coherent sense of my summit story. I felt my mountain was trying to teach me something but I couldn't grasp what it was. Until I went to Italy and climbed another. It was only then that I realised that this whole story is about truth. About the search for it, about its utter illusiveness. It was only then that I realised that learning to live in the liminal space of unknowing and multiple truths is one of the keys to peace and happiness. So please, read and remember that this will only ever be a version of my life and my mountainous musical adventure. Because there will always be *my* truth, *your* truth and *the* truth. And for the Italians – a nation of Roman Catholics – only God knows *the* truth.

And for me it will only ever be *Chomolungma* – Mother Goddess of the world.

When I was in Italy I listened to a lot of opera. One of the things I have loved about this adventure is I can now differentiate my Bellini[293] from my Puccini from my Rossini. And I'm a patsy for the pops – a bit of Pavarotti singing 'Nessun Dorma' or Maria Callas with her 'Vissi d'arte'. But it is a shame that so many of the female characters in opera seem to die such tragic deaths – although perhaps it's an explanation for why there are several opera choices on my 'To Die To Playlist'.

Verdi[294] is one of my dying favourites (that's Verdi not Monteverdi[295] – I also now know the difference). His *Requiem* has been chosen more than any of his operas and it is often

picked for final moments and funerals. Several castaways
have asked for the 'Dies Irae' but there's no peace in the
'wrath of God' – it sounds like a nuclear explosion to me. I'd
much rather have his 'Chorus of the Hebrew Slaves' from his
opera *Nabucco.* Apparently, when Verdi died, thousands of
Italians came to pay their respects and when his coffin was
brought out they spontanously broke into this song. I love
stories like this. It was one of my castaway friends – the
cartoonist Osbert Lancaster – who told it to me. I may have
worked in the theatre for a long time but what I love most is
real life theatre. Just as long as no one comes out and plays
Modest Mussorgsky or Verdi's 'Dies Irae' when I'm dying.
Save that for the encore – please.

8

Franz Schubert:
String Quintet in C

Ever since I was a very young child, I've been obsessed with death. I was always frightened that my parents, who were older than all my friends' parents, were going to die. And my grandparents all had such dramatic deaths – accident, suicide, even murder, I think that's played a part too. One of the very few things I know about my maternal grandfather was that he was shot during the war while undertaking humanitarian work for the Red Cross. And this makes me think of the wisdom of two of my best ever castaway friends – the death row lawyers Bryan Stevenson and Clive Stafford Smith – who both told me that *'everyone is more than the worst thing they've ever done'*.

I think that's true of my paternal grandfather – he was more than just the man who contributed towards my mum's birth and then abandoned her. He was also a man who was murdered while trying to help people. And every man in this story – and every woman too – is more than the worst thing they have ever done. I want to believe that. I do believe it. They've made me the person who I am.

Of all my grandparents, only my maternal grandmother, Mima, died of old age – she was ninety when she passed away peacefully, in a care home. And both my parents got beyond ninety (my mum's still going). So I've got good genes, and had nothing to worry about as a child.

Nevertheless, I always relate to people who are as fixated with mortality as I am. And one of my very last walking companions on this adventure was the founder of the Hospice Movement Cicely Saunders who made death her vocation. We spent some time together on the day of Queen Elizabeth II's funeral on 19 September 2022. I suggested we took a memorial walk together as a way of paying our respects. She told me that death is an important part of all our lives and there may be a lot to do to get ready for it: *'You can sum up what you've been, you can reconcile yourself with some of the situations that you may be unhappy with.'*

I told her that this book I'm writing is a kind of reconciliation – it's the third and last part of a trilogy of stories about my life. Because I'm not Maya Angelou. I can't write seven. And besides there's very little I'm unhappy about any more.

And then Cicely played me some Schubert[296] – his *'Auf dem See'*/'On The Lake' – which she said she played over and over again as she was coming out of the bereavement that defined her life. She said it's so lovely you almost want to dance to it. And I thought of the water. And then I thought of Schubert in his superlativeness maybe to dance to but definitely to die to.

Without *Desert Island Discs*, I'm not sure I'd have found Schubert. I'd heard his name but I didn't really know who he was. I definitely didn't know that what makes his String Quintet in C, a perfect track to die to, is the double cello. But now, thanks to this adventure, I know many things. Like I know what a crampon is. And I know about lieder. I know what to do with a jumar. And I don't mix up my Schubert with my Schumann.[297]

Schubert's String Quintet in C – in which he replaced the viola with a second cello is by far the most taken track of his on the show – beating his trouts (he wrote two of them), pieces of music for a Wonderful World. His Quintet was composed in 1828 just a few months before he died and it's said he never heard it played. In fact, the first known public performance of it was over twenty years after his death. So it's as if he was writing his own track to die to – and it was only after he'd passed away that he gave it to everyone else to play.

When the pianist Mitsuko Uchida chose it as we were walking together through the Winter Gardens in Regent's Park, she said: *'If death were this, it would be so wonderful.'* And on a mountain high and far away, the actress Patricia Routledge looked at me and simply said: *'It's peace and trust and submission.'*

Schubert, like Sandy Denny, was just thirty-one when he died. His compositions achieved little public recognition while he was alive. He was lauded too late to ever know what contribution he'd made to human life. First ascents of mountains are very different to creating art. Great art will always be subjective and acknowledgement of it often elusive. But with a mountain, you can plant your flag, take a picture, post it on social media.

I know not everyone will get or like my story. Some will say there's too much music and not enough mountains. Others will say there're too many mountains and not enough music. But it's made me into an Adventure Activist and this is what I want the world to know: some adventures are high and far away like climbing *Chomolungma*. Some are closer to home and in your head, like listening to every episode of *Desert Island Discs*. But an adventure, whatever it is, wherever it takes you, will always change your life for the better. So go on as many as you can because death is always following you, close behind.

My Songs to Die To Shortlist

Here is my shortlist to die to (which are different from my funeral music – that list is still behind the painting on the mantlepiece, in case you ever need it).

1. Dylan Thomas: 'Do Not Go Gentle Into That Good Night'

2. Henry Purcell: 'When I Am Laid in Earth', from *Dido and Aeneas*

3. Wolfgang Amadeus Mozart: Various

4. Monty Python: 'Always Look On the Bright Side of Life'

5. Leonard Cohen: 'Anthem'

6. Sandy Denny / Nina Simone: 'Who Knows Where the Time Goes'

7. Giuseppe Verdi: 'Chorus of the Hebrew Slaves', from *Nabucco*

8. Franz Schubert: String Quintet in C

Bonus Track! Death Cab for Cutie's 'I Will Follow You Into the Dark' – in memory of Jimmy Carr where this all started (Songs of Childhood, Chapter 1).

Coda

'*Some adventures are high and far away and some are closer
to home and in your head. But an adventure will
always change your life for the better.*'

–Jessica Hepburn

———————

After I summitted *Chomolungma*, I went to a desert island
in the Indian ocean. I swam with the fish. I told them I'd
swum 21 miles and I'd been in the water for 17 hours,
44 minutes and 30 seconds, so I knew something of their lives.
I then told them I'd also run 26.2 miles on the streets of
London. Climbed 8,848 metres to the top of *Chomolungma*.
And listened to and logged eighty years and 3,343 episodes of
Desert Island Discs. They said that they didn't understand what
those last three things meant but they had seen a desert island,
and it looked nice. I told them that my aim had been to come
here with eight discs. The fish asked what they were and I said
I was still undecided. I explained they're a bit like you – *too
many shapes, too many colours, it's too difficult to choose which I
like best.*

And they said: '*We get that. There are too many fish in the sea.*'
And I replied: '*I hope there's another.*'

So, I'm afraid I haven't decided my own final list of eight yet and I hope you're not disappointed. But I did choose eight discs for each of my grandparents, my parents, Peter and Molly – all informed by my castaway listening. I considered listing them for you here but I haven't because I don't want to risk this story becoming the length of my *Desert Island Discs* notes – currently 200,000 words and counting. But maybe you can write your own list or your family's. And don't worry if you've never met some of your family – it hasn't worried me.

I will always harbour a dream that one day I might get to go to the 'real' desert island myself – the one that was created by Roy Plomley in 1942. I know I'm only a small somebody but I might be the show's biggest superfan and I reckon I'm the only person to have climbed *Chomolungma* fuelled by the music and wisdom of all its castaways. Besides, I've got the rest of my life to get there. I think the oldest castaway was Dr Bill Frankland at 103 – the man who introduced the world to pollen. And if I do get there to join him, I promise I'll finalise my list of eight. I've done the research now.

One of the things I love most about *Desert Island Discs* is that it's a kaleidoscope of British twentieth-century social history (and now the twentieth-first century, too). From art to sport; science to religion; politics and the Press, and more. Its castaways have informed our lives and I feel privileged to have met them all. In fact I have learnt more from them than anyone else I know and I've also loved meeting their music. That's why I wanted to ensure they were all somehow included in this story. Hence the endnotes.

I do hope you haven't found all the citations too annoying. As I said at the beginning, you don't have to read them, if you don't want to. They are there for committed list lovers like me. But through them every guest on the show since 1942 is referenced in some way. (Even Frederick Coutts, who ended up being the one and only castaway I couldn't link to an artist or song that was in the story, so I've had to create an endnote especially for him. I'm choosing 'O Boundless Salvation',[298] which he saved from the waves and is a perfect song for this Coda.)

And on the subject of salvation, I also want to thank *Chomolungma* – Mother Goddess of my world (the 'my' isn't a typo. I know she's Mother Goddess of *the* world). It's been a privilege to meet her too. I sat on her summit and for that I will always be grateful. But in the end what was more important was the mountain she became in my mind. She has taught me everything I need to know about life and death, and has helped me to know the importance of living both with joy.

A friend of mine sent me a biscuit when I got back home on which she'd stamped these words in icing:

> *Tell the story of the mountain you climbed.*
> *Your words could become a page in*
> *someone else's survival guide.*

They are the words of the poet and musician Morgan Harper Nichols. She hasn't visited the island or been chosen in disc yet but her words are so true (*my* true, *your* true, *the* true). I have written this story to help me but I hope it will help you too. It's an adventure story – with a difference – maybe it's more like a pilgrimage.

And it wouldn't be right, and it wouldn't be me not to finish with some music. It's not a final list of eight, but it is a final list of three – my favourite number. When I ask people what they think is the most chosen popular song on *Desert Island Discs*, clever people often say Frank Sinatra's 'My Way'. It's a good guess. Ol' Blue Eyes being the most chosen popular singer on the show and living life 'your way' being such an important sentiment.

But no. The crown of the most chosen popular song in the show's first eighty years goes to a woman. Edith Piaf and her song, *'Je Ne Regrette Rien'*.[299] I'm so glad that alongside all the men at the top of the desert island palm tree this title was won by a woman. And I can honestly say I have no regrets about how I've lived my life, even though I'm only fifty-two years young and hope I'm not going to die yet. But if I do tomorrow, that's OK. *Je Ne Regrette Rien*. I know which music I'll play.

And the very last piece of music that I want to play you now is Beethoven's Symphony No. 5. Which is possibly the most famous piece of classical music ever written, even though he's not the most chosen classical composer and it's not the most chosen classical track. (And you know what they are don't you? – you've read my book, you've reached the Coda – if you've forgotten you'll find the answers in Songs of Faith & Survival, Chapter 3 and Songs to Die To, Chapter 3.)

Anyway, one sunny Saturday I was listening to the writer John Updike on the Regent's Canal tow path. He chose Beethoven's Symphony No. 5 saying he thinks it's a beautiful piece because in the final movement it's as if the music doesn't want to end. It's almost like a life struggling to stay alive. It keeps saying the same thing. You think it's over and then it's not, it goes back and says it again as if Beethoven's anxious he's got the message across. And if it's good enough for Beethoven, well, it's good enough for me. So, I know this is at least the third time I've said this but I'm going to say it again because I'm anxious to get the message across before I end: *'Some adventures are high and far away and some are closer to home and in your head. But an adventure will always change your life for the better.'*

I'm sitting on the terrace of a restaurant in San Marino as I write this. It's the end of my trip to Italy – the one where I climbed Vesuvius and learnt about the Italians' attitude to truth. Its tiny capital sits on the summit of a hill. I think I'll always like being high up; it feels homely now.

I'm sitting with a Negroni, alone, quietly talking to myself as I type. I check my spreadsheet because I'm thinking: wouldn't it be perfect poetry if John Updike had saved his Beethoven from the waves and I could finish my story with that. My heart descends for a moment when I see that he didn't. He saved from the waves Benny Goodman's 'Sing, Sing, Sing'.[300] But that's OK. It's a sign.

Endnotes

These endnotes are not an essential read. They're for the committed list lovers/music fans/*Desert Island Discs* devotees among you. Consider them an optional reading adventure, if you choose to take it.

The reason I've done them is because during all my listening I created an algorithm of 300 different artists/songs that can be cross-referenced in some way to each and every castaway in the eighty years from 1942 to 2022. (That's over 3,000 people and nearly 30,000 song choices). I believe it could be the definitive soundtrack of British life over the last century. It's also my way of evidencing I listened to and logged them all (because unlike my sea/street/summit achievements this bit of the adventure is uncertifiable). And – as I wrote in the Coda – it's how I ensured every *Desert Island Discs* castaway is part of this story.

It's been quite an adventure working out how to present the evidence for you without it becoming too long and boring. In the end I decided to list the algorithm in summary form here (with a few fun facts). So you'll have to trust me that it works or you can contact me via my website – **www.jessicahepburn.com** – for the forensics. If you give me the name of a castaway, I'll tell you how they relate to the list. Or if you give me the name of a song or artist, I'll tell you which castaway has chosen it. There are probably alternative algorithms that could achieve the same thing. This is just mine, full of my favourite music. I wonder, though, if at least one of your desert island discs choices is on the list below. Either the specific piece of music, or at the very least the artist who composed, played or sang it. Because if it is, then I reckon my algorithm works and this could be the ultimate playlist for human life.

Just call me Dr Desert Island Discs.

1 **Death Cab for Cutie: 'I Will Follow You Into the Dark'** was chosen once by Jimmy Carr.

2 **Diana Ross and the Supremes** were chosen nearly twenty times. Of the songs in this story, **'Baby Love'** four times; **'Ain't No Mountain High Enough'** three times (it's preferred to the **Marvin Gaye and Tammi Terrell** original chosen once).

3 **George Gershwin and Ira Gershwin's** music (as individual artists and as brothers) has historically been a very popular choice on the show. Of the songs in this story, **'A Foggy Day (in London Town)'** was chosen over ten times, **'They Can't Take That Away From Me'** seven times and **'Summertime'**, from the opera *Porgy and Bess*, circa thirty times.

4 **Vangelis' 'Chariots of Fire'** was chosen nineteen times – it's their most taken track.

5 **Blondie** was chosen over ten times. **'Sunday Girl'** twice.

6 **George Michael** (as a solo artist, as part of **Wham!**, and in collaboration with other singers), was chosen over ten times, **'Careless Whisper'** twice.

7 No one has taken **Joe Jackson** to their desert island yet – but should!

8 **David Bowie** was chosen over seventy times. Of the songs in this story, **'Life on Mars'** ten times – his most taken track; **'Space Oddity'** six times and **'Starman'** four times. **'Ashes to Ashes'** hasn't been taken.

9 **Paul Weller** and his bands **The Jam and The Style Council** were chosen over ten times. **'You're The Best Thing'** once by Marianne Elliot.

10 **Bruce Springsteen** was chosen over thirty times. **'Born to Run'** five times – his most taken track.

11 **Gilbert & Sullivan's** music has been chosen over a hundred times. *The Pirates of Penzance* nine times.

12 **Robbie Williams' 'Angels'** was chosen four times.

13 **Bernard Cribbins' 'Right Said Fred'** was chosen three times.

14   'The Lord is My Shepherd (aka 'Psalm 23', aka 'The Crimond') has historically been one of the most chosen hymns on the show.

15   Tracy Chapman's 'Fast Car' was chosen twice.

16   Music from Mikis Theodorakis' film, *Zorba the Greek*, was chosen seven times.

17   Beethoven is the second most chosen classical composer on the show. Of the music in this story, his Symphony No. 9 was chosen over a hundred times; Symphony No. 5 forty times; Symphony No. 1 three times; The 'Emperor Concerto' (aka Piano Concerto No. 5) fifty times; 'Moonlight Sonata' (aka Piano Sonata No. 14) over twenty times; 'Für Elise' seven times; *Fidelio* forty times; and String Quartet No. 13 was chosen thirty times.

18   Winston Churchill speeches were chosen over twenty times. The castaway favourite is 'This Was Their Finest Hour' from 18 June 1940.

19   Chopin's music was chosen over 250 times and since it became the first piece to be taken to the island, his Etude in C Minor, known as the 'Revolutionary', has been taken nine times.

20   Beatrice Lillie songs were chosen four times by Anton Dolin, Elisabeth Welch, Peter Bull and Peter Katin.

21   Λόλα Τσακίρη' 'Slowly Slowly' was chosen once by Peter Bull.

22   Songs from Frank Loesser's *Guys and Dolls* were chosen nearly thirty times and 'Sit Down, You're Rockin' the Boat' five times within that total. When Stubby Kay himself was cast away, he chose the show's title song.

23   Judy Collins' 'My Father' was chosen five times.

24   Songs from Lionel Bart's *Oliver!* were chosen over ten times, although 'Food, Glorious Food' has never been taken. When Lionel Bart was cast away, he took 'As Long as He Needs Me' from the show, sung by Shirley Bassey.

25   Songs from Lin-Manuel Miranda's *Hamilton* were chosen four times.

26   Songs from John Kander and Fred Ebb's *Cabaret* were chosen over ten times – most people ask for Liza Minnelli to sing Sally Bowles.

27   'The Lord's Prayer was chosen over ten times in various versions.

28   Mahalia Jackson was chosen over ten times. 'How Great Thou Art' once by Maya Angelou.

29   Songs from Charles Strouse and Martin Charnin's *Annie* were chosen four times.

30   Songs from Alan Parker and Paul Edwards' *Bugsy Malone* were chosen once by Len Goodman who took 'Fat Sam's Grand Slam'.

31   Richard Lumsden's 'Some of Your Planes' was chosen once by Emma Thompson.

32   Roger Daltry's 'When the Music Stops' was chosen once by Alan Parker. The Who have been taken over ten times as a band.

33   'Our House' by Crosby, Stills and Nash was chosen once by Michael Quinn. If you thought this was going to be a reference to the song of the

same name by the north London band **Madness** (and being a Camden girl it really should have been) then FYI nobody has chosen the song yet, although the band has been chosen ten times.

34 **Burt Bacharach's 'A House Is Not a Home'** was chosen three times.

35 **The Bells of Big Ben** was chosen once by James Blades. Other bells have been taken by John Betjeman (**Thaxted Church**), Noel Streatfield (**St Paul's Cathedral**) and Peggy Makins (**Canterbury Cathedral**).

36 'The London I Love' by George Posford and Harold Purcell was chosen three times (twice in the **Maxine Daniels'** version).

37 **Noel Coward** is one of the show's most selected artists, chosen well over a hundred times. Of the songs, in this story, **'London Pride'** was taken seven times; **'Mad Dogs and Englishman'** over twenty times.

38 **The Kinks' 'Waterloo Sunset'** was chosen seven times – and is their most taken track.

39 **Flanagan and Allen** were chosen over forty times. Of the songs in this story, **'Underneath the Arches'** over twenty – and is their most taken track; and **'Maybe It's Because I'm a Londoner'** was chosen five times.

40 **Ralph McTell's 'Streets of London'** was chosen twice.

41 **John Cage's '4' 33'** was selected and saved once by Ian McMillan.

42 **Denim's 'New Potatoes'** was selected and saved once by Charlie Brooker.

43 **Dylan Thomas'** writing in disc form was chosen over sixty times. *Under Milk Wood* was taken over thirty times and is his most selected work. **'Do Not Go Gentle Into That Good Night'** six times. Several castaways have also asked for his work as their one book of choice.

44 Every castaway gets given the complete works of **William Shakespeare** to take to their island but some have also taken him in disc form. Of his plays, *Hamlet* is the most popular and of his sonnets it's No. 18 – **'Shall I Compare Thee to a Summer's Day?'**.

45 **William Wordsworth's** poem 'The Old Waggoner' (which references The Swan in Keswick where my grandfather stayed) hasn't been taken to the island but four people have taken another of his poems as one of their discs.

46 **Edward Elgar** is the most chosen English classical composer on the show. Of the music in this story, his *Enigma Variations* were chosen over seventy times, particularly **'Nimrod'** the ninth; **The Pomp and Circumstance March No. 1** which was was set to lyrics by A.C. Benson to become the patriotic song **'Land of Hope and Glory'** over sixty times. The **Cello Concerto in E Minor** (superlatively played by Jacqueline du Pré) over fifty times. Penelope Wilton chose his **Serenade for Strings in E Minor**.

47 **Ralph Vaughan Williams** is particularly loved for three pieces of quintessentially 'English' music. His **Fantasias** on **'Greensleeves'** and on **'A Theme by Thomas Tallis'** (the Renaissance English composer). And – the Radio 4 listeners' choice – **The Lark Ascending**. All three pieces were chosen nearly thirty times each.

48 **Gustav Holst's** *The Planets* in which each of the seven movements of the suite is named after a different planet was chosen over forty times. **'Jupiter: the Bringer of Jollity'** – which was set to the poem **'I Vow To Thee My Country'** by Cecil Spring Rice – was chosen the most.

49 **Benjamin Britten** is the second most selected English composer. His opera *Peter Grimes* is his most chosen piece taken over thirty times and mainly for its **'Sea Interludes'**.

50 **'Jerusalem'**, the poem by **William Blake**, which was set to music by **Hubert Parry**, was chosen nearly fifty times.

51 **Billy Bragg** was chosen nine times. Of the songs in this story, **'Levi Stubbs' Tears'** once by Malcolm Gladwell. **'Waiting for the Great Leap Forward'** twice.

52 The Welsh folk song **'Cyfri'r Geifr'/'Counting the Goats'** was chosen once by George Guest.

53 **'We'll Keep a Welcome'** by **Mai Jones**, with lyrics by **Lyn Joshua and James Harper** was chosen over ten times, including by **Shirley Bassey** (who has also been chosen herself over twenty times).

54 **Tom Jones** was chosen over ten times and his version of the **Curly Putnam** song **'Green, Green Grass of Home'** five times and is his most taken track.

55 The Welsh National Anthem **'Land of My Fathers'** was chosen nearly twenty times.

56 **'Myfanwy'** composed by **Joseph Parry** was chosen over ten times.

57 **Bryn Fon's 'Angen y Gan'** was chosen once by Nigel Owens.

58 Eric Coates' **'By the Sleepy Lagoon'** – the theme tune of *Desert Island Discs* since 1942 – was chosen three times.

59 The Irish folk song **'Londonderry Air'**, also known as **'Danny Boy'**, with lyrics by **Frederic Weatherly**, was chosen over thirty times.

60 The Irish folk song **'Carrickfergus'** was chosen seven times, in versions by Ireland's own **Chieftains**, **Clancy Brothers**, **Dubliners**, **James Galway**, **Séan Ó Riada** and **Van Morrison**.

61 **Val Donnican's 'Paddy McGinty's Goat'** was chosen once by Douglas Bader.

62 **Rodgers and Hammerstein** are the kings of the modern musical – their show tunes were chosen well over a hundred times. Of the songs in this story, *Oklahoma* was taken nearly thirty times, particularly for its opening number **'Oh What a Beautiful Morning'**. Songs from the musical *Carousel* were taken over thirty times. This is in part due to the fact that **Gerry and the Pacemakers'** version of **'You'll Never Walk Alone'** from the musical has become a Liverpool football club home anthem chosen twelve times in itself. The show's 'conditional love song', **'If I Loved You'**, was also taken six times. Songs from *The Sound of Music* were chosen over thirty times. **'Climb Ev'ry Mountain'** is a favourite (of castaways and mine) and has been taken in various versions from the **Peggy Wood** film original to the **Sammy Davis Jr** cover. **'Something Good'**, sung by

Julie Andrews and Christopher Plummer in the film (and both former castaways FYI), once by Jilly Cooper.

63 **Joy Division** was chosen eight times. After Ian Curtis' death, the band became **New Order;** who were taken three times.

64 The Geordie folk song **'The Blaydon Races'** was chosen four times.

65 The Yorkshire folk song **'On Ilkla Moor Baht 'at'** was chosen six times.

66 **Kate Bush** was chosen over twenty times, **'Wuthering Heights'** six times – her most taken track.

67 **'The Skye Boat Song'** was chosen over ten times.

68 **Mendelssohn's 'Hebrides Overture' (aka 'Fingal's Cave')** was chosen nearly twenty times.

69 **The Royal Scots Dragoon Guards'** bagpipe version of **'Amazing Grace'** was chosen fifteen times.

70 **The Proclaimers** were chosen over ten times. Of the songs in this story **'I'm Gonna Be (500 Miles)'** (the contender for the best long distance walking song ever) was taken five times and **'Sunshine on Leith'** three times.

71 **Tim Minchin's 'White Wine in the Sun'** was chosen once by David Tennant.

72 Australia's unofficial national anthem **'Waltzing Matilda'** was chosen over ten times.

73 **Rolf Harris' 'Tie Me Kangaroo Down, Sport'** was chosen twice.

74 **John Betjeman's** poem about Captain Matthew Webb, entitled **'A Shropshire Lad'**, was chosen twice.

75 **Matthew Arnold's** poem, **'Dover Beach'**, was chosen once by Peter Quennell.

76 **The Spice Girls** were chosen three times for their break-through song **'Wannabe'**, which includes the inimitable lyric: *'really, really want'*.

77 **Madonna's 'La Isla Bonita'** was chosen three times and is – perhaps surprisingly – her most taken track.

78 **Harry Belafonte's 'Island in the Sun'** was chosen six times and is his most taken track.

79 **Charlie Rich's 'I Feel Like Going Home'** was chosen once by Tim Minchin.

80 **Nick Cave and the Bad Seeds' 'Love Letter'** was chosen twice.

81 **Declan O'Rourke's 'Marrying the Sea (Til Death Do Us Part)'** was chosen once by Anne-Marie Duff.

82 **Debussy's** music has been chosen nearly 200 times. His **'Clair de Lune'** is my personal favourite.

83 **Marlene Dietrich's 'Falling in Love Again'** was chosen seven times and is her most taken track; **'Peter'** once by Oleg Gordievsky.

84 **Wagner's** music has been chosen over 500 times. Of the four operas in his 'Ring Cycle' *Die Walküre* is the most selected followed by *Götterdämmerung*. **Brünnhilde's Immolation'** (aka the Closing Scene) of the latter was taken over ten times. *The Flying Dutchman* was taken three times.

85 **Robert Burns'** '**My Love Is Like a Red Red Rose**' was chosen nine times and is his most taken work. '**Green Grow the Rashes O**' twice, once sung by **Michael Marra** and chosen by Liz Lochhead, and once sung by **Jean Redpath**, chosen by Jackie Kay.

86 **Mozart** is the most chosen artist in *Desert Island Discs'* history. His works have been taken nearly 1,000 times. His opera *The Marriage of Figaro* is his most popular piece of music taken over 120 times. Of the other music in this story, his love song '**Là ci darem la mano**' from his opera *Don Giovanni* has been taken over twenty times. The 'goodbye' song '**Soave sia il Vento**' is the most chosen song from his opera *Cosi Fan Tutte* taken nearly forty times. His '**Eine Kleine Nachtmusik' (aka Serenade 13 in G Major)** was taken nearly thirty times. His **Clarinet Concerto in A** was taken over forty times (just beating his also popular **Clarinet Quintet in A**). And his **Requiem in D** was taken nearly forty times.

87 **Bob Marley** songs were chosen over 60 times. '**Redemption Song**' over ten times and is his most taken track. '**Buffalo Soldier**' once by Jilly Cooper.

88 **Tammy Wynette's** '**Stand By Your Man**' was chosen twice. John Cleese also chose Tammy Wynette's autobiography of the same name as his book choice.

89 **Kylie Minogue** songs were chosen twice.

90 **Sarah McLachlan's** '**Angel**' was chosen twice.

91 **Nina Simone** was chosen nearly sixty times. Of the songs in this story, '**Feeling Good**' nine times and is her most taken track, '**Mississippi Goddam**' three times, '**Here Comes the Sun**' twice, '**Who Knows Where the Time Goes**' once by John Malkovich. '**Sinnerman**' once by Tim Robbins. NB: '**Single Woman**' has not been taken (as of the time of writing this).

92 **Van Morrison** was chosen over fifty times. Of the songs in this story, '**Brown Eyed Girl**' six times, and '**Have I Told You Lately That I Love You**' four times.

93 **Bette Midler's** '**Wind Beneath My Wings**' was chosen twelve times and is by far her most taken track.

94 **Michael Jackson and his Jackson 5 brothers** were chosen nearly twenty times. '**ABC**' was taken once by Rachel Whiteread.

95 **Joni Mitchell** was chosen over forty times. '**A Case of You**' ten times and is her most taken track.

96 **Marvin Gaye** was chosen nearly forty times. '**Let's Get It On**' twice.

97 **Rachmaninov's Piano Concerto No. 2** is his most chosen piece of music taken over eighty times. In fact, it's the show's all-time most selected piece of piano music, as well as the theme tune to the film *Brief Encounter*.

98 **Nat King Cole** was chosen over eighty times. Of the songs in this story, '**When I Fall in Love**' over ten times; '**Let There Be Love**' five times; '**L-O-V-E**' three times, '**Nature Boy**' four times.

99 **Aretha Franklin** was chosen nearly forty times. '**(You Make Me Feel Like) a Natural Woman**' (written by **Carole King** – see endnote 100 below), which Aretha first made a hit, three times.

100 **Carole King** was chosen five times, just once singing '**(You Make Me Feel Like) a Natural Woman**' by Karen Brady. Her song '**You've Got a Friend**' was also chosen five times (once sung by her, and four times in the version by **James Taylor** (see endnote 123), which she sings on too because both songs were recorded in 1971 with shared musicians.

101 'Our Song' was **David Gray's** '**Please Forgive Me**'. It has never been chosen but '**Sail Away**' from the same album – *White Ladder* – has been taken twice.

102 **Roberta Flack's** '**The First Time Ever I Saw Your Face**' (by **Ewan MacColl** see endnote 107) was taken six times and is her most taken track. '**Until It's Time For You to Go**' once by Sue Townsend.

103 **Blur** were chosen three times, including twice for '**Country House**', the song which won the 'Battle of Britpop'.

104 **Oasis** were chosen over ten times. '**Don't Look Back in Anger**' is currently their most taken track.

105 **Pulp's** '**Common People**' was chosen nine times, beating any other single Britpop track. They are also hard on the heels of Oasis for the most chosen Britpop band.

106 **Johnny Cash's** version of the **Bonnie Prince Billy** song '**I See a Darkness**' was chosen twice. The **Bonnie Prince Billy** original once.

107 **Ewan MacColl's** '**The First Time Ever I Saw Your Face**' is his most selected song but it has never been taken in the original, not even by Peggy Seeger whom he wrote it for. Castaways prefer Roberta Flack's version (see endnote 102). However, Peggy did take Ewan singing '**The Joy of Living**', and his '**Manchester Rambler**' was taken once by Peter Melchett.

108 **Jack Teagarden's** '**A Hundred Years From Today**' was chosen once by Sue Townsend.

109 Songs from **Leonard Bernstein and Stephen Sondheim's** *Westside Story* were chosen fifty times. (For more on Stephen Sondheim, see endnote 220.)

110 **Joan Baez** was chosen nearly forty times. Her version of the folk song '**Black is the Colour of My True Love's Hair**' selected and saved once by Patricia Neal. Joan Baez was cast away in 1993 and took herself singing '**Diamonds and Rust**' – the song she wrote about her love affair with Bob Dylan. There's so much about this fact I love.

111 **Charles Trenet's** '**La Mer**' was chosen over twenty times – it's by far his most taken track.

112 **Leoš Janáček's String Quartet No. 2**, also known as '**Intimate Letters**', was the music used in the film version of *The Unbearable Lightness of Being* and was chosen five times.

113 **Olivier Messiaen's** music was chosen over ten times. '**L'Ascension**' once by Ed McBain.

114 **Tony Bennett** was chosen nearly twenty times. '**When Joanna Loved Me**' once by Ed McBain.

115   **Florrie Forde's** musical hall number, 'The Old Bull and Bush', was chosen once by Paul Hogarth.

116   **Beverley Knight's** 'Fallen Soldier' was chosen once by Doreen Lawrence.

117   **Glen Campbell** was chosen ten times, 'Wichita Lineman' three times.

118   **Arvo Pärt's** music was chosen seven times.

119   **Bill Evans** was chosen as a lead artist six times. 'Lucky to Be Me' once by Anne Reid.

120   **Charlie Parker** was chosen as a lead artist over thirty times. 'Parker's Mood' is his most taken track.

121   **Bob Dylan's** songs were chosen well over hundred times, sometimes sung by him, sometimes sung by other people. Of the songs in this story, his own version of 'Make You Feel My Love' was taken once by Jeremy Irons. **Adele's** version was taken once by Tony Robinson (for more on Adele see endnote 133). And the Norwegian singer **Ane Brun's** version was taken once by the former Norwegian prime minister Jens Stoltenberg. 'Blowin' in the Wind' was taken over ten times, sung by Dylan and others.

122   **J.J. Cale** was chosen three times. 'Magnolia' once by John Simpson.

123   **James Taylor** was chosen over ten times. 'Don't Let Me Be Lonely Tonight' once by Barbara Dickson.

124   **John Martyn** was chosen nine times. 'Couldn't Love You More' once by Anthony Minghella.

125   **Keith Jarrett** was chosen over ten times, predominately for his legendary 'Koln Concert'. Kazuo Ishiguro took him playing the jazz standard 'Blame It on My Youth'.

126   **Neil Young** was chosen over ten times. 'Harvest Moon' once by Kate Moss.

127   **Miles Davis** was chosen over forty times. The music from his seminal album *Kind of Blue* is most popular with castaways, with 'Blue in Green' being the most taken track.

128   **Nick Drake** was chosen seven times. 'River Man' twice.

129   **Pat Metheney** was chosen four times. 'Always and Forever' twice.

130   **Simon & Garfunkel** songs were taken over eighty times – as a duo, solo and cover versions. Their most taken track is 'Bridge Over Troubled Water'. 'Was a Sunny Day' was taken once by Glenys Kinnock.

131   **Tom Waits** was chosen twenty times. 'The Piano Has Been Drinking' twice.

132   **Sting and The Police** songs were chosen twenty times. Their most taken track is Sting's 'Fields of Gold'.

133   **Adele** was chosen seven times. 'Skyfall' is currently her most taken track and for details of her version of 'Make You Feel My Love' see endnote 121.

134   **Elvis** was chosen over ninety times. Of the songs in this story, 'Are You Lonesome Tonight?' (the laughing version) twice and the non-laughing version another four times. 'Hound Dog' was taken four times.

135 **Charles Penrose's 'The Laughing Policeman'** was chosen six times.

136 **Joyce Grenfell and Norman Wisdom's 'Narcissus (The Laughing Record)'** was chosen six times.

137 **Bob Newhart** sketches have been a popular choice for making castaways laugh. **'Introducing Tobacco to Civilisation'** was taken most at seven times, followed by **'The Driving Instructor'**.

138 **Tony Hancock** sketches have been a popular choice for making castaways laugh. **'The Test Pilot'**, featuring Kenneth Williams, was taken seven times. Neck and neck with **'The Blood Donor'**.

139 **Queen** was chosen over thirty times. **'Bohemian Rhapsody'** was selected seven times and is their most taken track. NB. The actress Anita Dobson is married to Queen guitarist Brian May.

140 **Doug O'Brien's 'Rotterdam 82'** was chosen once by Mervyn King.

141 **David Baddiel, Frank Skinner and the Lightning Seeds' 'Three Lions'** was chosen three times, including by David Baddiel himself (cast away in 2018). David said he had asked Frank Skinner (who was cast away in 2010) whether he'd taken the song. Frank apparently said he didn't because that would be embarrassing – instead he'd taken another football song **'Back Home'** by the England 1970 World Cup Football squad. David's response was he didn't care about embarrassing and was taking it – and that seems totally fine to me too.

142 **Ennio Morricone's 'Gabriel's Oboe'** – the main theme from *The Mission* – was taken three times.

143 **Pachelbel's Canon in D Major** was chosen nearly twenty times.

144 The **Adagio in G Minor for Strings and Organ** created by the twentieth-century musicologist **Remo Giazotto** from a fragment of music by the eighteenth-century composer **Albinoni** was chosen twenty times.

145 **Samuel Barber's Adagio for Strings** was chosen over ten times.

146 **Brahms'** music was chosen over 250 times but his **Cello Sonata No. 2 in F Major** just three times by Betty Driver and two cellists, Anita Lasker-Wallfisch and Jacqueline du Pré.

147 **Victor Borge's 'Phonetic Punctuation'** was chosen three times.

148 A track of **Edward Lear's** poem **'The Owl and the Pussycat'** was chosen twice.

149 **Elton John's** music was chosen over sixty times – sung by himself or others. Of the songs in this story, **'The Circle of Life'** (with lyrics by **Tim Rice**), from *The Lion King*, twice. **'I'm Still Standing'** (with lyrics by **Bernie Taupin**) four times.

150 **Ella Fitzgerald** was chosen circa 150 times, making her the most selected female artist on the show. **'Ev'ry Time We Say Goodbye'** by **Cole Porter** is her most taken track, chosen over twenty times. Her version of the song **'Skylark'**, by **Hoagy Carmichael and Johnny Mercer**, was taken once by John Cooper Clark.

151 **Frank Sinatra** was chosen over 250 times, singing over 100 different songs, making him the most selected solo artist on the show ever. Of the songs in this story, **'My Way'** is his most taken track, chosen thirty times. His version of the song **'Moon River'**, by **Henry Mancini and Johnny Mercer**, was taken once by Wangari Maathai. (NB: The most popular version is **Audrey Hepburn's** from the film *Breakfast at Tiffany's*).

152 **Led Zeppelin's 'Stairway to Heaven'** was chosen seven times. It's the band's most taken track.

153 **Pharrell Williams' 'Happy'** was chosen three times by Edna Adan Ismail, Esther Rantzen and Sarah Millican.

154 **Finlay Quay's 'Even After All'** was chosen once by Steve Backshall.

155 The **Gerry and the Pacemakers** song **'Ferry across the Mersey'** has never been chosen (people prefer **'You'll Never Walk Alone'** – see endnote 62 – but the real life sound of foghorns on the Mersey was selected and saved by Roger McGough. Other interesting sound choices include Anthony Steele (the sounds of Piccadilly Circus); Reverend Awdry (creator of Thomas the Tank Engine who took two tracks of trains); and Eric Porter (a montage of noises he'd be glad to leave behind).

156 **The Beatles (John Lennon, Paul McCartney, George Harrison and Ringo Starr)** have been chosen more than any other popular artists on the show – nearing 400 times. Of the songs in this story, **'Here Comes the Sun'** was taken eleven times and my personal favourite version, sung by **Nina Simone**, taken twice. **'Blackbird'** was taken five times (Ali Smith took the Julie Fowles version – I like it a lot but prefer the original). **'Eleanor Rigby'** and **'Penny Lane'** were chosen fourteen times each, **'Strawberry Fields'** seven times, **'Yellow Submarine'** three times and **'Maxwell's Silver Hammer'** once by the Duchess of Kent. **'Good Day Sunshine'** was taken once by novelist Ken Follett. John Lennon's **'Imagine'** was taken twenty-six times. Paul McCartney's **'Mull of Kintyre'** was chosen five times. McCartney was cast away in 1982; he took John Lennon's **'Beautiful Boy'**, as did Yoko Ono cast away in 2007 (they are currently the only two people to take it). Their manager, Brian Epstein, was cast away in 1964, and took **'She's A Woman'**. George Martin, their producer, was cast away twice – in 1982 and 1995. The first time, he took **'Here, There and Everywhere'** (written by McCartney) and **'In My Life'** (written by Lennon), the second time, he took **'I Want to Hold Your Hand'** (written by them both).

157 **Leyla McCalla's 'Manman'** was chosen once by Elizabeth Anionwu.

158 **Maurice Chevalier's 'Louise'** was chosen five times, but he is most requested for his role in **Lerner and Loewe's** musical *Gigi*, particulary for **'Thank Heaven for Little Girls'**. Indeed.

159 **Ed Sheeran** was chosen four times and was cast away himself in 2017, aged twenty-six. He said it felt like the peak of his career and that as a kid he had listened to the show every weekend. (He also said that he was planning on being cast away again when he was aged forty or fifty, so watch this space.)

160 **Amy Winehouse** was chosen nine times, mainly for songs on her second and final studio album, *Back to Black*.

161 **Stevie Wonder** was chosen over fifty times. Of the songs in this story, **'I Just Called to Say I Love You'** has been chosen over ten times and is his most taken track. **'Sir Duke'** three times; and **'Isn't She Lovely'** three times too.

162 **Mahler's** music has been chosen over 150 times. His **Symphony No. 9** was taken over ten times but his **Symphony No. 5** is the most popular.

163 **Glenn Miller** was chosen nearly sixty times. **'Moonlight Serenade'** and **'In the Mood'** are his most taken tracks.

164 **Count Basie** was chosen nearly thirty times. **'The Kid From Red Bank'** and **'Lil' Darlin'** are his most taken tracks.

165 **(Sir) Duke Ellington** was chosen over eighty times. **'Mood Indigo'** is his most taken track. My personal favourite is **'In a Sentimental Mood'**, featuring **John Coltrane** – taken by one of my best castaway friends David Mitchell (who took the archive of *DID* as his luxury), as well as British King of Jazz Ronnie Scott (so I reckon I'm in good company).

166 No one does an opera pop like **Puccini** – his music has been taken over 300 times. Of the songs in this story, **'O Mio Babbino Caro'** from *Gianni Schicchi* has been taken over twenty times; **'Nessun Dorma'** from *Turandot* and **'Vissi d'Arte'** from *Tosca* forty times a piece.

167 **Bobby Hebb's** 'Sunny' was chosen once by Penelope Wilton.

168 The music of the **Gamelan Orchestra** was chosen eight times.

169 **Ravi Shankar's** music was chosen nearly twenty times. When he was cast away himself in 1971, he took **Abdul Karim Khan,** one of the founders of Indian classical music.

170 **Ismaël Lô's** 'Tadieu Bone' was chosen once by Tidjane Thiam.

171 **Bono and U2** were chosen nearly twenty times. **'One'** is their most taken track.

172 **Angelique Kidjo** was chosen four times.

173 The South African National Anthem **'Nkosi Sikelel' iAfrika'** was chosen nearly twenty times, more than any other national anthem, even the UK's (which has only been taken thrice).

174 **Miriam Makeba** was chosen twenty times. **'Pata Pata'** five times and is her most taken track.

175 **Erik Satie's** music was chosen over twenty times. His *Three Gymnopédies* is by the far his most taken track. It's one of my all-time favourite 'threes' too.

176 **Buena Vista Social Club** was chosen six times – their track **'Chan Chan'** was taken every time.

177 **Antonio Carlos Jobim's** song, **'The Girl From Ipanema'**, was chosen over ten times in various versions but mainly in the rendition featuring **Astrud Gilberto**, which first appeared on the seminal jazz album *Getz /Gilberto*. It was composed by American saxophonist **Stan Getz**, Brazilian guitarist **João**

ENDNOTES

Gilberto (Astrud's husband at the time) and Jobim himself. João Gilberto was also the father of the singer **Bebel Gilberto** (from his second marriage to the singer Miucha). Bebel was chosen once by Mario Testino.

178 **Whitney Houston** was chosen ten times and **'I Will Always Love You'** is neck and neck with **'One Moment in Time'** as her most taken track.

179 **Franz Lehár's** *The Merry Widow* is his most chosen operetta – taken over twenty times. Followed by *The Land of Smiles*.

180 **Stormzy's 'Wiley Flow'** – which features Everest/*Chomolungma* – was taken once by Simon Reeve.

181 **ABBA** was chosen nearly thirty times. **'Dancing Queen'** over ten times and is by far their most taken track.

182 **Tchaikovsky's** music has been chosen over 300 times. Of his three ballets, *Swan Lake* was chosen the most (over fifty times) followed by *Sleeping Beauty* (over thirty times), then *Nutcracker* (over twenty times).

183 **'Wheels on the Bus'**, an American folk song written by **Verna Hills**, was chosen once by Dorothy Byrne.

184 **Stacey Kent** was chosen twice – by Kazuo Ishiguro, singing the **Gershwin brothers'** number **'They Can't Take That Away From Me'** (see endnote 3), and by Peter Bonfield, singing the **Bernice Petkere** number **'Close Your Eyes'** (one of my personal favourite Stacey songs).

185 **Engelbert Humperdinck (1)** – the German composer – was chosen over ten times, almost entirely for his opera *Hansel and Gretel*. And **Engelbert Humperdinck (2)** – the British singer – was chosen four times, including by himself when he was cast away in 2004. He gave me one of the most loved songs of my 'Sea Playlist' – **'All This World and the Seven Seas'**.

186 The music of the Austrian composer **Johann Strauss** was chosen over 100 times, predominantly for his Viennese waltzes, **'The Blue Danube'** being the castaway favourite.

187 The music of the German composer **Richard Strauss** was chosen over 200 times. Of the songs in this story, *Der Rosenkavalier* his most popular piece. **'Also Sprach Zarathustra'**, which became the theme tune to the iconic film *2001: A Space Odyssey*, has been taken over ten times, including by science fiction writer Arthur C. Clarke, who wrote the screenplay of the film, and movie star Tom Hanks, who described it as the 'wow moment' of his life which inspired him to want to be in cinema. He saved it from the waves.

188 The poet **Samuel Taylor Coleridge** was chosen four times in disc form primarily for his 'Ancient Mariner'.

189 The composer **Samuel Coleridge-Taylor** was chosen seven times, including by Chi Chi Nwanoku, founder of Chineke!, the UK's first orchestra primarily comprised of musicians of colour. His trilogy of canatas, *Hiawatha*, is his most taken piece but Chi Chi took his **Ballade in A Minor**.

190 **Ike and Tina Turner's 'River Deep Mountain High'** was chosen six times but Tina's most taken track is **'The Best'**.

191   The folk song **'Red River Valley'** was chosen once by Edmund Hillary.

192   **'Leaving on a Jet Plane'**, written by **John Denver**, was chosen four times. **The Peter, Paul and Mary** version was taken on three occasions, the **John Denver** original once.

193   **Vera Lynn** was chosen over thirty times. She's particularly popular for songs about saying hello and goodbye. Her version of **'Now is the Hour'** was taken once by Edmund Hillary but her signature song **'We'll Meet Again'** is her most taken track.

194   **Bobby McFerrin's 'Don't Worry, Be Happy'** was chosen once by Winnie Byanyima. Not to be confused with his father **Robert McFerrin** – who was an opera singer and the first African American to perform at the Met and who has been taken by several castaways, most often singing Gershwin's *Porgy and Bess* (see endnote 3).

195   **Manu Chau's 'Bongo Bong'** was chosen once by Alexandra Shulman.

196   **B.B. King's 'Better Not Look Down'** was chosen three times.

197   **Imagine Dragons' 'On Top of the World'** was chosen once by Fiona Hill.

198   **The Carpenters' 'Top of the World'** was chosen three times.

199   **'The Happy Wanderer'** was chosen six times, including by Alfred Wainwright.

200   **Bach** was the third most chosen classical composer on the show (after Mozart and Beethoven). His most taken work is his *St Matthew Passion*. Of the songs in this story, his six *Brandenburg Concertos* were taken nearly a hundred times in total. And his *Goldberg Variations* were taken over forty times. Five of my very best castaway friends who specifically asked Glenn Gould to play them for them are Anthony Minghella, Clare Tomlin, David Almond, Edna O'Brien and Steve McQueen.

201   **Dave Brubeck** and his band were chosen over thirty times. **'Take Five'** over ten times and is their most taken track.

202   **John Legend** was chosen three times.

203   Songs from the musical *Singin' in the Rain* featuring Gene Kelly, Debbie Reynolds and Donald O'Connor were chosen over twenty times. The title track is by far the most popular choice but **'Good Morning'** and **'Moses Supposes'** have been taken too.

204   The hymn **'Morning Has Broken'**, made into a popular song by **Cat Stevens** (who later changed his name to **Yusuf Islam**), was chosen six times.

205   **'A Nightingale Sang in Berkeley Square'** by **Manning Sherwin and Eric Maschwitz** was chosen over ten times in over ten different versions. **Barbara Cartland's** rendition (my favourite) was taken once by A.N. Wilson.

206   **Frederick Delius' 'On Hearing the First Cuckoo in Spring'** was chosen nearly twenty times.

207   **Fleetwood Mac's 'Albatross'** was taken twice; and **'Songbird'** once by Kirsty Young.

ENDNOTES

208 **Real Birdsong**
Nightingales and Lancaster Bombers – taken twice.
Nightingales (on their own without any bombers) – taken three times.
Blackbird – taken six times.
Skylarks – taken twice.
Curlews – taken twice.
Pink footed geese – taken once by James Robertson Justice.
Mistle thrush – taken once by Redmond O'Hanlon.
Burchell's coucal – taken once by Lyall Watson.
Laughing kookaburra – taken once by Arthur Bliss.
Woodlark – taken once by Percy Edwards.
Sparkie Williams' 1958 Champion talking budgerigar – taken once by Sandy MacPherson.
Dawn Chorus – taken over ten times.

209 **Haydn's 'Song of the Quail'** was chosen once by Ludwig Koch. **'The Creation'** is his most taken piece made all the more moving to me by professor of fertility Robert Winston who told me that Haydn was in a childless marriage and when the piece was first performed the audience rose, clapped and called,'Father Haydn to the front!' It shows there are many ways to procreate.

210 **Pablo Casals' 'El Cant Dels Ocells'/'Song of the Birds'** was chosen five times.

211 **Roy Rodgers' 'Four Legged Friend'** was chosen twice.

212 **The Stooges' 'I Wanna Be Your Dog'** was chosen once by David Byrne. (NB: Byrne's band **Talking Heads** were chosen over ten times).

213 **Andrew Lloyd Webber's** music has been chosen over fifty times. *Cats* is his most taken piece of work. This is basically because of one song, **'Memory'**, sung by the Cat Grizabella, based on **T.S. Eliot's** poems, with lyrics by Trevor Nunn. The song was selected over ten times, including by Nunn himself. Plus, Gillian Lynne, who choreographed the show, chose **'The Jellicle Ball'**. And Douglas Reeman didn't choose the musical but did chose a reciting of the T.S. Eliot poem **'The Song of the Jellicles'**.

214 **Rossini's 'The Cat Duet'** was taken four times, including by Judith Kerr, who picks it for all the cats who inspired her best-selling books about Mog (it's one of my all-time favourite episodes). *The Barber of Seville* is Rossini's most chosen opera.

215 **Ravel's 'The Cat Duet'** from *L'Enfant et les Sortilèges* was taken three times. *Daphnis and Chloé* is Ravel's most chosen piece of music.

216 **The Incredible String Band's 'The Hedgehog Song'** was chosen once by Rowan Willams (former Archbishop of Canterbury).

217 **Beatrix Potter's 'Tale of the Flopsy Bunny'** was chosen once by Hugh Grant (Hollywood actor).

218 **Michael Flanders and Donald Swann's 'The Hippopotamus Song'** was chosen three times, including by Ian Hislop (the satirist). Their **'Hippo

Encore' was also taken once as well. And politician Ann Widdecombe asked for the sound of real hippos in the African Bush.

219 **Randy Newman's 'Simon Smith and his Amazing Dancing Bear'** was chosen four times – three times in the version by Alan Price, which made the song a hit, and once sung by Randy Newman himself. Of the other songs in this story, **'I Think It's Going to Rain Today'** was chosen once by Jamie Cullum (who also sang it live on the show).

220 The musical *A Little Night Music* is **Stephen Sondheim's** most chosen composition (not including *Westside Story* for which he wrote the lyrics – see endnote 109). This is largely because of the popularity of one particular song – **'Send in the Clowns'** – which has been chosen over ten times, including by Glynis Johns for whom he wrote the song to sing. Sondheim was cast away in 1980 and 2000 – he took his *Pacific Overtures, Sweeney Todd* and *Sunday in the Park with George.* He didn't take *Westside Story.* He said he was embarrassed about the standard of the lyrics.

221 **Mercury Rev's 'The Dark is Rising'** was chosen once by Colin Pillinger.

222 **Maria Muldaur's 'Midnight at the Oasis'** was chosen once by Jancis Robinson.

223 **Toploader's 'Dancing in the Moonlight'** was chosen twice.

224 **Spiritualized's 'Ladies and Gentlemen We Are Floating in Space'** was chosen once by Samantha Morton.

225 The film composer **John Williams** has mostly been chosen for the theme to the film *Schindler's List.* But Warwick Davis chose his main title theme to the *Star Wars* films – for memories of playing several characters in the films himself.

226 **Pink Floyd** was chosen over thirty times and over ten castaways took tracks from the album *The Dark Side of the Moon.*

227 **John Holt's 'Help Me Make It Through the Night'** was chosen twice.

228 **Max Boyce's 'The Ballad of Morgan the Moon'** was chosen once by Ruth Jones.

229 **'Show Me the Way to Go Home'** was chosen once by Henry Longhurst.

230 The song **'Autumn Leaves'/'Les Feuilles Mortes'** was chosen over ten times, mostly in the orginal French version sung by **Yves Montand.** In an attempt to big up 'Autumn' further, have a listen to **Frank Chacksfield's 'Autumn Concerto'** chosen by Percy Merriman.

231 **Vivaldi's** *Four Seasons* is his most chosen piece of music taken over forty times.

232 **Stravinsky's:** *Rite of Spring* is is by far his most chosen piece of music, taken over forty times.

233 **'White Christmas' by Irving Berlin** was chosen fifteen times, nearly exclusively in the **Bing Crosby** version, although Jan Morris took **Bryn Terfel's** rendition of the song.

234 Christmas Carols have historically been a popular choice with **'Silent Night'** being the most taken, followed by own personal favourite **'In the Bleak Midwinter'**, which has been taken over ten times (words by **Christina Rossetti** – my favourite version is the **Harold Darke** setting sung by the **King's College Cambridge Choir)**. NB: Frank Oz took **'God Rest Thee Merry Gentlemen'**.

235 **Victor Hely-Hutchison's** *Carol Symphony* was chosen twice.

236 **'The Twelve Days of Christmas'** was chosen once by Ronald Lockley.

237 **Don McLean's 'American Pie'** was chosen seven times and is his most taken track.

238 **'Stormy Weather' by Harold Arlen and Ted Koehler** was chosen nine times in various versions. My own personal favourite **Lena Horne's** was taken by Ian McKellan (along with the story he told about hearing her singing it live).

239 **Morecambe and Wise's 'Bring Me Sunshine'** was chosen over ten times, including by Ernie Wise himself, when he was cast away alone in 1990, after Eric Morecambe's death. The pair of them were also cast away together in 1966.

240 **'Walking on Sunshine'** – the **Eddy Grant** song – was chosen once by Lawrence Dallaglio, and the **Katrina and the Waves** song was chosen three times. (It's a bit of a cheat to include them in the same entry, I know!)

241 **Electric Light Orchestra's 'Mr Blue Sky'** was chosen four times

242 **Willie Nelson's 'Blue Skies'** was chosen once by Bill Gates.

243 **Kathleen Ferrier's 'Blow the Wind Southerly'** was chosen over twenty times and is her most taken track.

244 **Ann Peebles' 'I Can't Stand the Rain'** was chosen twice.

245 **Scott Walker's 'It's Raining Today'** was chosen once by Thom Yorke – another of my all-time favourite episodes of the show, even though I've never been a big **Radiohead** fan (NB as a band, they were chosen nearly twenty times).

246 **Prince's 'Purple Rain'** was chosen three times and is his most taken track.

247 **The Weather Girls' 'It's Raining Men'** was chosen three times.

248 **Jim Henson/Kermit the Frog's 'Rainbow Connection'** was chosen once by David Mitchell (the comedian, not the writer). Other Rainbow songs include **'Look to the Rainbow'** (sung by **Fred Astaire** and **Petula Clark**), taken once, and **Terry Riley's 'A Rainbow in Curved Air'**, taken twice.

249 **'Over The Rainbow' by Harold Arlen and Yip Harburg** was chosen nearly thirty times in various versions. **Judy Garland** is, of course, the castaway favourite, taken over twenty times. **Israel Kamakawiwo'ole's** version was taken three times. **Eva Cassidy's** version was taken once by Ruthie Henshall. And **Meco's** disco version has was also chosen once by Fay Weldon.

250 **Paul Robeson** was chosen over ninety times. **'Ol' Man River'** (from the **Kern and Hammerstein** musical *Showboat*) nearly twenty times and is his most taken track.

251 **Charles Aznavour's 'She'** was chosen five times, including by **Herbert Kretzmer** who co-wrote the song.

252 **Lou Reed** and **Velvet Underground** were chosen collectively nearly twenty times. **'Ocean'** was chosen once by Helen McDonald.

253 **Laurie Anderson** was chosen twice.

254 **REM's 'Find the River' was** taken once by Doug Allen.

255 **Jimmy Cliff's 'Many Rivers to Cross'** was chosen three times and is his most taken track.

256 **Gary Bartz and NTU Troop's 'I've Known Rivers'** was chosen once by Sonita Alleyne.

257 **Louis Armstrong's 'What A Wonderful World' by Bob Thiele and George David Weiss** is by far his most taken track, chosen nearly thirty times (including by himself). **'Blueberry Hill'** was taken three times.

258 **'Thanks for the Memory' by Ralph Rainger and Leo Robin** was chosen nine times, mainly in the original version sung by **Bob Hope and Shirley Ross**. Bob Hope was cast away in 1961 and he took the song himself.

259 Songs from *Les Miserables* by Claude-Michel Schonberg and **Herbert Kretzmer** were chosen over twenty times. **'I Dreamed a Dream'** is the most taken track. Michel Schonberg took two tracks from the show when he was cast away (the **'Prologue'** and **'The End of the Day'**). Kretzmer didn't, but see endnote 251.

260 **Acker Bilk's 'Stranger on the Shore'** was chosen over ten times and is by far his most taken track.

261 **Otis Redding's '(Sittin' on) the Dock of a Bay'** was chosen six times and is his most taken track.

262 **Blind Faith's 'Can't Find My Way Home'** was chosen once by Conrad Anker.

263 **Rimsky Korskov's 'Flight of the Bumble Bee'** was taken five times. *Scheherazade* is his most chosen piece of music.

264 **Gavin Bryars' 'Jesus' Blood Never Failed Me Yet'** was chosen three times.

265 **The Smiths' 'Please Please Let Me Get What I Want'** was taken twice and the band were chosen nearly twenty times.

266 **The Rolling Stones' 'You Can't Always Get What You Want'** was taken nine times and the band were chosen nearly eighty times.

267 **USA for Africa's 'We Are the World'** was chosen three times.

268 **Handel's** *Messiah* currently holds the record as the show's most chosen single piece of music chosen over 120 times.

269 **The Muezzin's 'Call to Prayer'** was chosen once by Jeremy Farrar.

270 **Kanye West** was chosen six times. On my faith playlist I've got **'Jesus Walks'**, taken by Jasvinder Sanghera, and **'God Is'**, taken by Helena Morrissey.

271 **Nirinjan Kaur's 'Triple Mantra'** was chosen once by Russell Brand.

272 **Gregorian Chants** were chosen over ten times. James MacMillan took the monks of Santo Domingo de Silos singing '**Salve Festa Dies**'.

273 **Miley Cyrus'** '**The Climb**' was chosen once by Jo Malone.

274 **Tasha Cobbs Leonard's** '**You Know My Name**' was chosen once by Amanda Khozi Mukwashi.

275 '**My Man**', which was first sung by **Fanny Brice,** then made a hit by **Billie Holiday,** and then sung by **Barbra Streisand** playing Fanny Brice in the film *Funny Girl,* was chosen four times. Billie Holiday's version was chosen three times and Barbra Streisand's once. Billie Holiday's most taken track is '**Strange Fruit**' which has always seemed to me to be a strange song to take to your desert island because of its savagery. Barbra Streisand's is another song from *Funny Girl* – '**People**'.

276 **Beyoncé** songs were chosen eleven times – ten different tracks with '**Crazy in Love**' taken twice.

277 **Jay-Z** (Beyoncé's husband) was chosen three times.

278 **Gloria Gaynor's** '**I Will Survive**' was chosen seven times.

279 **Labi Siffre's** '**Something Inside So Strong**' was chosen four times.

280 **Keala Settle's** '**This Is Me**' from *The Greatest Showman* was chosen once by Nick Webborn.

281 **Baz Luhrmann's** '**Everybody's Free (To Wear Sunscreen)**' was chosen once by Chris Boardman.

282 **The Beach Boys'** '**Good Vibrations**' was chosen five times and the band have been taken over thirty times.

283 **The The's** '**This is the Day**' was chosen twice.

284 **Dire Straits** were chosen nearly thirty times and the original version of their song '**Brothers in Arms**' was taken once by David Davis. However an alternative version of it, sung by **Ronnie Drew,** was also taken by Ralph Steadman. The BBC's website says that Frances Edmonds took it as well but she didn't – if you listen to the episode you'll hear she took '**Walk of Life**', their most taken track.

285 **Modest Mussorgsky's** '**Night on the Bare Mountain**' was chosen five times. *Boris Godunov* is his most selected piece of music.

286 **Henry Rowley Bishop's** song '**Home Sweet Home**' was chosen once by Fred Streeter.

287 **Henry Purcell's** '**When I Am Laid in Earth**' (aka '**Dido's Lament**'), from his opera *Dido and Aeneas,* was chosen nearly thirty times and is his most taken piece of music.

288 **Billie Eilish's** '**Everything I Wanted**' was chosen twice.

289 **Monty Python's** '**Always Look On the Bright Side of Life**' was chosen eight times.

290 **Leonard Cohen** was chosen over fifty times, sometimes sung by him, sometimes sung by other people. **'Anthem'** was taken three times.

291 **'Who Knows Where the Time Goes'** was chosen four times: twice in the **Sandy Denny/Fairport Convention** original, once in the **Nina Simone** version by John Malkovich, once in **Judy Collins'** version by Whoopi Goldberg.

292 **Elvis Costello's** 'Everyday I Write the Book' was chosen three times and is his most taken track.

293 **Bellini's** most chosen opera is *Norma* and the top track from it is **'Casta Diva'**.

294 **Verdi's** *Requiem Mass* is his most chosen piece of music (yes, even more than *La Traviata* which is his most chosen opera). The mass was taken over seventy times and the **'Dies Irae'** is the most popular section in it. His **'Chorus of the Hebrew Slaves'**, from *Nabucco*, was taken over thirty times and is basically the only song selected from the opera unless you're Harry Enfield who took the **'Prelude'**.

295 **Monteverdi's** most chosen opera (and now my own favourite) is *The Coronation of Poppea*.

296 **Schubert** is the most chosen classical composer after Mozart, Beethoven and Bach. His **String Quintet in C** is his most selected piece, taken nearly eighty times. His **'Trout Quintet'** nearly thirty times and the lied **'The Trout'** over ten times. **'Auf Dem See/On The Lake'** was taken once by Cicely Saunders.

297 My favourite **Schumann** is **'Träumerei'** (Dreaming), from his *Scenes of Childhood*, although his **Piano Concerto in A Minor** is his most taken track.

298 **'O Boundless Salvation'**, sung at the Salvation Army Meeting of Thanksgiving on 2 July 1965 at Westminster Abbey, London, was selected and saved from the waves by Frederick Coutts.

299 **Edith Piaf's** *'Je Ne Regrette Rien'* was the show's most chosen popular song, taken forty-eight times in total.

300 **Benny Goodman's** 'Sing, Sing, Sing' was chosen five times, including by John Updike.

Acknowledgements

Firstly thank you to everyone who has helped bring this book into being – particularly the amazing team at Quarto Publishing who I have loved working with including Denise Bates, Phoebe Bath, Laura Bulbeck, Viviane Basset, Victoria Gilder, Lewis Laney, Paileen Currie, Aruna Vasudevan, Philip Parker, Ramona Lamport, Rohana Yusof, David Meikle, Jude Hodgsonhann, Aisling May, Hannah Chow and Priya Mistry for her beautiful cover design. Also special thanks to my agent Charlie Brotherstone for introducing me to them all.

To my family – my grandparents, parents, sister, nieces, aunt, uncle, cousins. And my childhood and university friends and first loves, especially Beth, Tara, Vicky, Ella, Dan and Leo (who have all appeared in the pages of my books) – the older we get, the more important the people we knew when we were young become.

To my Lyric family – especially Sean, Kim, Lyndel and Tracey – and to Imogen who over the last few years has taught me so much about Living Big and Brave. To Amy Belson for offering me a bigger boat. And special thanks to Janet Ellis for hosting a trilogy of book launches.

To my fertility family – especially the following for doing so much to champion my writing and work from the beginning, and still: Anya Sizer, Caroline Stafford (Kitsch Hen Biscuiteer Extraordinaire), Francesca Steyn, Gabby Vautier, Kate Brian, Laura Biggs, Lisa Faulkner, Jacky Boivin, Jody Day, Joyce Harper, Natalie Silverman, Stephanie Phillips and Zeynep Gurtin.

Also so much love to Alexandra W, Alice R, Annie Lou S, Barbara S, Best Fertility, Big Fat Negative, Bindi S, Carmel D, Catherine H, Cat S, Charlotte G, Dee A, Diane C, Emma C, Fee D, Fiona G, Foz F, Full Stop Podcast, Geeta N, Kat B, Kate D, Kazuko H, Hannah V-J, Harriet C, Helen G, Helen Louise J, IVF Babble, Izzy J, Jon & Mette, Julia L, Julienne B, Kelly D-S, Lesley P, Lorna M, Lucy S, Megumi F, Monique KK, NAFM, Natalie H, Nina B, Pippa M, Rosalyn S, Sarah B, Sarah E, Sarah H, Sheila L, Sophie M, Sophie S, Susan B, Tabitha M, Titania K, Tone JM, Tracey S, Vicky D, Victoria F, Veronique B and the Worst Girl Gang Ever. And please forgive me if I've not mentioned you – my fertility family is HUGE and I love you all.

To my *Chomolungma* Family – especially Adele Pennington (and Jim); Jon Gupta; Jeff Smith; James Barber and everyone at the Altitude Centre; the Ramblers and the LDWA (especially Kate C, Gill M, Joan W and Sue T); and ALL the expedition companies, guides, support staff and fellow team members who were part of my journey to the top of the world. And in loving memory of Annelise Massiera.

To my Channel family – especially Alice, John and everyone at SwimQuest, my dearest friend Katie Barlow plus everyone else listed in *21 Miles:* the book. And to Anoushka Warden, Erebus Pictures and Sheila David who are working hard to make *21 Miles:* the movie.

And a special shout out to my Pond to Peak sister – Anna Brown.

To my *Desert Island Discs* family – all the castaways and presenters as well the BBC for granting me permission to write

ACKNOWLEDGEMENTS

about, use quotes and audio clips from the show. Special thanks to John Goudie, Nigel Gibson, Paula McGinley and Sue Dickson; and to Andi Beckham and Ellen Evers (from Getty Images) for going above and beyond to help make it happen! And special love to the castaways Ann Daniels, Benjamin Zephaniah and Maxine Peake.

I'm also very grateful to Doug O'Brien and Richard Lumsden for giving me permission to quote the lyrics from their fabulous songs – 'Rotterdam 82' and 'Some of Your Planes' (and FYI, I've since found out you can download 'Rotterdam 82' via the Bandcamp website). And reprinted by permission of Hal Leonard Europe Ltd: 'Brothers in Arms' - Words and Music by Mark Knopfler. Copyright © 1985 STRAITJACKET SONGS LIMITED. All Rights Administered by ALMO MUSIC CORP. All Rights Reserved & Used by Permission. Also, thanks to John Hooper for kind permission to reference his book *The Italians*. And to Morgan Harper Nichols for permission to quote her beautiful words about mountains.

I also want to acknowledge the following people for their personal friendship and professional support in various ways that have directly contributed to this book and my work of the last few years: Alexandra Lamont, Alison Collantine, Anna Cooling, Belinda Kirk, Beth Kempton, Caroline Crewe-Read, Carolyn Braby, Cristina Colombo, Daniela Capetti, David Bond, Darren Brady, David Beidas, David Greig, Di Westaway, Donna Ferguson, Emily Sweet, Emma Gannon, Gianvito Petruzzelli, Jacque Price Rees, Kitty Stewart, Joanna Lal, Julie Spence, Justine Solomons, Lyn Carpenter, Marilyn Daish, Matthew Johnston, Neil Adleman, Nicky Moran, Mel Rosenblatt, Polly Courtney, Penny Hearne, Sarah Williams, Sara Tasker, Sheree Vickers, Sofia Sciardo and Armando Tumulo, Richard Townsend, TEAfilms, The McGraths, The Orrs and Zohar Glouberman.

And finally, to my dear friend Anna Disley (Executive Director of New Writing North) for being my first and perfect reader. Thank you for that beautiful list you sent me which I will always treasure.

And to Peter, with my gratitude and love always – for making me a writer, and giving me his permission to write my truth.